Interest Rate Swaps and Their Derivatives

Interest Rate Swaps and Their Derivatives

A Practitioner's Guide

AMIR SADR

John Wiley & Sons, Inc.

Published by John Wiley & Sons, Inc., Hoboken, New Jersey.
Published simultaneously in Canada.

For general information on our other products and services or for technical support, please contact our Customer Care Department within the United States at (800) 762-2974, outside the United States at (317) 572-3993 or fax (317) 572-4002.

Wiley also publishes its books in a variety of electronic formats. Some content that appears in print may not be available in electronic formats. For more information about Wiley products, visit our Web site at www.wiley.com.

Library of Congress Cataloging-in-Publication Data:

Sadr, Amir, 1963–
    Interest rate swaps and their derivatives: a practitioner's guide / Amir Sadr.
        p. cm. – (Wiley finance series)
    Includes bibliographical references and index.
    ISBN 978-0-470-44394-1 (cloth)
    1. Interest rate swaps.   2. Interest rate futures.   3. Derivative securities.   I. Title.
    HG6024.5.S32 2009
    332.63'23–dc22   2009008840

Printed in the United States of America

10 9 8 7 6 5 4 3 2 1

Contents

Preface

The market for interest rate swaps and their derivatives has experienced tremendous growth since its beginning in the early 1980s, and swaps are now a key component of capital markets. While trading in swaps and their derivatives was initially the domain of major money-center banks, most investment and commercial banks these days run a swaps and options desk alongside their cash and repo desks.

"RATES" MARKET

The "rates" market consists of swaps, flow options (caps/floors, European swaptions), Bermudan swaptions, some semi-exotics (CMS/CMT products), and exotics (structured notes,...). While at some point, Bermudan swaptions were considered exotics, their popularity and volume has made them into an integral part of the interest-rate options market.

While a newcomer to a typical broker-dealer trading floor can find ample background material on the bond and repo markets, he is often overwhelmed by the instruments and the technical requirements to understand swaps and their derivatives. For bonds and repos, a typical analyst can use a Bloomberg terminal or the financial toolkit in Excel, or even an HP-12 calculator to get up and running. However, for swaps and options, he has to typically master the in-house derivatives system with many moving parts and nonstandard terms. The analyst can quickly become discouraged, and think of swaps and options to be the domain of quants and tech-savvy individuals who can handle such seeming complexity. Some of this complexity is merely the terms used in the swaps market: receiving/paying in swap lingo instead of buying/selling cash bonds—economically the same things—while for the options and exotics markets the complexity is real. The goal of this book is to break down some of this complexity.

BACKGROUND

This book came about over the past 15 years as alongside my day time Wall Street job, I periodically taught an evening course on interest-rate swaps and options at NYU's School of Continuing and Professional Studies. Each semester, I was asked what a good book would be to accompany the course. My answer has always been, "I have yet to find a book," and instead I would use notes gathered from various sources that I would pass out in the class. Moreover, in my last trading job, I was assigned to mentor the entry-level analyst class in their rotation on the fixed income (repo, treasury, swaps, options) desks, and was asked to assemble a required reading list for them. Again, I would have liked to recommend one book that would most directly and expeditiously get the analysts up to speed both in theory and more important the practice—so that we could extract the most work out of them!—but I still could not find such a book or training manual, and would end up recommending various chapters from a selection of books.

The final straw, so to speak, came when the head of trading asked me to organize a couple of lectures to educate and familiarize our "cash" traders (treasury, swap, repo, agency) and generalist sales force on the workings of options and exotics desk, where I was a trader. These lectures and their orientation to front-line staff on a trading floor finalized the orientation of this book, where the goal is to demystify in the quickest way what actually happens on the trading floor, and help people understand the concepts.

While there are many books on fixed-income and interest-rate derivatives, they generally suffer from being either too elementary and bond-centric, mentioning swaps in passing, or too technical and focused on exotics and the myriad implementation issues and algorithms used to tackle them. The exotics area is the most challenging part of the market, and holds an understandable pull for quants, academics, and technically-oriented individuals. Their pricing and risk issues remain challenging, although most of the challenge is not in the theory, but in the efficient implementation of the theory. Rather than focusing on exotics, the goal of this book is the more mundane task of adequately and thoroughly covering the mainstream products—swaps, flow options, Bermudans, semi-exotics—as they are traded by showing the common pricing techniques, while showing how to generalize the concepts to other nuanced products.

The main audience for this book is the current or aspiring practitioners in interest-rate products. These would be traders, salespeople, marketers, structurers, and operations, finance, risk management, and IT professionals involved in rates products. Indeed, this mix has usually been the main audience of my class at NYU, where people who are already involved in some aspect of interest-rate products want to have the theory and practice demystified for them.

With this broad target audience in mind, the level of mathematics is kept to only what is needed, and special effort is made to not lose the audience with overly technical discussions. Still, this being a book on rates derivatives, it requires a college-level of math with some calculus and probability, although most concepts are broken down as much as possible into their intuitive and pictorial elements. Fundamental results are motivated and expressed in simple settings, illustrated in examples for actively traded products, and their generalized versions are simply stated without proof. As much as possible, technical discussions are avoided and delayed. For example, Ito's Lemma is only introduced in the final two chapters when discussing HJM-type models. Even at this level, in Appendix A, we show how to think of Ito's Lemma as a simple extension of Taylor Series with a quirky (but easy to remember) multiplication rule. This in my experience is the most productive way of understanding rates products for the target audience.

BOOK STRUCTURE

The book is organized in three parts, following closely the layout of different trading desks on a typical USD fixed income trading floor: repo and cash (treasury) desks, swaps desk, options desk, with the exotics and structured products desk alongside or part of the options desk.

Part 1. Cash, Repo, and Swap Markets

Part 1 deals with cash, repo, and swap products, namely all instruments that are not volatility-based (Euro-dollar convexity adjustment being an exception) and do not require the options machinery. The techniques for pricing these instruments are quite similar, and are pretty much the idea of financing cost, discount factors, and projection of forward curves.

Chapter 1 begins by a quick review of fixed-income basics: time value of money, future and present value, price-yield formula, forward prices, and sensitivity measures such as PV01, PVBP, and convexity. This chapter can be considered as "all you need to know about bonds" to proceed to swaps and options. The U.S. Treasury bond market is the main example used to illustrate these concepts, and many of its quote conventions and nuances are explained in detail. As financing is the main driver of all fixed-income products, the repo market as it pertains to the U.S. treasuries is discussed in detail. We present popular trades such as *Curve* (slope of the treasury curve), *Curvature* (weighted butterfly), and *Carry* trades.

Chapter 2 covers the pricing of plain-vanilla interest-rate swaps. The main pricing difference between bonds and swaps is that swaps require the whole term structure of interest rates, while for bonds there is a single yield-to-maturity. We present the contractual cash flow structure of a typical swap, and show that pricing interest-rate swap requires access to a discount factor and *projected* forward curve. As long as the swap counterparties' funding is the same as the swap's floating index, one can use the same discount curve for both projection and discounting. Using this setup, we show how to extract a discount factor curve from the variety of quoted market instruments, and discuss the nuances of curve construction methods while highlighting the main tradeoff between smooth forwards versus having reasonable prescribed hedges.

Chapter 3 delves into actual swap market instruments (cash rates, futures, par-swap rates) using U.S. swap market as its prime example. USD swaps are usually quoted and traded as spreads to treasuries, and we present typical broker screens, trading mechanisms (rates/spreads), and different ways of trading spreads: headline spread, matched-maturity spread, and asset-swap spreads. As swaps are priced off of a curve built from a blend of input instruments, we show how the bond sensitivity measures such as PV01 and convexity have to get extended to bucket-PV01 and gamma-ladder in Swap-Land. An advantage of swaps is they are bilateral OTC contracts, with the ability to customize their cash flows, requiring the counterparties to negotiate and agree on all the cash flow details. We present some of these date minutiae and considerations when constructing a swap's cash flows.

Chapter 4 discusses *Basis Swaps* and the need for the separate extraction of a forward curve distinct from the discount curve for their pricing and risk management. In particular, one needs to first extract a discount curve from swaps keyed to one's funding index, and then use this discount curve to extract the forward curve for other indices, from which one arrives at the discount curve based on them. Historically, Libor rates have been used synonymously as risk-free rates, but with the recent banking turmoil, careful attention is being paid on Libors of different tenors (1m, 3m, 6m). We discuss the issues related to Libor-Libor basis swaps, and show why this basis is not merely driven by supply and demand dynamics.

We present OIS swaps in the final section and discuss their growing importance and relevance to swap markets. Most credit support agreements (CSA) for swaps specify OIS rather than Libor rates for margining any mark-to-market value. We present the view that OIS rates should then be considered the funding index for plain-vanilla swaps, and swaps are in reality basis swaps. This view is still being debated in the markets, and has yet to be universally adopted.

Part 2. Interest-Rate Flow Options

With the cash and swap products out of the way, Part 2 covers the options markets for flow products. These include options on futures (Euro-dollar) contracts, caps and floors, and European swaptions. As with any option product, the pricing and risk management of these requires dealing with volatility as the main risk factor.

Option trading in general has been delegated to the more technically oriented staff, and has enjoyed a mystique of being understood only by whiz-kids and sophisticated traders who are able to understand the plethora of the associated Greek letters. We will show that one does not need to have a Ph.D. in math, or be fully proficient in stochastic calculus and Ito's Lemma to understand options. While the original Black-Scholes option pricing formula was derived using these advanced techniques, the modern approach is *Risk-Neutral Valuation*, which can be easily explained in a simple binomial setting.

Chapter 5 introduces the basic concept of option replication in a simple binomial setting suggested by Cox-Ross-Rubinstein, and follows its simple extension into a two-period setting to illustrate the concept of *dynamic* replication. This is surprisingly the main idea of option pricing, and it is said (and shown in Chapter 5) that the binomial model is all you really need to understand the theory of derivatives. The binomial model naturally leads to the framework that has become known as *risk-neutral valuation*, which can be summarized as follows: Option prices are the prices of their self-financing dynamic replicating portfolios, and can be obtained as the risk-neutral *expected* discounted value of their payoffs. This framework applies to all options, be it equity, FX, or interest rates, and all option models are (simple or elaborate) specialized applications of it. Risk-neutral valuation remains the main option pricing framework for the rest of the book.

Chapter 6 presents Black-Scholes-Merton and Black's Formulae, the main pricing models used for European-style options. These formulae are shown to be the result of risk-neutral valuation when the uncertainty about the underlying asset changes (absolute or percentage) are modeled via a Normal distribution. For interest rate flow options, the main pricing model is Black's Formula; originally the Log-Normal version, and in recent years supplanted by the Normal version. Black's Formula is obtained by evaluating an integral (through some tedious algebra), and without resorting to stochastic calculus or the dreaded Ito's Lemma. We present the standard formulas for calls/puts and digital options, and their sensitivities (Greeks) for both Normal and Log-Normal dynamics, and review general option concepts such as put-call parity, gamma versus theta, and the far reach of the call-formula.

Chapter 7 shows how Black's formulae as used for interest-rate flow options such as ED options, cap/floors, and European swaptions. We use the liquid instruments in USD options markets and present in detail how these are traded in practice. As most option quotes imply different volatilities for different strikes, we present the SABR model, which is the most commonly used model for capturing skews and smiles. Most flow options desks also make markets in *Constant-Maturity-Swap* (CMS) products: CMSs, cap/floors, and curve cap/floors. While these products should properly be priced within a term-structure model, one usually tries to resort to simple analytical approximation formulae for them, and we present the commonly used analytical formulae and techniques. We discuss popular trades such as conditional curve trades using a pair of swaptions, and contingent spread trades implemented as a bond option and a swaption pair.

Part 3. Interest-Rate Exotics

Black's Formula and simple analytical formulas are all one needs to price and risk-manage interest-rate *flow* options. For the next class of products—Bermudan options serving as a poster child—there are no simple analytical formulae, and one has to resort to more complex computational algorithms. As these products depend on a variety of interest rates, one has to use models that capture the dynamics of the whole term structure. The framework for pricing these options remains risk-neutral valuation, but applied to the whole term structure, and with multiple underlyings spanning the full maturity spectrum.

The first attempts to develop models for exotics were based on the evolution of the short rate as the state variable in a risk-neutral setting, and have become known as short-rate models, with Hull-White and BDT/BK models the most commonly deployed ones. As the short rate spans the term of any longer rate, the dynamics of all rates could be related back to the future evolution of the short rates. The typical implementation of short-rate models admits a recombining tree (lattice) format, which lends itself easily to the pricing of Bermudan options.

Chapter 8 introduces the common short-rate models used in practice and highlights the main features of their dynamics. Using the BDT model—not the most commonly used model in practice any more, but a good conduit to expose the common ideas and techniques—we show the typical discretization of the process dynamics into a discrete-time setting, and how to satisfy the no-arbitrage requirement imposed in a risk-neutral setting, namely *inverting the yield curve*. While brute-force trial and error works for inverting the yield curve, we discuss the more computationally efficient *Forward Induction* technique using Arrow-Debreu prices. Having inverted the yield curve, we can at each future node extract discount factors to compute option payoffs that depend on par-swap rates, swap values, forward rates, and so on, and discount these back to today to arrive at option values. Most short-rate models have free parameters (local volatility, mean-reversion) that can be tweaked so that the market price of liquid options can be recovered. This process of tweaking the free parameters is called calibration, and in general is a computationally hard problem. No matter, having constructed a calibrated arbitrage-free short-rate lattice, we are well on our way to price any complex payoff.

The previous steps are common to all short-rate lattice models, and are particularly suited for non-path-dependent options. For Asian (path-dependent) options, we need to keep track of the evolution of interest rates from today up to the time of its terminal payoff. While this can *conceptually* be done in a lattice implementation, the computational burden quickly becomes exorbitant, and one instead resorts to simulation methods, which unfortunately suffer from run-to-run variability (simulation noise). There are many techniques for reducing simulation noise, and variance reduction is a specialized discipline with many implementation tricks. We present the simplest such technique (antithetic) to provide a taste.

Chapter 9 presents Bermudan-style options, which confer to the holder the option to choose an exercise time within an exercise window. We show that this exercise option can still be handled within the risk-neutral valuation framework, but one has to *search* for the optimal exercise policy. As this class of problems has been studied in dynamic programming disciplines, there exists an algorithmic way—*backward induction*—of extracting the option value under this optimal exercise policy. We discuss the common Bermudan cancelable swap structures and show how to use backward induction in a lattice model to price them.

As there are models that don't admit a lattice implementation due to their non-Markovian dynamics—an up-down move does not end up in the same state as a down-up move—and are usually implemented as a simulation model, we discuss the challenges of pricing Bermudan options for these models. This is still an active area of research, and while certain algorithms have become the standard (LSM, boundary extraction), there is still room for further improvement.

Chapter 10 introduces the full term-structure models of HJM, which explicitly evolve the full term-structure in a risk-neutral setting. We recall that a short-rate model *implicitly* evolves the full term-structure, but with HJM models, the term-structure is the explicit evolved quantity. We present the discrete-time, discrete-tenor version of the HJM models, and show how to ensure that they are arbitrage-free in a risk-neutral setting. This version, despite the seemingly complex notation, is relatively simple to understand and renders itself to algorithmic implementation as a computer program (simulation model). HJM models also offer an intuitive and flexible way of modeling volatilities via the forward-forward volatility surface, and can easily be extended to multifactor settings to drive the correlations of various forward rates. We show the volatility signature of flow products on the forward-forward volatility surface, and present approximations for swaption vols and correlations that can aid in calibration.

We show the continuous-time version of the HJM model for instantaneous forward rates in Appendix C. While an elegant framework for interest-rate products, HJM models are generally non-Markovian and need to get implemented as a simulation model, making them challenged for Bermudan options.

Chapter 11 revisits the issue of numeraires, and shows in a simple binomial setting how to change them. The technique of changing numeraires has been invoked to provide new insights (and justification) for using Black's model for interest-rate flow options, the main objection to it being that it ignores the required stochastic discounting, and that it treats forward rates as assets (they are not). By switching numeraires to a discount bond with maturity coinciding with the option payout, one arrives at the *forward measure*, under which both common practices are justified. Furthermore, by assuming Normal/Log-Normal terminal distribution under this forward measure, one can fully recover Black's formula as used for interest-rate flow options.

The forward measure lens provides theoretical justification—albeit a tortured one—of market practice, and has given rise to the subclass of HJM models which focus on the evolution of discrete-tenor forward rates through this lens. These Brace-Gartarek-Musiela (BGM) Market models have gained popularity since they initially provided the hope for easy calibration to the readily available cap or swaption vols. We discuss how these hopes were somewhat premature, since when one needs to price the usual multi-rate exotics, the elegant forward-measure structure of various forward rates breaks down when considered under any unified measure, and the Market model becomes non-Markovian, requiring simulation implementation with the associated Bermudan pricing issues. In this way, they share the same gains and pains of a typical discrete-tenor HJM model viewed through the more intuitive money-market measure.

At this point, a typical reader should realize that modeling topics are becoming more nuanced, and are best handled in other books that do proper technical justice to them. At the same time, the discussions in this chapter should allow one to become somewhat conversant and gain a working knowledge and appreciation of the main features of these models and their related issues.

ACKNOWLEDGMENTS

The learning has never stopped for me on Wall Street, and I am grateful to the following individuals who have taught me new things: David Heath, Sean Hamidi, Joseph Langsam, James Tilley, Wei-Tong Shu, Charbel Aburached, Andrew Gunstensen, Craig Gustafson, Sergio Kostek, Peter Ritchken, Darrell Duffie, David Moore, Charles Henry, Morris Sachs, Stephen Siu, E.G. Fisher, Michael Sussman, John Mannion, Tim Dann, James Mather, Hongbing Hsu, Mitchell Stafman, Robert Wahl, Leslie Harris, George Nunn, Elan Ruggill, Tom Fitzmaurice, Gerald Cook, Joseph Vona, John Kuhn, Hugh Bush, Rohit Apte, Marc Braunstein, David Kwun, Joe Mastrocola, Steve Bredahl, Raymond Humiston, Brian Ciardi. Special thanks to GCM's ISD team for having put up with me for the past (and who knows, next?) decade, and to all my NYU students over the years who have kept my feet to the ground. Final thanks to my editors at John Wiley & Sons: Bill Falloon, Laura Walsh, Meg Freeborn, Kevin Holm, and Jay Boggis for patiently walking me through this project and correcting my many typos. All remaining errors are mine, and I welcome any corrections, suggestions, and comments sent to asadr@panalytix.com.

About the Author

Amir Sadr received his Ph.D. in 1990 from Cornell University with thesis work on the Foundations of Probability Theory. After working at AT&T Bell Laboratories until 1993, he started his Wall Street career at Morgan Stanley, initially as a Vice President in Quantitative Modeling and development of exotic interest rate models, and later on as an exotics trader in Derivative Product Group. He founded Panalytix, Inc., in 1997 to develop financial software for pricing and risk management of interest-rate derivatives. In 2001, he joined Greenwich Capital as Managing Director for proprietary trading. He joined HSBC in 2005 as Senior Trader in charge of CAD exotics and USD inflation trading. His latest role was the COO of Brevan Howard US Asset Management in Connecticut.

List of Symbols and Abbreviations

$\alpha(T_1, T_2)$	accrual fraction for calculation period $[T_1, T_2]$ according to some day-count
w	generic random future path
σ, σ_N	log-volatility, normal volatility
bp	1% of 1%, 0.0001
$CT[n]$	U.S. current n-year Treasury
$d, d_{1,2}$	moneyness, $d = \frac{F-K}{\sigma\sqrt{t_e}}$, $d_{1,2} = \frac{ln(F/K)}{\sigma\sqrt{t_e}} \pm 1/2\sigma\sqrt{t_e}$
$D(T), D(t, T)$	discount factor at time t (today, if omitted) for maturity T
$f(t, [T_1, T_2])$	simple forward rate at time t (today if omitted) for the forward deposit period $[T_1, T_2]$
$f(t, T)$	instantaneous forward rate at time t (today if omitted) for the forward deposit period starting at T
$F_A(t, T), F$	forward price of asset A at time t (today, if omitted) for forward delivery date $T > t$
$f_c(t, [T_1, T_2])$	continuously-compounded forward rate at time t (today if omitted) for the forward deposit period $[T_1, T_2]$
FV, PV	future value, present value
$LN(\mu, \sigma^2)$	Log-Normal random variable
$M(t, w)$	money market (unit currency rolled over at successive short rates) account numeraire, $M(t, w) = e^{\int_0^t r(u,w)du}$
$N(\mu, \sigma^2)$	A Normal random variable with mean μ, and standard deviation σ
$N(x)$	cumulative distribution function of a standard ($N(0, 1)$) Normal random variable
$N'(x)$	$\frac{1}{\sqrt{2\pi}}e^{-x^2/2}$
$P(C, y, N, m), P$	price of a bond with coupon rate C, paid m times/year, with N remaining coupons, with yield y
P_{Clean}, P_{Dirty}	clean, dirty price of a coupon bond
$PV01$	present value change due to an "01" (1 bp) change in yield
$PVBP$	present value change due to a 1 bp change in coupon, present value of a 1 bp annuity
$Var(X)$	variance of a random variable X

w	accrued fraction (according to some daycount) of the periodic coupon for bond calculation
$y(T)$	zero rate (according to some payment frequency and daycount) for a zero-coupon bond maturing at T
$y_c(T)$	continuously-compounded zero rate for a zero-coupon bond maturing at T
ATMF	at the money forward option, $K = F_A$
CDF	cumulative distribution function
DF	(probability) density function
MF	modified following roll convention
P&L, P+L	profit and loss
r.v.	random variable
RMS	root-mean-square average
RTP, RTR	right-to-pay (payer), right-to-receive (receiver) swaption
YTM	yield to maturity
100M	100 million, sometimes written as 100MM, where M stands for 1000's
100-nnm	price quote convention for U.S. treasuries, $100 + nn/32 + (m/8)/32$ in percentage points. A '+' for 'm' stands for 4.
$f'(x)$, $f''(x)$	first, second derivative of f with respect to x

Interest Rate Swaps and Their Derivatives

Cash, Repo, and Swap Markets

Bonds: It's All About Discounting

Before we delve into all the good stuff (swaps and options), let us review some fixed income basics.

TIME VALUE OF MONEY: FUTURE VALUE, PRESENT VALUE

Following the classical fixed income gospels, we remember that the *Future Value*, *FV*, on a horizon date of an investment *PV* at an annual interest rate of *r*, *compounded m* times a year, for *N* whole compounding periods is

$$FV = PV(1 + r/m)^N$$

For example, if $m = 1$, we have annual compounding $FV = PV(1 + r)^N$, and N is the number of years until the future horizon date. If $m = 2$, we have semiannual compounding (standard for U.S. Treasury securities) $FV = PV(1 + r/2)^N$, and $N = 2T$ is the number of whole semiannual periods until the horizon date (*T* years from now).

The above formula can be easily generalized to incorporate horizon dates that are not a whole number of compounding periods away. We compute *T* as the number of years between the investment date and the horizon date, according to some day count basis, and come up with:

$$FV = PV(1 + r/m)^{Tm}$$

From college math courses, we recall that as you increase the compounding frequency, the above, in the limit, becomes

$$\lim_{m \to \infty} FV = PVe^{rT}$$

and *r* is then referred to as the *continuous* compounding rate.

An alternative to using compounded rates is to use *simple* or noncompounding interest rates:

$$FV = PV(1 + rT)$$

where T is the number of years (can be fractional) to the horizon date. Simple interest rates are usually used for *Money Market* instruments, that is, with maturity less than 1 year.

In order to compute how much money needs to be invested today at interest rate r, compounded m times a year, for T years to get FV at maturity, one simply inverts the above equation to come up with *Present Value, PV*:

$$PV = \frac{FV}{(1 + r/m)^{Tm}}$$

and in the limit:

$$\lim_{m \to \infty} PV = FVe^{-rT}$$

By setting FV to 1, PV becomes today's price of unit currency to be received at time T, that is, present value of $1, and we will denote it by *Discount Factor, D*:

$$D(T) = \frac{1}{(1 + r/m)^{Tm}} \to e^{-rT}$$

This would be price of a security that returns unit dollar at maturity (T years from now), that is, the price of a T-maturity zero-coupon bond, and provides an (implicit) yield r, compounded m times a year.

Note that while interest rates r can be quoted in different ways, the actual investment (PV dollars in, FV dollars out) remains the same. In order to compare different investments, one would need to compare them using the same metric, that is, interest rates with the same quote convention. However, in order to value investments, all we need are discount factors.

Discount factors are the fundamental building blocks for valuing fixed income securities. Given a series of known cash flows $(C_1, \ldots, C_N)$ to be received at various times $(T_1, \ldots, T_N)$ in the future, if we know the discount factor $D(T_i)$ for each payment date T_i, then today's value of this package is:

$$PV(\text{Portfolio of Cash flows}) = \sum_{i=1}^{N} C_i D(T_i)$$

PRICE-YIELD FORMULA

For example, today's price P of a T-year bond paying an annualized coupon rate C, m times a year (so $N = T \times m$ payments left) is

$$P = \sum_{i=1}^{N} \frac{C}{m} D(T_i) + D(T_N)$$

The standard bond pricing formula is based on *Flat Yield* assumption: it assumes that there is a *single* interest rate called *Yield-to-Maturity* (YTM) y applicable for all cash flows of the bond, regardless of how far the payment date is. With this assumption, $D(T_i) = 1/(1 + y/m)^i$, and we get the classical bond pricing formula:

$$P(C, y, N, m) = P = \sum_{i=1}^{N} \frac{C/m}{(1 + y/m)^i} + \frac{1}{(1 + y/m)^N}$$

$$= \frac{C}{y} \left(1 - \frac{1}{(1 + y/m)^N}\right) + \frac{1}{(1 + y/m)^N}$$

The above formula is for when there are $N = T \times m$ *whole* future coupon periods left. For a bond in the middle of a coupon period, the discount factors get modified as $D(T_i) = 1/(1 + y/m)^{i-w}$ where w measures the *accrued* fraction (measured using some day-count convention: Act/Act, Act/365, ...) of the current coupon period:

$$P = \sum_{i=1}^{N} \frac{C/m}{(1 + y/m)^{i-w}} + \frac{1}{(1 + y/m)^{N-w}}$$

$$= \frac{1}{(1 + y/m)^{-w}} \left[\sum_{i=1}^{N} \frac{C/m}{(1 + y/m)^i} + \frac{1}{(1 + y/m)^N} \right]$$

$$= (1 + y/m)^w \left[\frac{C}{y} \left(1 - \frac{1}{(1 + y/m)^N}\right) + \frac{1}{(1 + y/m)^N} \right]$$

The above formula is the *Dirty Price* of a bond, that is, how much cash is needed in order to purchase this bond. One needs to always remember that *dirty price of a bond is the discounted value of its remaining cash flows*. The standard price/yield formulae simply express this via assuming a flat yield and expressing all discount factors as a function of this (hypothetical) yield y. Figure 1.1 shows the graph of Price as a function of YTM. As can be seen, when yield equals the coupon rate, the price of the bond is *Par* (100%).

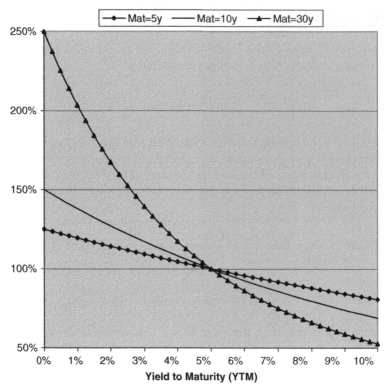

FIGURE 1.1   Price-Yield Graph for a 5% Semiannual Coupon Bond

Also, longer-maturity bonds exhibit a higher curvature (*convexity*) in their price-yield relationship.

The graph of a dirty price of a bond versus time to maturity T is discontinuous, with drops (equal to paid coupon) on coupon payment dates. This makes sense, since the present value of *remaining* cash flows should drop when there is one less coupon. For bond traders focused on quoted *price* of a bond, this drop in price (while real in terms of PV of *remaining* cash flows) is artificial in terms of worthiness/value of a bond, and they prefer a smoother measure. By subtracting the *accrued interest*, wC/m from the dirty price, one arrives at the *Clean/Quoted Price*:

$$P_{Clean} = P_{Dirty} - w\frac{C}{m}$$

$$= (1 + y/m)^w \left[\frac{C}{y} \left(1 - \frac{1}{(1+y/m)^N} \right) + \frac{1}{(1+y/m)^N} \right] - w\frac{C}{m}$$

Note that when coupon rate equals yield, $C = y$, the term in the square brackets becomes 1, and the formula simplifies to

$$P_{Clean} = (1 + y/m)^w - w\frac{y}{m}$$

On coupon payment dates the accrued fraction w equals zero, and the price is *par*: $P = 1 = 100\%$. In between coupon payment dates, even when $C = y$, the price is not exactly par. This is because the above formula is based on the *Street Convention* where fractional periods are adjusted using the formula suggested by compounded interest rates: $1/(1 + y/m)^{-w} = (1 + y/m)^w$. If instead, we had used *simple* interest rates for first period, we would get the clean price using the *Treasury Convention* (TC):

$$P_{Clean,TC} = P_{Dirty,TC} - w\frac{C}{m}$$

$$= (1 + wy/m)\left[\frac{C}{y}\left(1 - \frac{1}{(1 + y/m)^N}\right) + \frac{1}{(1 + y/m)^N}\right] - w\frac{C}{m}$$

and then the price of a bond when $C = y$ would be par (100%) at all times.

Figure 1.2 shows the evolution of the clean and dirty prices for a 2y 5% semiannual coupon bond as we get closer to maturity while holding yields constant for 3 yield scenarios: $y = 7.5\%$ leading to a *Premium bond* $(C < y)$, $y = 2.5\%$ leading to a *Discount* bond $(C > y)$, and $y = 5\%$ leading to a par $(C = y)$ bond. Notice the *Pull-To-Par Effect* for the bond regardless of the assumed yield scenario: A discount bond gets pulled *up* to par, while a premium bond gets pulled *down* to par.

In order to flesh out the calculation details, for the remainder of the chapter, we will focus on the 2y U.S. Treasury note issued on 1-Oct-2007, with *CUSIP* (Committee on Uniform Security Identification Procedures) number 912828HD5, shown in Table 1.1. From Announcement date till Auction date, these 2-year notes will be considered *When-Issued* (WI) and trade based on yield since the coupon rate is only known at Auction time. After the auction they start trading based on price, and become the *current* 2y-notes, replacing the old 2y-note. Until the Issue Date, they will have a forward settlement date of Mon 1-Oct-2007, and thereafter they will have a $T + 1$ settlement date. The 4 coupon dates are: 31-Mar-2008, 30-Sep-2008, 31-Mar-2009, and final coupon and redemption on 30-Sep-2009. Note that U.S. treasury securities follow *month-end* convention, so if the maturity is at month-end, then the (assumed) coupon dates are also at month-end (March-31st, rather than March-30th).

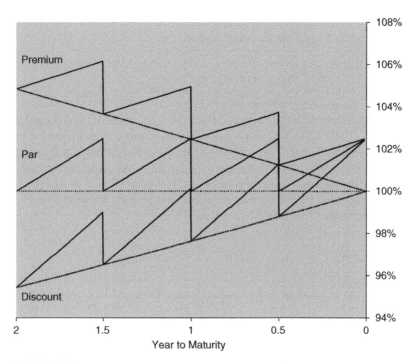

FIGURE 1.2 Clean/Dirty Price Evolution for a 2y 5% Semiannual Coupon Bond in Unchanging Yield Scenarios

Example 1. On Tue, 2-Oct-2007, the current 2y U.S. Treasury (CT2 from now on) is trading at clean price of 100-02+ for (T+1) settlement date of Wed 3-Oct-2007:

$$P_{Clean} = (100 + 2.5/32)/100 = 100.078125\% = 1.00078125$$

TABLE 1.1 *Current* U.S. 2y Treasury Note for Oct 2007

CUSIP	912828 HD 5
Announcement Time	Mon, 24-Sep-2007, 11 a.m.
Auction Size	$18 Billion
Auction Date	Wed, 26-Sep-2007, 1 p.m.
Maturity Date	30-Sep-2009
Issue Date	Mon 1-Oct-2007
Dated Date (Interest starts accruing)	Sun 30-Sep-2007
Coupon Rate (Determined at Auction Time)	4% Semiannual

Although this bond's issue date is Mon, 1-Oct-2007, it starts accruing interest (*dated date*) on Sun, 30-Sep-2007, and hence has 3 days of accrued interest on settlement date. U.S. Treasury securities use the "Actual/Actual" convention for fractional first periods and accrued interest:

$$
w = \frac{\text{Actual number of days from LastCpn/DatedDate to Settlement Date}}{\text{Actual number of days in current coupon period}}
$$

$$
= \frac{\text{3-Oct-2007} - \text{30-Sep-2007}}{\text{31-Mar-2008} - \text{30-Sep-2007}} = \frac{3}{183}
$$

Its accrued interest is then $(.04/2) \times (3/183)$ and the dirty price is:

$$
P_{Dirty} = P_{Clean} + w \times C/2 = 1.00078125 + (3/183) \times .04/2 = 1.001109119
$$

Its semiannual yield (3.95866%) is computed by backing out (trial and error, or Newton-Raphson root-search method) the y that solves:

$$
1.001109119 = \frac{.04/2}{(1+y/2)^{1-w}} + \frac{.04/2}{(1+y/2)^{2-w}}
$$

$$
+ \frac{.04/2}{(1+y/2)^{3-w}} + \frac{.04/2}{(1+y/2)^{4-w}}
$$

$$
+ \frac{1}{(1+y/2)^{4-w}}
$$

$$
= (1+y/2)^{\frac{3}{183}} \left[\frac{.04}{y} \left(1 - \frac{1}{(1+y/2)^4} \right) + \frac{1}{(1+y/2)^4} \right]
$$

If you bought \$50M face/principal of this treasury on 2-Oct-2007, then you need to pay \$50,055,455.94 ($= 50,000,000 \times 1.001109119$) to seller on 3-Oct-2007 by 3 p.m. (before the Fed-Wire closes).

True Yield

The standard bond price formula assumes that coupons are paid on specific dates, even if they are holidays. In reality, a coupon is paid on the next good business day after the assumed coupon date. Since one is paying the same amount up front, but getting the coupons later, the standard yield backed out from the bond equation potentially overstates the yield. This overstatement is more relevant for short-term bonds (sometimes referred to as *short coupons*), say with maturity less than 2 years, and especially when the maturity date falls on a holiday, and can be as high as a few basis points. *True yield* (sometimes referred to as yield adjusted for *bad days*) is the typically lowered yield when actual payment dates are taken into consideration. The usual formula used to back out the true yield is:

$$P_{Clean} = \sum_{i=1}^{N} \frac{C/m}{(1 + y/m)^{t_i}} + \frac{1}{(1 + y/m)^{t_N}} - wC/m$$

where

$$t_i = \frac{\text{Number of Days from Settlement Date to } T_i}{365/m}$$

and T_i is the i-th true (holiday-adjusted) future payment date. Note that this replaces the exponent term for the i-th cash flow from $i - w$ to t_i, and can lead to a potentially different yield, even if all nominal payment dates are good business days. For example, for the CT2 in Example 1, even though all its nominal coupon dates fall on good business days, the True Yield using the above formula gives 3.95316% versus 3.95866% using the standard formula. As such, the above formula should mainly be used to back out the true yield *adjustment*.

Zero-Coupon Bonds

Treasuries can be stripped into principal (P-strip) and coupon strips (C-strip) to come up with single cash flows. One can buy these as zero-coupon bonds by paying an up-front fee (quoted price) and receiving the principal at maturity. Their yield is quoted using the standard bond equation, but with the coupon set to zero:

$$P_{Zero} = \frac{1}{1 + y/m^{N-w}}$$

where N is the number of hypothetical coupon periods left if the bond was paying periodic (m coupons per year) coupons, and w is the hypothetical accrued fraction. Similar to coupon bonds, we can also compute the true yield of zeros.

PV01, PVBP, CONVEXITY

Much space is wasted in the bond gospels on Macaulay Duration (sometimes abbreviated to Duration): "In 1938, Frederick Macaulay constructed a measure.... In practice, nobody cares about Macaulay Duration! All we care about is the price sensitivity to changes in interest rates, that is, the derivative of the PV to yields/rates. It is the standard to consider price changes due to 1 basis-point (bp, $0.0001 = 1\%$ of 1%) move in yields/rates, giving rise to *PV01*: present value of 1 basis-point increase in interest rates, sometimes called *risk*, or DV01 for dollar-centric folks. For a bond,

$$PV01 = \frac{dP}{dy} \times 0.0001$$

In Bond-land, PV01 is defined as the negative of the previous equation, so that a positive PV01 signifies a long position in the bond. We will stay with the true definition for the rest of the book, so a positive PV01 implies one is short the market.

Since accrued interest does not depend on yield y, the P in the above can either be the dirty or the clean price of a bond. A little bit of algebra gets us

$$P'(y) = (1 + y/m)^w \left[\frac{C}{y^2} \left(\frac{1}{(1 + y/m)^N} - 1 \right) + \frac{N}{m} \left(\frac{C}{y} - 1 \right) \frac{1}{(1 + y/m)^{N+1}} \right]$$
$$+ \frac{w}{m+y} P_{Dirty}(y)$$

Modified Duration is defined as the *percentage* change in bond price, that is,

$$\text{Modified Duration} = -\frac{1}{P_{Dirty}} \frac{dP}{dy}$$

and has unit of years. While it makes sense for bonds, since swaps can have zero PV, it does not extend to swaps, swaptions, ..., and that's why we will stay with PV01.

A concept similar to PV01, but not identical to it is *PVBP* : Present value of 1 bp. This is the change in the price due to changing the coupon rate by 1 bp:

$$PVBP = 0.0001 \times \frac{dP_{Dirty}}{dC}$$

Since PVBP is the *change* in price, it is equivalent to PV'ing a 1 bp per annum annuity, paid m times a year, it is also called the *Annuity Formula*:

$$PVBP = 0.0001 \times \frac{(1 + y/m)^w}{y} \left(1 - \frac{1}{(1 + y/m)^N}\right)$$

For par bonds $(C = y)$, receiving 1 bp extra in coupon is almost equivalent to yields dropping by 1 bp, and that's why PV01 and PVBP are (wrongly) used interchangeably in practice. For nonpar bonds, the difference can be significant, see Figure 1.3, and the appropriate formula should be used depending on the application.

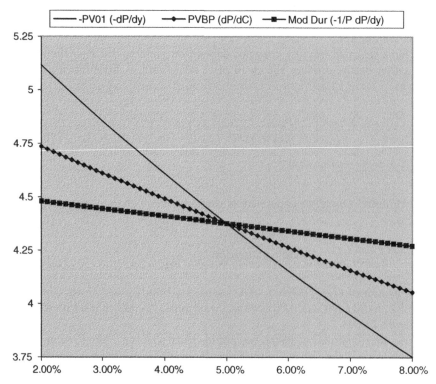

FIGURE 1.3 PV01, PVBP, Modified Duration for a 5y, 5% Semiannual Coupon Bond

The *convexity* of a bond is a measure of the curvature of the price-yield graph, and is defined as $\frac{d^2 P}{dy^2}$, that is, the rate of change of PV01:

$$
\text{Convexity} = \frac{d^2 P}{dy^2} = \frac{-w}{(m+y)^2} P_{Dirty} + \frac{w}{m+y} \frac{dP}{dy}
$$

$$
+ \frac{N(N+1-w)}{m^2} \frac{1-C/y}{(1+y/m)^{N+2-w}} - \frac{2CN/(my^2)}{(1+y/m)^{N+1-w}}
$$

$$
+ C \frac{(1+y/m)^w}{y^3} \left(1 - \frac{1}{(1+y/m)^N} \right) \left(2 - \frac{wy}{m+y} \right)
$$

PV01 and convexity can be used via a Taylor Series expansion (see Appendix A) to estimate the price change due to a small change (Δy) in yields:

$$
P(y+\Delta y) - P(y) = \frac{\partial P}{\partial y}(y)\Delta y + 1/2 \frac{\partial^2 P}{\partial y^2}(y)(\Delta y)^2 + \text{Higher Order Terms}
$$

$$
\approx \text{PV01} \times \frac{\Delta y}{0.0001} + 1/2 \times \text{Convexity} \times (\Delta y)^2
$$

In practice, one is primarily interested in the PV01, ignoring the convexity effect except for long maturity bonds, or for large rate movements. Using only the first order term in the Taylor series expansion, one gets

$$
\Delta P = P(y+\Delta y) - P(y) \approx P\,V01 \times \Delta y
$$

where Δy is expressed in basis points. The change in price, ΔP, is usually expressed in *cents*, that is, units of 1/10,000, or for a principal of \$100 = 10,000 cents. For example, when holding a \$1,000,000 face of a security, and the price changes by 5 *cents*, one has made \$1,000,000 × 5 × 0.0001 = \$500.

For U.S. Treasuries, units of 1/32 of 1% (1/3200) (also called treasury ticks, or ticks for short) are usually used. In this case, when holding a \$1,000,000 face of a bond, and the price moves by 1 tick, one has made \$1,000,000 × 1 × (1/3200) = \$312.50 = 3.125 cents. Therefore, each U.S. Treasury tick (1/32 of 1%) equals 3.125 cents.

Since we will be dealing with interest rate derivatives later, we will stay with cents, sometimes called bp's upfront, or just bp's. Using the previous first order approximation, one can relate the changes in yields to

TABLE 1.2 U.S. Treasury *Currents* for 3-Oct-2007 Settlement

U.S. Treasury	Mat. Date	Cpn Rate	Clean Price	Yield	PV01 (cents)	Mod. Dur (yrs)	Conv.
CT2	30-Sep-2009	4%	100-02+	3.95866%	1.898	1.90	4.59
CT3	15-May-2010	4.5%	100-10	3.96541%	2.483	2.41	7.47
CT5	30-Sep-2012	4.25%	100-24	4.08233%	4.495	4.46	23.43
CT10	15-Aug-2017	4.75%	102-19	4.42213%	8.050	7.80	75.76
CT30	15-May-2037	5%	109-05	4.44093%	17.457	15.72	401.58

P&L: *Each 1 bp change in yields translates to approximately PV01 cents change in value.*

Table 1.2 shows an example of PV01s and convexities of benchmark U.S. Treasuries.

Example 2. Continuing with Example 1, let us compute the above sensitivity measures for U.S. CT2 trading at 100-02+ ($y = 3.95866\%$) for settlement on 3-Oct-2007 with dirty price of 100.1109119%. Using the previous formulae ($N = 4$, $w = 3/183$, $C = .04$), we get:

$$\frac{dP}{dy} = -1.89834$$

$$\text{PV01} = 0.0001 \times \frac{dP}{dy} = -0.0189834\%$$

$$= -1.89834 \quad \text{cents}$$

$$\text{Modified Duration} = -\frac{dP/dy}{P_{Dirty}} = 1.89624 \; years$$

$$\text{PVBP} = 0.0001 \times \frac{dP}{dC} = 0.01905432\% = 1.90543 \; cents$$

$$\text{Convexity} = \frac{d^2 P}{dy^2} = 4.592691$$

We can estimate the price change due to a small, say 10 bp, change in yields:

$$P(y + 10 \; bp) - P(y) \approx PV01 \times 10 + 1/2 \times \text{Convexity} \times (0.10\%)^2$$

$$= -0.0189834\% \times 10 + 1/2(4.592691)(0.10\%)^2$$

$$= -0.18960\%$$

leading to an estimate of $P(y + 10\ bp) = 99.88852049\%$. Compared to actual $P(y + 10\ bp) = 99.88852026\%$, we see that the difference is quite small (0.0007% of 1/32nd, or \$0.22 for \$100M face!).

PV01 is the basic measure of market risk, either for outright purchase and sale of U.S. treasuries, or for trades based on the *slope* of the yield curve.

Example 3. Yield Curve Trade Using prices in Table 1.2, we observe that the 2's-10's curve is trading at 46.35 bp ($= 4.42213\% - 3.95866\%$), which a trader might feel is too flat compared to their historical relationship. The trader can express a yield curve steepening view by buying CT2 and selling CT10 in PV01-equal amounts, that is, 4.2413 ($= 8.050/1.898$) units of CT2 for each unit of CT10. For example, if one buys \$424.13M CT2 versus selling \$100M of CT10, one is long a spread-PV01 risk of \$80,500 ($= \$100M \times 8.050 \times 0.0001$) per each 1 bp steepening of 2's-10's treasury yield curve.

Another common trade is a *butterfly* trade which is a way of expressing a view on the difference between slopes of the yield curve at different points, that is, on the *curvature* of the yield curve. For example, if one feels that 2's/5's is too flat compared to 5's/10's (5-year yields are too low in relationship to 2y, 10y yields), one can buy a 2-5-10 butterfly by buying CT2, selling CT5, and buying CT10 so that each spread leg (CT2-CT5, CT5-CT10) is PV01-equivalent.

Example 4. Butterfly Trade Using prices in Table 1.2, the 2-5-10 butterfly is trading at

$$-21.6\ bp = (4.42213\% - 4.08233\%) - (4.08233\% - 3.95866\%)$$

which a trader might think is too low compared to history. A simple trade would be to buy the butterfly by buying the 2's-5's curve and selling 5's-10's curve in equal spread-PV01 amounts: buy N_1 CT2 versus selling N_2 CT5 (2's-5's curve), while simultaneously buying N_2 CT5 versus buying N_3 CT10 (5's-10's curve), so that

$$N_2/N_1 = PV01(2y)/PV01(5y)$$
$$N_2/N_3 = PV01(10y)/PV01(5y)$$

For example, for a \$100M sale of CT5, one has to buy \$118.38M CT2 and \$27.92M CT10 for an equal-weight butterfly trade.

A more common trade is to volatility-weight each curve leg. For example, if a regression analysis shows that for each 1 bp movement in 2's-5's, there is typically a 0.8p movement in 5's-10's, then one would weight the butterfly so that

$$PV01(2's - 5's)/PV01(5's - 10's) = 0.8$$

that is, one has to overweight the 5's-10's leg due to its lower volatility, resulting in purchase of \$105.23M CT2 and \$31.02M CT10 for a sale of \$100M CT5.

In general, a *regression-weighted butterfly* between 3 points of yield curve is expressed as

$$\frac{m}{1+m} \times (y_2 - y_1) - \frac{1}{1+m} \times (y_3 - y_2)$$

where m is the regression slope of $y_3 - y_2$ versus $y_2 - y_1$:

$$(y_3 - y_2) = m(y_2 - y_1) + b + Error$$

with the principals satisfying:

$$N_1 = \frac{PV01_2}{PV01_1} \times \frac{m}{1+m} N_2$$

$$N_3 = \frac{PV01_2}{PV01_3} \times \frac{1}{1+m} N_2$$

REPO, REVERSE REPO

While *real-money* investors buy/sell bonds by tendering/receiving the requisite funds on settlement date, most trading desks will instead borrow/lend the requisite funds by entering into a *repo, reverse repo* transaction, that is, a collateralized loan. A typical purchase of a bond is then followed by *selling it in repo*: lending the bond, and borrowing funds in a loan collateralized by that bond. A typical short sale of a bond is followed by *buying it in a reverse repo*: borrowing the bond and lending funds in a loan collateralized by that bond.

Let us consider a typical overnight repo transaction for a 1-day holding (buy at T/sell at T + 1) of a UST bond; longer holding periods can *conceptually* be reduced to this case via a series of 1-day holding periods, where the bond position is closed out and reopened at same price on each intermediate date. Of course, if the plan is to hold the bond for a period longer than one day, then one can finance it in a *term repo* transaction.

On trade date T, a dealer buys a UST bond from Bank A for the gross price of $P(T)$ for settlement $T_1 = T + 1$, which means that the transaction has to be settled by 3 p.m. (when the Fed-Wire closes) on T_1. On the morning of T_1—typically before noon for *cash*/same-day settle to secure funds by that day's 3 p.m.—the repo desk will *fund* this position by selling/delivering the bond as collateral for an overnight $[T_1, T_2 = T_1 + 1]$ loan for $P(T_1^*)$ to a repo counterparty, while simultaneously agreeing to buy the bond back on T_2 for $P(T_1^*) \times (1 + r/360)$. The *repo rate* r is the financing cost of this bond and follows the money market convention in each currency, Act/360 in USD. Notice that the amount owed to Bank A $P(T)$ on T_1-settlement does not necessarily equate the amount of funds secured by the repo desk $P(T_1^*)$ for that time, resulting in residual cash balance, $P(T_1^*) - P(T)$, which is typically funded at some rate r_{Cash} different than the repo rate r. After a 1-day holding period, on T_1 the dealer closes out the position by selling it to Bank B for the gross sale price of $P(T_1)$, to be settled at T_2.

The sequence of cash flows on the *opening leg*, settled on T_1 by 3 p.m. are as follows: Receive bond from Bank A, Deliver cash $P(T)$ to Bank A, Receive cash $P(T_1^*)$ from repo counterparty in exchange for delivering bond as collateral. The sequence of cash flows on the *closing leg*, settled on T_2 by 3 p.m. are as follows: Pay $P(T_1^*) \times (1 + r/360)$ to repo counterparty, receive bond (collateral) back, deliver bond for $P(T_1)$ to bond-buyer (Bank B), and clear the residual cash balance

$$[P(T_1^*) - P(T)] \times r_{\text{Cash}}/360$$

resulting in a net P&L of:

$$\text{Daily P\&L} = [P(T_1) - P(T)] - P(T_1^*) \times r/360$$
$$+ (P(T_1^*) - P(T)) \times r_{\text{Cash}}/360$$

If only the purchase price is financed, $P(T) = P(T_1^*)$, then the daily P&L becomes

$$\text{Daily P\&L} = [P(T_1) - P(T)] - P(T) \times r/360$$

that is, the net of the *capital gains*, $P(T_1) - P(T)$, versus the (repo) *financing cost*. In practice, since the residual cash term—even if the amount borrowed is not exactly the purchase price—is very small compared to the other terms, it is usually ignored, and the previous simplified equation is considered as the daily P&L of a bond.

In a repo transaction, the terms *seller, buyer, lending, borrowing* can be confusing. The best way to remember is to follow the security (bond) at the opening leg of the transaction. After buying a bond, it is funded in a repo transaction by *selling, lending* it, and receiving cash. As such, the bond buyer becomes the repo-seller. Conversely, after a short sale of a bond, one has to *buy, borrow, reverse-in* the bond from a bond-lender in exchange for lending them cash. Hence, the expression "Lend Low, Borrow High": When *lending* the bond and receiving cash, the lower the repo rate, the better; when *borrowing* (reversing-in) the bond and lending cash, the higher (reverse-)repo rate, the better.

Example 5. Continuing with U.S. Treasury CT2, let a leveraged investor buy $100M face of the bond at a clean price of $P = 100 - 02+$, on trade date Tue, 2-Oct-2007, so he owes $100,110,911.89 to the seller by 3 p.m. on settlement date Wed, 3-Oct-2007. On Wed morning, when the repo trader is looking to fund this position, let us assume that the bond has increased in value and is trading at clean price of 100-05, and the repo trader funds the $100M position overnight (Wed night) in a *cash* (same day) settlement repo agreement at a repo rate of 3.4%. The gross price based on Wed clean price 100-05 for Wed settlement (not Thu, since cash-settlement on repo) is:

$$\$100M \times [(1 + 0.05/32) + 3/183 \times .04/2] = \$100,189,036.89$$

By 3 p.m. on Wed, $100M face of the bonds are received for payment of $P(T) = \$100,110,911.89$, and then delivered to repo counterparty in exchange for a loan of $P(T_1^*) = \$100,189,036.89$, incurring a positive cash balance (overborrowing) of $78,125. Let the overnight cash rate applied to this balance be the Fed-Funds rate, say 3.50%.

During the trading day on Wed, assume the bond is increasing in price, and the leveraged investor decides to sell the $100M face of the bond at clean price of 100-08, for Thu, 4-Oct-2007 settlement. The gross price to be received on Thu 4-Oct-2007, by 3 p.m., is

$$\$100M \times [(1 + .08/32) + 4/183 \times .04/2] = \$100,293,715.85$$

On Thu by 3 p.m., the repo counterparty delivers the bonds back, receives

$$\$100,198,499.18 = \$100,189,036.89 \times (1 + .034/360)$$

and the bonds are then delivered to the buyer after receiving $100,293.715.85. The capital gains are:

$$\$100,293,715.85 - \$100,110,911.89 = \$182,803.96$$

while the repo financing cost is $9,462.30, and the interest on positive cash balance is $7.60, resulting in 1-day P&L of $173,349.26 = $182,803.96 − $9,462.30 + $7.60.

FORWARD PRICE/YIELD, CARRY, ROLL-DOWN

The price-yield formulae were based on *spot* ($T + 1$ for U.S.) transactions. If instead one wants to agree on a *Forward Price* today, but take ownership of a bond at a later (forward) date, one is entering into a *forward* transaction. Since the forward price has to be set today, one resorts to a cash-and-carry argument to arrive at the fair forward price.

The forward seller can conceptually buy the bond today, finance it to the forward delivery date, and deliver the bond to buyer, receive the previous agreed-upon forward price, settle the financing cost, and be free. Also, if there are any coupon payments before the forward date, then a (fair) seller needs to future-value these coupon payments to the forward date. Hence the fair forward price, FP, of a bond is:

$$FP_{Dirty} = P_{Dirty} + \text{Financing cost} - FV(\text{Coupon Income})$$

As bonds are usually financed via repo markets, the future value of any coupon income is calculated using the repo rate, r. Hence, for UST bonds, we have:

$$FP_{Dirty}(T_{Fwd}) = P_{Dirty} \times (1 + r\frac{T_{Fwd} - T_s}{360}) - \sum_{i=1}^{M} \frac{C}{2}(1 + r\frac{T_{Fwd} - T_i}{360})$$

where $T_1, \ldots, T_M$ are the payment dates of the intermediate coupons (if any) from the settlement date T_s to the forward date T_{Fwd}.

The *forward yield* is the implied YTM of the forward price using the forward settlement date.

The *price carry* (sometimes called dollar-carry, or just carry), is the difference between the current (spot) clean price and the forward clean price:

$$\text{Price Carry} = P_{Clean} - FP_{Clean}(T_{Fwd})$$

while the *yield carry* (again sometimes just called carry), is the difference between the forward and spot yields:

$$\text{Yield Carry} = \text{Forward Yield} - \text{Spot Yield}$$

Example 6. Continuing with UST CT2 with $P = 100 - 02+$, $y = 3.95866\%$ with gross price of 100.11091% as of the spot settlement date 3-Oct-2007, let us compute its forward price/yield 6 months forward, for forward settlement date 3-Apr-2008, using an Act/360 repo rate of 3.75%. Note that there is a coupon payment on 31-Mar-2008 between the spot and forward settlement dates. We have

$$FP_{Dirty}(\text{3-Apr-2008}) = 1.001109119 \times \left(1 + 3.75\% \frac{N_1}{360}\right) - \frac{4\%}{2}\left(1 + 3.75\% \frac{N_2}{360}\right)$$

$$= 100.018651\%$$

where $N_1 = 183$ is the number of days from spot to forward settlement dates, and $N_2 = 3$ is the number of days from next coupon date to forward date. On the forward date, the accrued interest would be for 3 days (31-Mar-2008 to 3-Apr-2008), out of 183 days (31-Mar-2008 to 30-Sep-2008) and is computed as

$$w_f = \frac{4\%}{2}\frac{3}{183} = 0.032787\%$$

leading to the forward clean price of

$$FP_{Clean}(3 - Apr - 2008) = FP_{Dirty}(3 - Apr - 2008) - w_f = 99.985864\%$$

and forward yield of 4.00963%.

If there are no intermediate coupon payments between settlement date and forward date, we can simplify the general forward price formula as:

$$FP_{Clean}(T_{Fwd}) = P_{Clean} + r\frac{T_{Fwd} - T_s}{360} - \frac{C}{m}\frac{T_{Fwd} - T_s}{D}$$

where D is the actual number of days in the current coupon period.

If the yield carry is positive, then one can buy the bond spot, finance it in repo to forward date, and as long as its actual yield on the forward date is lower than the forward yield, one can close out the position by selling the bond for a net profit. Hence, the yield carry is a measure of the cushion in yield movements (from spot) for a long position in this bond to be profitable. A high positive carry is a signal that yields have to move by a lot from their spot (today's) values before a long position in a bond loses money. Note that when analyzing carry strategies, one should focus on yield rather than price carry as the latter ignores the pull-to-par effect.

In general, for a positively sloped yield curve where spot yields are higher than repo rates (after adjusting for the difference in their quote convention, Act/Act vs. Act/360), purchasing a bond and earning the higher yield while financing it via the lower repo rate leads to *positive carry*. This investment strategy is sometimes called "riding the yield curve" which in essence is equivalent to betting against the forward yields: the ride is profitable if future yields turn out to be lower than what was implied by the forwards.

Yield carry is sometimes called the amount of unfavorable *parallel shift* in the yield curve before one loses money. This is not exactly correct, since it ignores the *roll-down effect*, that is, it ignores the fact that the bond on the forward date has a shorter maturity than when bought today. Therefore one is comparing the spot yield of a longer bond to the forward yield of a shorter bond. To compare apples to apples, one then computes the *yield roll-down* (sometimes just called roll-down) as the difference between spot yield of the bond, to the spot yield of another bond whose maturity is shorter by the length of the investment horizon (Forward Date - Spot Date):

$$\text{``n'' – Month Roll-Down} = y(T) - y(T - \text{``n''-Months})$$

where T is the maturity of the bond under consideration, and $y(T)$ its YTM. The amount of parallel shift protection is the sum of yield carry and yield roll-down.

Example 7. Continuing with U.S. Treasury CT2 with clean price quoted at $P = 100 - 02+$, $y = 3.95866\%$ on trade date 2-Oct-2007, and settlement date 3-Oct-2007, let us compute its forward price/yield 3 months forward, for forward settlement date 3-Jan-2008, using a repo rate of 3.5%, quoted Act/360. Since there is no intermediate coupon between settlement date and forward date, we can compute the forward clean price as

$$FP_{Clean}(3\text{-Jan-}2008) = P_{Clean} + 3.5\% \frac{N}{360} - \frac{4\%}{2} \frac{N}{D}$$

where N is the actual number of holding days (3-Oct-2007 to 3-Jan-2008), and D is the number of days in the current coupon period (30-Sep-2007 to

31-Mar-2007). We get $N = 92$, $D = 183$, and

$$FP_{Clean}(\text{3-Jan-2008}) = 1.00078125 + 3.5\% \frac{92}{360} - \frac{4\%}{2} \frac{92}{183}$$
$$= 0.99967105$$

leading to a forward yield of 4.01678%. The price carry is 0.11102% or 3.55 ticks, and the yield carry is 5.81 bp's. If there was a bond today with maturity 30-Jun-2009, with a yield of 3.92866% (3 bp's lower), then the 3m-roll-down would be computed as 3 bp, for a total of 8.81 bp parallel shift (carry + roll-down) protection.

A quick formula to estimate yield carry is

$$\text{Forward Yield} - \text{Spot Yield} \approx \left(\text{Spot Yield} - \text{Repo Rate} \times \frac{365}{360} \right) \times \frac{\Delta T}{PV01 - \Delta T},$$

where ΔT is the length of holding period in years, and 365/360 is to convert the Act/360 repo rate to Act/365 which is an approximation for Act/Act. Applying this formula to Example 7, we estimate yield carry as

$$\left(3.95866\% - 3.5\% \times \frac{365}{360} \right) \times \frac{0.25}{1.898 - 0.25} = 6.22 \; bp$$

which is not that far from the correct value (5.81 bp's). Note that in this approximate formula, we need to use yields rather than coupon rates to incorporate the pull-to-par effect.

Repo-Adjusting Specials

When the repo rate for a certain treasury issue is different (typically lower) than other treasury issues, it is said to be trading *special*. This is usually due to high demand for a particular issue that has been shorted and needs to be borrowed in a reverse-repo. Since the lender of the issue is borrowing money, the extra demand for the particular treasury drives down the repo rate, and he can pay a lower interest for temporarily availing the scarce treasury issue. For all nonspecial treasury issues, their repo rate is the *general collateral* (GC) rate.

Many investors demand to be invested in *current* treasuries (2y, 5y, 10y, . . .) and roll their holdings into a new current after each auction. Therefore, current treasuries usually trade special until they are replaced by a new current, when they become the old issue. For example, since new 2y treasury notes are issued every month, the current CT2 is replaced by a new issue in 1 month, and becomes the *Old 2*, and after another month becomes the *Old Old 2, double-old*, and so on.

Issues trading special are generally bid up, and hence their yields are lower than comparable nonspecial issues. For relative-value strategies, when comparing yields of a special issue versus comparable non-special issues, the yield can artificially appear to be lower. A common method to adjust for its specialness is to repo-adjust its yield as follows: One first assumes that after passage of some time, the issue will not trade special any more and will join the GC pool. For example, it is plausible to assume that the current CT2 will not trade special in 3 months when it has become the triple-old 2y. With this assumption, one computes the 3m-forward price of CT2 using its 3m special term repo rate, and then backs out an implied price today if instead one had used the 3m GC term repo rate. The resulting price is then converted to yield, and is called its *repo-adjusted yield*.

Example 8. Continuing with U.S. Treasury CT2 with clean price of $P = 100 - 02+$, $y = 3.95866\%$ for settlement date 3-Oct-2007, its forward price for forward settlement date 3-Jan-2008, using a repo rate of 3.5% is 0.99967105 ($y = 4.01678\%$). If the 3m GC rate is 3.75%, we can back out its today's clean price that would give the same forward price:

$$P_{Clean} = 0.99967105 - 3.75\% \frac{92}{360} - \frac{4\%}{2} \frac{92}{183}$$
$$= 1.000142$$

resulting in repo-adjusted yield of 3.99233%, which is 3.37 bp higher than its unadjusted yield (3.95866%). A quick and dirty way of getting a ballpark estimate for the adjustment is

$$\text{Yield Adj.} \approx (\text{GC Rate} - \text{Special Rate}) \times \frac{365}{360} \times \frac{\text{Holding Period (yrs)}}{P\,V01}$$
$$= (3.75\% - 3.50\%) \times \frac{365}{360} \times \frac{0.25}{1.898}$$
$$= 3.43\ bp$$

CHAPTER **2**

Swaps: It's Still About Discounting

A plain-vanilla fixed-for-floating *Interest Rate Swap* (IRS) is an over-the-counter (OTC) agreement between 2 counterparties to periodically exchange interest payments on a hypothetical loan, where one counterparty, the fixed-rate payer, pays a periodic fixed coupon, while the other counterparty, the floating rate payer, pays a variable amount that periodically resets on a benchmark interest rate index, for example, 3-month London Interbank Offered Rate (Libor) for USD, which is considered to be the funding index for banks. As opposed to a bond, each counterparty only pays the *interest payments* on the hypothetical loan, and no principal payment is made either at the beginning or end of the swap, hence the name *interest rate swap*. Figure 2.1 shows the cash flows of a simple 1-year USD swap with fixed-rate C.

When talking about plain-vanilla fixed-for-floating swaps—*swaps* from now on—the point of reference is the fixed rate. If one is receiving the fixed rate (floating-rate payer), one is said to be *receiving in a swap* or simply *receiving*. Similarly if one is the fixed-rate payer, then one is *paying in a swap*, or simply *paying*. Receiving in a swap is akin to being long a bond, since one is receiving a coupon and paying periodic financing (3m-Libor rather than overnight or term repo). Similarly, paying in a swap is akin to being short a bond.

The stream of cash flows made by each counterparty (fixed/floating payer) is referred to as a *leg*, and a swap's cash flows are considered to be made up of a *fixed leg* and a *floating leg*. For each leg of a swap, the first/last date that interest begins/ends accruing is called the *effective date* and *maturity date* respectively. Commonly both legs of a swap have the same Effective and Maturity dates, and these are then referred to as the swap's effective/maturity dates. Also the interest payments are based on hypothetical loans with same principal, referred to as the *notional* of the swap.

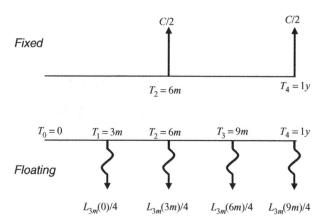

FIGURE 2.1   Simplified Cash Flows of a 1y USD Swap

Each leg of a swap is comprised of contiguous *calculation periods*, so a 1y USD swap has 2 semiannual calculation periods on the fixed leg, and 4 quarterly calculation periods on the floating leg. To value an IRS, one needs to compute the net PV of the fixed and floating legs. While this is straightforward for the fixed leg as it is a series of known cash flows, pricing the floating leg seems to require forecasting the unknown payment, and then discounting it to today. We shall soon see that this is not the case, and an IRS can be priced without resorting to *forecasting* future interest rates.

DISCOUNT FACTOR CURVE, ZERO CURVE

As in any other fixed-income product, pricing a swap boils down to discounting the series of future cash flows for each leg. As opposed to a bond where the PV of all cash flows are related to a single yield by making a flat yield assumption, in Swap-land the term structure of interest rates is respected, that is, it is recognized that deposits for different terms/maturities earn different interest rates, and there is no *single* interest rate or yield-to-maturity that is applicable to *all* cash flows. The collection of interest rates for all different terms is referred to as the *term structure* of interest rates, and is typically represented as a *curve*, showing the dependence (graph) of interest rates versus maturity.

The purest way of representing the term structure of interest rate is via a discount factor curve that reflects the counterparties' funding. Let $D(T)$ denote the present value of a dollar to be received in time $T \geq 0$ based on our financing. Then $D(0) = 1$, and as long as interest rates cannot become negative, $D(\cdot)$ is a nonincreasing function—a dollar earlier is better than a dollar later—that is, $dD(T)/dT \leq 0$

$$(0 \leq T_1 \leq T_2) \qquad 1 = D(0) \geq D(T_1) \geq D(T_2)$$

Other names for this curve are zero-coupon bond price (ZCBP) curve, discount curve, and discount function. Once we have this curve, we could in principle price any stream of *known* (and some unknown!) future cash flows.

While quite useful and necessary for pricing future cash flows, a specification (or a graph) of the discount curve does not reveal much to the naked eye. For example, knowing that the price of a 1-year dollar is 95 cents ($D(1y) = 0.95$), and $D(2y) = 0.90$, does not say much about the relative attractiveness of these prices. Consequently, we measure the rate of return of these 2 investments by computing their yield-to-maturity. The price of a T-dollar is $D(T)$, or equivalently, a dollar invested today will be worth $1/D(T)$ at future time T. Assuming periodic compounding of m times a year (semiannual $m = 2$ for U.S.) at a constant reinvestment yield $y(T)$, we have:

$$(1 + y(T)/m)^{mT} = 1/D(T)$$

The yields $y(T)$ are called the *zero* rates. Massaging the previous equation gives

$$D(T) = \frac{1}{(1 + y(T)/m)^{mT}} \qquad \Leftrightarrow \qquad y(T) = m(D(T)^{\frac{-1}{mT}} - 1)$$

Therefore, for USD ($m = 2$), $D(1y) = 0.95$ is equivalent to $y(1) = 5.19567\%$ and $D(2y) = 0.90$ implies $y(2) = 5.33802\%$, so a 2-year investment has a higher return than a 1-year investment. A graph of $y(T)$ versus the maturity T is called the *zero curve*.

As we increase the compounding frequency, we get *continuously compounded zero rates*:

$$D(T) = \lim_{m \to \infty} \frac{1}{(1 + y(T)/m)^{mT}} = e^{-Ty_c(T)} \qquad \Leftrightarrow \qquad y_c(T) = -\frac{1}{T} \ln D(T)$$

FORWARD RATE CURVE

While the zero curve gives good information about the market *average rates* from today to any future date, one can extract even more information from it (or the equivalent of the discount curve) via *forward rates*. A forward rate-lock agreement is an agreement for a loan starting in the future, but with the interest rate of the loan agreed upon today. If both counterparties to the loan agree on some rate, and shake hands on the loan with *no exchange* of money today, that rate is called the break-even or *forward rate*. One might think that in order to come up with it, we ought to have a good idea as to what the future interest rates would be. After all, if we agreed to some rate today and in future the prevailing interest rates were very different, one side would be very happy, while the other side would feel foolish, and unemployed.

Before losing all hope though, we can appeal to a simple replication argument to compute forward rates. Specifically, assume that the underlying future loan is for the period $[T_1, T_2]$ in the future, and the interest is computed on a simple basis. Starting with \$1 today, it will be worth $FV(T_1) = 1/D(T_1)$ at T_1, which can then be reinvested at the locked rate $f([T_1, T_2])$ until T_2, so the terminal value of \$1 investment is

$$1/D(T_1) \times (1 + f([T_1, T_2]) \times \Delta T)$$

at T_2, where ΔT is the duration of the loan period in years according to the rate's day-count. Alternatively, a \$1 investment can be guaranteed to be worth $FV(T_2) = 1/D(T_2)$ at T_2. Lack of arbitrage requires that these should be worth the same amount in the future:

$$\frac{1}{D(T_1)} \times (1 + f([T_1, T_2]) \times \Delta T) = \frac{1}{D(T_2)}$$

or equivalently,

$$D(T_2) = D(T_1) \times \frac{1}{1 + f([T_1, T_2]) \times \Delta T}$$

leading to the following formula for simple forward rates:

$$f([T_1, T_2]) = \frac{D(T_1)/D(T_2) - 1}{\Delta T}$$

A similar argument leads to

$$f_c([T_1, T_2]) = \frac{\ln(D(T_1)/D(T_2))}{\Delta T}$$

if the rate f_c is quoted with continuous compounding.

For a given tenor/term, ΔT, say 3 months, a graph of $f([T, T + \Delta T])$ versus T, is called the *forward-ΔT rate curve*.

If there is no uncertainty about future interest rates, say if God came and told us what the 3-month financing rates would be in 3 months and every 3 months thereafter, then the forward-3m rates have to equal these God-given known rates. If not, for any quarterly period, one would borrow at the lower rate (whichever one: locked rate or God-given rate), and lend at the other (higher) rate, creating a sure profit. *The forward rate curve then is the implied path of short-term rates if interest rates are deterministic.*

In the presence of uncertainty, the realized future interest rates can differ from the previously-locked forward rates. For realistic (random) interest rates, the forward rate curve can still be interpreted as the *expected* future interest rates; however, this interpretation is only a first-order understanding of them, and further qualifications need to be made.

Forward Rates and Discount Factors

We saw that knowledge of the discount factor curve determines all forward rates. Conversely, given a sequence of forward rates spanning a series of dates $0 = T_0 < T_1 < T_2 < \ldots$, one can iteratively use the above relationship to compute discount factors: $D(T_0) = D(0) = 1$,

$$D(T_{n+1}) = 1 \times \frac{1}{1 + f([T_0, T_1])\Delta T_0} \times \cdots \times \frac{1}{1 + f([T_n, T_{n+1}])\Delta T_n}$$

$$= \prod_{i=0}^{n} \frac{1}{1 + f([T_i, T_{i+1}])\Delta T_i} \qquad \Delta T_i = T_{i+1} - T_i$$

using simple rates, or

$$D(T_{n+1}) = e^{-\sum_{i=0}^{n} f_c([T_i, T_{i+1}])\Delta T_i}$$

for continuously compounded forward rates. Once again, the Forward Rate curve and the discount factor curve are interchangeable, and knowledge of one completely determines the other.

Instantaneous Forward Rates

If we let the period of a forward loan go to zero, we can compute the *instantaneous* forward rate, $f(T)$. Starting from simple forward rates, we have

$$
\begin{aligned}
f(T) &\equiv \lim_{\Delta T \to 0} f([T, T + \Delta T]) \\
&= \lim_{\Delta T \to 0} \frac{D(T)/D(T + \Delta T) - 1}{\Delta T} \\
&= - \lim_{\Delta T \to 0} \frac{1}{D(T + \Delta T)} \times \frac{D(T + \Delta T) - D(T)}{\Delta T} \\
&= - \frac{1}{D(T)} \frac{dD(T)}{dT} \\
&= - \frac{d}{dT} \ln D(T)
\end{aligned}
$$

We could get the same result if we started from continuously compounded forward rates:

$$
\begin{aligned}
f(T) &\equiv \lim_{\Delta T \to 0} f_c([T, T + \Delta T]) \\
&= \lim_{\Delta T \to 0} \frac{\ln(D(T)/D(T + \Delta T))}{\Delta T} \\
&= - \lim_{\Delta T \to 0} \frac{\ln D(T + \Delta T) - \ln D(T)}{\Delta T} \\
&= - \frac{d}{dT} \ln D(T)
\end{aligned}
$$

Discount factors can be recovered from instantaneous forward rates via:

$$
D(T) = e^{- \int_0^T f(u)du}
$$

Using this, we can relate instantaneous forward rates to continuously compounded zero rates, since $D(T) = e^{-Ty_c(T)}$:

$$
\begin{aligned}
f(T) &= - \frac{d}{dT} \ln D(T) \\
&= \frac{d}{dT}(Ty(T)) \\
&= y(T) + T \frac{dy_c(T)}{dT}
\end{aligned}
$$

or equivalently,

$$y_c(T) = \frac{1}{T} \int_0^T f(u)\,du$$

From the above, we observe that *zero rates are the average of forward rates.*

PAR-SWAP CURVE

With the forward rates in place, we are now ready to tackle swap valuation. Focusing on the 1y swap shown in Figure 2.1, we can easily price the fixed leg, as the fixed-payer makes 2 known semiannual payments $C/2$ with per unit notional with payments in 6 months, and 1 year's time. Armed with a discount function $D(T)$, it is easy to evaluate the fixed leg per unit notional ($T_2 = 6m$, $T_4 = 1y$):

$$PV(FixedLeg) = C/2 \times (D(T_2) + D(T_4))$$

The obligation of the float-payer and its valuation are more complex. The 1-year duration of the swap is divided into four quarterly calculation periods, $\{[T_i, T_{i+1}]\}_{i=0}^3$ where $0 = T_0 < T_1 = 3m < T_2 = 6m < \cdots < T_4 = 1y$. At the beginning of each calculation period, $[T_i, T_{i+1}]$, the prevailing 3-month floating index $L_{3m}(T_i)$, is determined (rate-fixing), accrued for 3 months, and paid at the end of that period (T_{i+1}). Specifically, at T_{i+1}, the float-payer pays $L_{3m}(T_i)/4$ which we recognize as the interest component of 3-month forward loan at rate $L_{3m}(T_i)$.

If the floating index reflects the swap counterparties' funding rate, one can replicate this interest-only portion by ensuring that one owns unit currency at T_i, and owes unit currency at T_{i+1}. In this case, one can invest the unit currency at T_i at the prevailing 3-month rate, $L_{3m}(T_i)$, and use the proceeds, $1 + L_{3m}(T_i)/4$, as follows: pay $L_{3m}/4$ to settle the floating obligation, and pay the unit principal to whom he owed unit at T_{i+1}. Therefore, the economic value of the floating payment is $D(T_i) - D(T_{i+1})$, and the value of the floating leg can be computed as:

$$PV(FloatLeg) = \sum_{i=0}^{3}(D(T_i) - D(T_{i+1}))$$

$$= D(T_0) - D(T_4)$$

per unit notional. Note that with this static replication, we do not need to know (or care) what the future interest rates will be!

Putting it all together, the value to the receiver of a 1-year swap is

$$PV(Swap) = \left[\sum_{i=1}^{2} C/2 \times D(T_{2i}) \right] - (D(T_0) - D(T_4))$$

per unit notional, while the value to the payer is the negative of the above.

In general, the value of the fixed leg of N-year swap with annual fixed-rate C paid m times per year, with effective date T_0, maturity date T_{Nm} and payment dates $T_1 < \cdots < T_{Nm}$ is:

$$C \times \sum_{i=1}^{Nm} \alpha_i D(T_i)$$

where $\alpha_i = \alpha(T_i, T_{i+1})$ is the length of each calculation period in years, according to the specified day-count for the fixed leg (for USD swaps (SA, 30/360), $\alpha_i = 1/2$). The value of the floating leg is $D(T_0) - D(T_{Nm})$, giving the following formula for the value of a receiver swap:

$$\left[C \times \sum_{i=1}^{Nm} \alpha_i D(T_i) \right] - (D(T_0) - D(T_{Nm}))$$

per unit notional.

Par-Swap Rates

A *par-swap* is a swap whose value today is zero, and the *par-swap rate* is the fixed rate of this swap. For a swap with effective date T_0, maturity date T, since the value of the floating leg is simply $D(T_0) - D(T)$, we form the calculation periods for the fixed leg, $\{T_0, \ldots, T_M = T\}$ to compute the par-swap rate, $S(T_0, T)$, as the fixed rate that makes the value of the swap zero:

$$S(T_0, T) = \frac{D(T_0) - D(T)}{\sum_{i=1}^{M} \alpha_i \times D(T_i)}$$

A graph of $S(0, T)$ versus maturity T is called the *par-swap curve*.

A typical swap is spot-starting: $(T_0 = 0)$. If its effective date is in the future, $T_0 > 0$, then it is a *forward swap*, and its par-swap rate is called the *forward (par) swap rate*.

By letting the fixed frequency go to infinity, in the limit, we get

$$\lim_{m \to \infty} S(T_0, T) = \frac{D(T_0) - D(T)}{\int_{T_0}^{T} D(u) du}$$

Swap = Bond–Par Floater

The reason for calling a swap with zero value a "par swap" is as follows: For a spot starting $(T_0 = 0)$ par swap, note that by rearranging the preceding equation, we have

$$1 = \sum_{i=1}^{M} S(0, T) \times \alpha_i \times D(T_i) + D(T)$$

The right-hand side is the value of a T-maturity coupon bond with coupon rate $S(0, T)$, where the cash flows are discounted by a series of different spot/zero rates—$D(T_i) = 1/(1 + y(T_i)/2)^{2T_i}$ for semiannual zero rates— rather than assuming a single constant yield-to-maturity y. So, $S(0, T)$ is the coupon rate of a par-bond, that is, par-coupon rate, with *discounting along the curve* rather than flat.

The receiver in a swap is therefore economically long a fixed-coupon bond at par. Hence, an N-year swap is similar to an N-year bond, with similar duration characteristics. When a swaps's fixed rate is the same as market par swap rates, its value is zero, similar to the bond being worth par if its coupon rate is the same as market yields. *Par-swap rates are analogous to bond YTMs.*

Swap Leg's Floating Payment

As long as the floating index is the same as swap counterparties' funding index, since the funding index can be locked at the forward rate, we can replace its unknown future value by its locked forward value. Simple algebra shows that

$$\begin{aligned}
PV(Float\,Payment) &= D(T_i) - D(T_{i+1}) \\
&= (D(T_i)/D(T_{i+1}) - 1) \times D(T_{i+1}) \\
&= \frac{D(T_i)/D(T_{i+1}) - 1}{-\Delta T_i} \times (\Delta T_i) \times D(T_{i+1}) \\
&= f([T_i, T_{i+1}]) \times (\Delta T_i) \times D(T_{i+1})
\end{aligned}$$

Therefore, in order to value the floating leg's payments, it *mathematically suffices* to assume that its unknown floating rate is equal to the forward rate, accruing it for ΔT_i, and discounting this *assumed* cash flow by $D(T_{i+1})$. This is the usual practice, and is referred to as *discounting the forwards*. For this method to work, one has to ensure that the floating index's tenor and day-count exactly match the floating payment's—true for plain-vanilla swaps. For other swaps, this method fails and only provides a first-order approximation, requiring further adjustment to arrive at the correct value.

CONSTRUCTION OF THE SWAP/LIBOR CURVE

We have seen that as long as the floating index is the same as our funding index (driving our discount function), all we need is the discount curve $D(T)$ to price swaps and calculate swap rates. It would be nice if the market quoted $D(T)$ directly, saving market participants a lot of grief. Sadly, it is not the case. Note that we would like to have the daily discount factors for a good number of years, say 30 years, amounting to about 10,000 daily prices. In reality, at each point of time, there are active and liquid markets for at most 40 to 50 instruments that provide information about our funding index: cash and forward rates (FRAs), futures contracts, par-swap rates. From these input instruments keyed to our funding index, we need to extract their associated 10,000 discount factors! Obviously, the solution is not unique, and there are many ways of skinning this cat.

Bootstrap Method

A standard method of constructing the curve is to *bootstrap*: Arrange the traded instruments into increasing maturity, and starting with the shortest maturity, derive the discount curve up to its maturity, and move on to the next instrument. Since the next instrument may have cash flows that precede the prior instruments's maturities, we will use the already-constructed curve for these, and estimate the remaining discount factors.

A simple example will be useful. Assume we are quoted the market rates appearing in Table 2.1.

Starting with $D(0) = 1$, since the 3-month cash rate is quoted as 5%, this implies:

$$D(3m) = \frac{1}{1 + 5\%/4} = 0.98765$$

TABLE 2.1 Inputs for Bootstrap Method

3m Cash Rate	5%
$f([3m, 6m])$	5.1%
$f([6m, 9m])$	5.2%
$f([9m, 1y])$	5.3%
2y Swap Rate	5.4%
3y Swap Rate	5.5%

Recalling the relationship between discount factors and simple forward rates, we can recursively generate $D(6m)$, $D(6m)$, $D(1y)$:

$$D(6m) = D(3m)/(1 + 5.1\%/4) = 0.97522$$
$$D(9m) = D(6m)/(1 + 5.2\%/4) = 0.96271$$
$$D(1y) = D(9m)/(1 + 5.3\%/4) = 0.95012$$

The 2-year semiannual par-swap rate is quoted as 5.4%. Relating this to discount factors we have:

$$5.4\% = \frac{1 - D(2y)}{0.5(D(6m) + D(1y) + D(18m) + D(2y))}$$

At this point, it might seem that we are stumped, since we have one equation and 2 unknowns: $D(18m)$, $D(2y)$. In a sense we are, since as we pointed out, we are trying to estimate daily discount factors (in this case for 3 years, so about 1000 of them) from a handful (6) of quoted rates. Invariably, we have to use some interpolation scheme. A simple interpolation candidate would be linear interpolation in discount factors. In this case, $D(18m) = 1/2(D(1y) + D(2y))$, resulting in a single equation and a single unknown $D(2y)$:

$$5.4\% = \frac{1 - D(2y)}{0.5(0.975 + 0.950 + 0.5(0.950 + D(2y)) + D(2y))}$$

which after a little algebra gets us $D(2y) = 0.89879$, and $D(18m) = 1/2(D(1y) + D(2y)) = 0.92445$.

Continuing along in the same vein, we have

$$(3y) = 5.5\%$$
$$= \frac{1 - D(3y)}{0.5(0.975 + 0.950 + 0.924 + 0.898 + 0.5(0.898 + D(3y)) + D(3y))}$$

TABLE 2.2 Resulting DFs, Zero Rates, Swap Rates, and Forward-6m Rates for Bootstrap Method

Maturity T (years)	Discount Factor D(T)	Zero Rate SA, y(T)	Par-Swap Rate SA, S(T)	Fwd-6m Rate f([T,T+6m])
0	1.00000			5.08187%
0.25 (3m)	0.98765	5.03125%		5.18315%
0.5 (6m)	0.97522	5.08187%	5.08188%	5.28445%
0.75 (9m)	0.96271	5.13250%		5.42438%
1	0.95012	5.18314%	5.18184%	5.55222%
1.5	0.92445	5.30609%	5.30199%	5.71076%
2	0.89879	5.40718%	5.40000%	5.63691%
2.5	0.87415	5.45311%	5.44480%	5.80039%
3	0.84951	5.51095%	5.50000%	

which gets us $D(3y) = 0.84951$, and $D(2.5y) = 1/2(D(2y) + D(3y)) = 0.87415$. Table 2.2 summarizes the resulting discount factors, and zero, par-swap, and forward-6m rates.

Interpolation Methods

The above interpolation method (linear in discount factors), while simple, is one of the worst interpolation methods. The metric used to make this assessment is to look at the graph of implied 1-day or 3-month forwards. This graph is discontinuous, and highly jagged, forcing one to forecast excessively high implied rates, followed by excessively low implied rates (see Figure 2.3).

There are other simple methods that somewhat alleviate this problem. One such method is linear interpolation in $Ty_c(T) = \ln D(T)$, sometimes referred to as *log-linear* or *piece wise constant forwards* or *constant-daily-forwards* (CDF) method. This method is also *minimum height*, as it results in the lowest short-term forward rates.

For any given $T_1 < T < T_2$, if we linearly interpolate in the $Ty_c(T)$ space, we have:

$$(T_1 < T < T_2) \quad Ty_c(T) = \frac{T_2 - T}{T_2 - T_1} T_1 y_c(T_1) + \frac{T - T_1}{T_2 - T_1} T_2 y_c(T_2)$$

which, since $D(T) = e^{-Ty_c(T)}$, implies

$$(T_1 < T < T_2) \quad D(T) = D(T_1) \left(\frac{D(T_2)}{D(T_1)} \right)^{\frac{T - T_1}{T_2 - T_1}}$$

Since over each segment, $Ty_c(T)$ is linear, its derivative, the instantaneous forward rate, $f(T)$, becomes constant, and a graph of it versus T looks like a staircase (with discontinuity at segment points). Forward rates of longer tenor are averages of instantaneous forward rates, and also exhibit this staircase behavior, albeit slightly smoother. Other methods are linear interpolation in zero rates ($y_c(T)$-space), which looks similar to log-linear interpolation, or cubic spline interpolation in zero rates, which results in short-term forwards that are smooth (3rd-order polynomials), since they are derivatives of $Ty_c(T)$ where $y_c(T)$ is a cubic polynomial.

While the bootstrap method combined with an interpolation scheme is the usual method to construct a discount factor curve, there are other (global) methods that would fit a curve satisfying all the input constraints, and fall into the category of constrained optimization methods. Among these are minimum length methods that minimize the total variation of the instantaneous forward curve and lead to a smooth curve. Another approach is to posit a parametric shape for the forward, zero, or par-swap curve, and optimize the free parameters according to some metric while satisfying the input constraints either exactly, or within user-specified tolerances for each constraint.

Flow or Prop: Descriptive or Normative

The question usually arises as to which one is the "best" curve build method. While it might seem that we should insist on a continuous and smooth forward curve when building a curve and discard any discontinuous method, it turns out that smooth methods result in nonintuitive hedges (see discussion of partial PV01s in Chapter 3). Therefore, *when selecting a method, one has to decide on the right tradeoff between smoothness and the sensibility of the prescribed hedges.* Because each trader may have a different opinion on where the right tradeoff is, there has yet not emerged a universally accepted curve build method.

Another consideration in the choice of curve building is its target application. For a market-maker or a flow-trading desk at a broker/dealer, the source of profit is usually the bid-offer of traded instruments. For this group, the market is always right, and the constructed curve has to completely fit all traded instruments, even if one thinks that certain instruments trade rich or cheap. This is also the requirement imposed by control groups within a broker/dealer, so that each book is marked-to-market, so that the proper liquidation value of a book can be ascertained (at least in theory). With this constraint, the constructed curve has to be *descriptive* and perfectly fit the market, whether rational or irrational.

Another motivation when building a curve can be to determine the relative fair value of traded instruments. In this paradigm, not all instruments need to fit exactly, and one requires an exact fit for a subset, while using the difference between the modeled versus the market value as a rich/cheap trading signal. This *normative* view of curve construction is used by proprietary traders because it aids in determining where an instrument *should* trade in contrast to where it *does* trade relative to some benchmark instruments.

Which Curve to Focus On?

We have seen that the discount-factor curves, zero curves, forward rate curves, and par-swap curves are all inter related, and knowledge of one allows us to construct the other ones (with some interpolation if necessary). Since a par-swap rate is effectively a weighted average of the forward rates that cover the swap period, when constructing Libor curves, it is best to keep the smoothness requirements on the forward rate curve: A smooth forward rate curve implies an even smoother par-swap curve. At the extreme, one can focus on a daily or continuous graph of instantaneous forward rates, and require these to be smooth, or without implausible jaggedness or breaks. More practically, one can set the smoothness criteria on the daily graph of overnight forward rates, that is on the daily/daily forward rate curve. As forward rates drive zero rates, which in turn drive swap rates, if the daily/daily curve is smooth, then zero-rates are also smooth, and par-swap rates even smoother.

A graph of, say daily-daily, forward rates provides good information about other forward rates. As shown in Figure 2.2, if we want to consider various rates, say as of 1y forward, then all we need to do is to focus on today's forward curve from 1y onward. By shifting today's forward curve 1y to the left, we arrive at 1y-forward curve. Starting from that curve, we can then compute various (forward) swap rates. As shown—and this happens quite often in practice—the forward curve as of any forward date is flatter than today's forward curve, which explains why curve steepeners are usually implemented via forward swaps, as they provide better entry points.

A Comparison of Bootstrap Interpolation Methods

Regardless of curve build method, once we have the discount factor curve, we can then calculate any forward simple and swap rates, zero rates, and so on. As many of these (forward) rates are not directly quoted in the market, each dealer can end up with a different rate depending on their curve build method. This is illustrated in Table 2.3, where starting with the same market

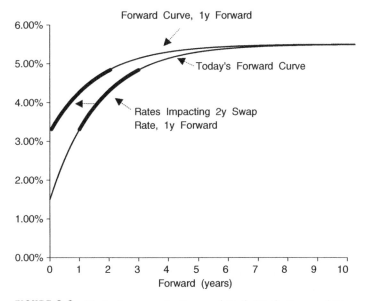

FIGURE 2.2 Today's versus 1y-Forward Daily/Daily Forward Curves

TABLE 2.3 *Calculated* Rates Due to Different Curve Build Methods

Rate	Fwd Start	Linear DFs	Log-Linear	Linear Zero Rates	Cubic Spline Zero Rates
3m Libor	Spot	5.34003%			
	1m	5.32988%	5.33499%	5.33595%	5.33679%
	3m	5.28472%	5.29691%	5.30549%	5.30320%
	1y	5.03734%	5.03753%	5.03520%	5.03108%
	5y	5.50086%	5.61922%	5.57882%	5.59013%
	10y	5.60586%	5.90029%	5.84643%	5.90156%
1y Par-Swap Rate	1m	5.33041%	5.33289%	5.33524%	5.33350%
	3m	5.27603%	5.27901%	5.28152%	5.27819%
	1y	5.16746%	5.16460%	5.16121%	5.16331%
	5y	5.73883%	5.73885%	5.73884%	5.73928%
	10y	**5.85160%**	**6.02845%**	5.99703%	6.02457%
5y Par-Swap Rate	Spot	5.40001%			
	1m	5.44203%	5.44490%	5.44389%	5.45123%
	3m	5.40624%	5.41197%	5.41000%	5.41047%
	1y	5.47118%	5.47065%	5.46985%	5.47044%
	5y	5.87379%	5.87381%	5.87380%	5.87388%
	10y	6.02774%	6.02823%	6.02818%	6.02835%

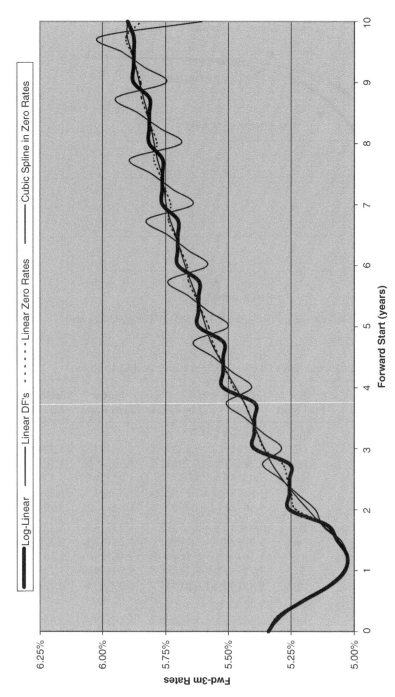

FIGURE 2.3 Forward Rates Due to Different Curve Construction Methods

inputs for the USD swap curve, we calculate different forward 3m-Libor and swap rates depending on the interpolation method.

For example, note that "1y par-swap rate, 10y forward" can be calculated to be anywhere between 5.85160% and 6.02845%—a variance of almost 18 bp—depending on which interpolation method is used in bootstrapping the curve.

The implied forward-3m rates due to different interpolation methods are shown in Figure 2.3. As alluded to before, the forward rates can loosely be considered as the expected value of future short-term interest rates. The U-shaped forward-3m curve in the front end illustrates the market expectation of declining interest rates (central bank easings) in the near future.

CHAPTER 3

Interest Rate Swaps in Practice

The previous chapter laid out the basic theory of pricing plain-vanilla interest rate swaps. As we saw, swap valuation boils down to extracting discount factors and using this discount factor curve to project and discount the cash flows. In this chapter, we consider the details of swap markets in practice using the USD market as our prime example.

In the United States, almost every major financial institution and corporation uses interest rate swaps. Like any other market instrument, swaps can be used for hedging or speculation. Commercial banks can use swaps to match the duration of their assets (long-term fixed rate loans) to their liabilities (short-rate deposits, CDs). Agencies use swaps and swap derivatives to fine-tune and hedge the duration of their mortgage portfolios in response to expected or realized prepayments, and for funding. Corporates typically follow a debt issuance (typically fixed-rate bonds) by swapping these to floating rates at opportune times (steep yield curves). Finally, speculators such as hedge funds and proprietary trading desks use swaps to express views or take advantage of level/slope/curvature of interest rate curves. Since swaps are over-the-counter (OTC) instruments, they are quite flexible and can be tailor-made to address one's needs.

MARKET INSTRUMENTS

For the USD swap market, the benchmark floating index is the 3-month London Inter-Bank Offered Rate (LIBOR), which is the prevailing 3-month interest rate for dollar-deposits between London banks. The default settlement date, also known as the *Spot Date*, is 2 London business days after trade date, rolled forward if necessary to be a good New York and London business day.

In order to construct a Libor discount factor curve (Libor curve), a collection of the following input instruments are used.

Cash Deposit Rates, Libor Fixings

Every day, at 11:00 a.m. London time, the British Bankers Association (BBA) polls various dealers for cash deposit rates for various terms: Overnight (O/N), Tomorrow Next (T/N) (although no longer quoted), 1 week, 2 week, 1M, 2M, 3M,..., 12M, and publishes the resulting averages for various currencies. When USD swaps are traded during the day, these Libor fixings (rather than their live quoted values) are used to construct the front end of the Libor curve.

For USD, all these rates are quoted simple (no compounding) Act/360. The O/N rate is for a deposit starting on trade date to the next London business day, while T/N (use O/N if not available) is for an overnight forward deposit starting on the next London business day and ending 2 London business days from trade date. These 2 rates provide the discount factor for spot date.

The other deposit rates, 1wk, 2wk, 1m,..., 12m are for deposits starting on the spot date for the corresponding term.

The typical BBA fixings used are O/N, T/N, and 3m, and to a lesser degree 1m, 2m, 6m, rates. Other rates are rarely used.

FRAs

An $n \times m$ *forward rate agreement* (pronounced n-by-m FRA \'*frä*\) is an agreement based on the economic value of a forward deposit starting n months from today, and maturing m months from today, with the payoff based on the difference between the actual "$m - n$"-month rate versus the agreed-upon deposit rate K. So a 2×5 FRA is based on the 3m (forward) rate, starting in 2m. At inception, the rate K is chosen so that the FRA has zero value, that is, K is equated to the forward rate. A seasoned FRA has positive or negative value, depending on how the fixed rate K compares to the current market forward rate. The payoff of $n \times m$ FRA occurs at rate fixing date—n-months from now—and uses the actual rate for fixing *and* discounting (called "FRA discounting"). For example, if one owns a 2×5 FRA struck at K, the payment in 2 months is:

$$\frac{\alpha \times (L_{3m}(2m) - K)}{1 + \alpha \times L_{3m}(2m)}$$

per unit of notional, where $\alpha \approx 1/4$ is the length (Act/360) of the [2m,5m] period.

While not as liquid as ED futures, FRAs are quoted and can be used as input instruments to a Libor curve. One can think of FRAs as the basic building block for swaps. A swap is just a portfolio of FRAs, with the difference that floating payments are paid at the end of each calculation period, while FRAs pay the discounted value of this floating payment at the beginning: These would be economically equivalent as long as the floating index matches the funding cost. Another difference is that swaps typically have 1 fixed flow for each 2 floating flows, for example, USD swaps are semiannual/quarterly on fixed/floating legs. Modulo these differences, a swap is simply a portfolio of FRAs, or equivalently a FRA can be considered as a single-period/reset swap. The quote convention for FRAs is sometimes in reference to the floating index: *buying, selling* a FRA is same as paying/receiving in the single period swap.

Euro-Dollar Futures

Euro-dollar contracts are exchange-traded derivative contracts traded in the International Money Market (IMM) pit of the Chicago Mercantile Exchange (CME, or "Merc"). Each contract settles on 2 London business days prior to the third Wednesday of the contract month based on that day's BBA Libor fixing.

3m-Euro-dollar contracts settling on the last month of each quarter (March, June, September, December) are actively traded and fairly liquid for the first 3y of contracts (12 of them). Later contracts (up to 40, 10y out) can be traded, but have diminishing liquidity. There are also 6 monthly 3m-Euro-dollar contracts for the first 6 months, and also 12 monthly 1m-Euro-dollar contracts, but these are not as liquid as "Quarterly 3m-Euro-dollar Futures Contracts" (ED futures from now on).

Each ED is based on the interest payment of a hypothetical $1M 90-day deposit starting on the third Wednesday of quarter-end. A Euro-dollar "tick" is the change in value of the contract due to a 1 bp change in the implied interest rate:

$$1 \text{ tick} = \$25 = \$1,000,000 \times 0.0001 \times \frac{90}{360}$$

ED futures trade based on price, and have an implied futures rate (100-Price). They are forward contracts and have 0 value at trade time. Other than opening a futures (margin) account and posting initial margin, and paying brokerage (about $1 per contract), no money is exchanged when trading them. So if ED1 is trading at 95.00 (implied futures rate 5%), and you buy 100 contracts, you pay no money (except $100 for brokerage). However, unlike true forward contracts (FRAs) which require no cash exchange until expiration, ED contracts are cash-settled daily.

At each day's end, the Merc computes that day's final settlement value based on the markets at the close, 2 p.m. Chicago time. Every open position will get cash-settled, akin to closing your ED position at settlement price, and immediately initiating an identical new position. For example, having bought 100 ED1 for 95.00, if that day's settlement value is 95.10 (implied rate of 4.90%), you have made 10 ticks, or $25,000 = 100 \times 10 \times \$25$, and this amount will be posted to your margin account. Until you close out the position (sell 100 ED1), each day an amount equal to the daily move (in ticks) times the number of contracts in your account is posted or taken from your futures account. When you close out the position (sell 100 ED1), the difference between the sale price and prior day's settlement value is used and posted/taken from your futures account.

ED futures are also referred to in colors. The first 4 contracts are called whites, the next 4 reds, followed by 4 greens, 4 blues, 4 golds, 4 purples, 4 oranges, 4 pinks, 4 silvers, and 4 coppers. So ED5 is sometimes referred to as first red, ED6 as the second red, ED9 as the first green, and so on.

A common trade is to buy/sell an ED *pack*: 1 contract in each series of a specific color. Buying/selling 1 red pack means buying/selling 1 ED5, 1 ED6, 1 ED7, and 1 ED8. The PV01 of a pack is $100.

Trading an *n*-year ED *bundle* is the trading of the first $4 \times n$ EDs. For example buying/selling 1 2y bundle is buying/selling of 1 ED1, 1 ED2, ..., 1 ED8 contract. The PV01 of an *n*-year bundle has $n \times \$100$.

Packs and bundles are quoted based on change on day. For example, "+3 (up 3) on day" means each contract in the pack is priced at prior day's close plus 3 ticks.

Future/Forward Convexity Adjustment

As stated, ED futures are not exactly forward rate contracts, as they have daily mark-to-market settlement, while true FRAs do not. For FRAs the P&L of the contract (the difference between the contracted value and the realized value) is only paid at the final settlement date, and hence its value today is the properly discounted value of this future settlement value. In contrast, the P&L of the future contract, while based on the same forward interest rate, is broken out into a series of daily P&Ls and paid daily without discounting. Since interest rates are highly correlated (overnight rates versus forward rates in our case), this daily settlement confers an advantage to a short position in the ED future contract, as he earns money and gets to reinvest it daily at overnight rates when interest rates are high, and loses money and hence has to borrow overnight money when interest rates are low. This systematic advantage for a short position does not go unnoticed by the market. The short is charged for this free lunch in the form of being required to sell the contract at a cheaper level than would have otherwise been if it was a true FRA. Therefore, the implied rate in the future contract (100 − *price*) is higher than the true forward rate, and this difference is known as the *future-forward convexity adjustment*. The size of convexity adjustment depends on the expected extra P&L of the short position over the life of the contract, which in turn depends on the volatility of the rates, and requires a model to calculate it. In general, it can be shown that the implied future rate is the expected rate at future's settlement (see Appendix B). A commonly used formula based on the Ho-Lee model is as follows:

$$\text{Implied Futures Rate} - \text{Forward Rate} = 1/2\sigma_N^2 t^2$$

for a future contract that settles in t-years, and has Normalized volatility of σ_N. As can be seen, the effect of the convexity adjustment gets larger (t^2 order) for later settlements, and this is one of the reasons that later contracts (3-years and out) are less liquid, as their value depends on the proper modeling of the convexity adjustment. Armed with a convexity adjustment model, one can construct a Libor curve purely based on a strip of ED futures, and calculate par-swap rate from this curve. The resulting par-swap rate is called the *strip rate*, and can be compared to quoted par-swap rates to potentially take advantage of differences.

Stub Rate, Interpolated Libor

The first ED future's settlement is rarely 1m or 3m away. One usually needs to obtain the discount factor for the ED1's settlement, and some brokers quote a *stub rate*, which is for a deposit starting on Spot Date, and maturing on the ED1's settlement date (2 London business days prior to the third Wed of the contract month).

An alternative is to interpolate BBA's Libor fixings to come up with the stub rate. Assume that ED1 settles 45 days from Spot Date. In this case, we can linearly interpolate 1M Libor and 2M Libor to come up with a plausible stub rate.

Par-Swap Rates

Par-swap rates for various maturities are quoted and are used to construct a Libor curve. In USD, the following maturities are quoted: 2y-10y, 12y, 15y, 20y, 25y, 30y. Longer par-swap rates (40y, 50y, 60y) are quoted as spreads to 30y rates. Also, USD par-swap rates are typically quoted as (swap) spreads to *current* treasuries with similarly quoted maturity

(CT2, CT3, CT5, CT10, CT30), or interpolated treasury yields for other maturities, though 12y spread is usually quoted as a spread to CT10. In most other currencies, the swap rates are directly quoted, and not as spreads to government yields. For 1y maturity, the swap rate is derived and calculated from the money market futures (ED for USD). As the 1y point is the cross over point between money market and capital markets, it is often quoted with a different frequency and/or day-count basis than other rates, so care needs to be taken when trading 1y swaps.

Regardless of the quote mechanics, one arrives at a series of par-swap rates.

SWAP TRADING—RATES OR SPREADS

USD par-swap rates are quoted as spreads to benchmark current (on-the-run) treasuries, and a typical broker swap screen is shown in Table 3.1, and the graph of the swap rates or spread versus maturity is known as the Swap and Spread curves, Figure 3.1. For example, a 2y spread market of 55-55.5 means that the dealer is willing to pay the yield of CT2 treasury, y_2, plus 55 bp, and receive y_2 plus 55.5 bp.

USD swaps can trade either as *rates* or *spreads*.

TABLE 3.1 A Typical USD Swap Broker Screen

	Treasury Cpn/Mat	Treasury Price	Treasury Yield (%)	Swap Spd (bp)	Swap Rate (%)
2y	4% 30-Sep-09	100-09/092	3.84235/3.84657	55/55.5	4.39235/4.40157
3y	4.5% 15-May-10	101-12/12+	3.92275/3.92917	58/58.5	4.50275/4.51417
4y			3.99967/4.00376	60/60.5	4.59967/4.60876
5y	4.25% 30-Sep-12	100-242/24+	4.07659/4.07835	65/65.5	4.72659/4.73335
6y			4.14498/4.14678	66/66.5	4.80498/4.81178
7y			4.21337/4.21521	67/67.5	4.88337/4.89021
8y			4.28176/4.28364	68/68.5	4.96176/4.96864
9y			4.35015/4.35207	69/69.5	5.04015/5.04707
10y	4.75% 15-Aug-17	102-19/19+	4.41855/4.42050	70/70.5	5.11855/5.12550
12y			4.41855/4.42050	71.5/72	5.13355/5.14050
15y			4.42360/4.42551	74/74.5	5.16360/5.17051
20y			4.42865/4.43052	75/75.5	5.17865/5.18552
25y			4.43370/4.43554	77/77.5	5.20370/5.21054
30y	5% 15-May-37	109-05/06	4.43876/4.44055	80/80.5	5.23876/5.24555

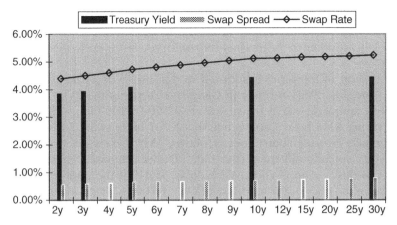

FIGURE 3.1 USD On-the-Run Treasury, Par-Swap, and Swap-Spread Curves

Trading in Rates

When one is trading *rates*, one is taking duration risk. For example, receiving in $100M 2y-swap has similar risk of buying $100M 2y treasuries. In this case, the inquiry should specify that swap *rates* are needed: "My client wants to receive in $100M 2y swaps. Rates! Where will you pay?" Dealer response: "Spreads are 55-55.5. With 2y treasury trading at 100-09/100-092 (3.84235%-3.84657%), I will pay 4.39235% (=3.84235% + 55 bp)." The reason that the dealer is using the offered side of the treasury (100-092 price, 3.84235% yield) is that he is paying in the swap, so he has short duration risk. U.S. swap traders are not in the business of taking duration risk (that belongs to the cash/treasury desk), only spread risk. As soon as the trade is done, the trader will cover his short and buy treasuries, that is, lift the offer of 100-092. This will leave him with spread risk, where he is paying the bid side (55 bp) of the swap-spread market. With enough 2-way flows, he will try to pay the bid side of the swap-spread market, and receive the offered side, and make a living out of the bid-offer spread (of the swap-spread market).

Trading in Spreads

On the other hand, one can directly enter into a *spread* trade by entering into a swap and simultaneously providing the treasury hedge.

Buying a spread is the simultaneous purchase of treasuries (called cash), and paying in swaps. This is also called *paying in spreads*. *Selling* a spread is the simultaneous sale of treasuries, and receiving in swaps. This is called *receiving in spreads*. To remember it, always recall that in a *spread* trade, whatever you are doing to the treasury (buy/sell), you are doing to the spread (buy/sell).

The amount of treasuries is adjusted so that the PV01 of the treasury position (using the PV01 formula in Chapter 1) matches the PV01 of the swaps. For example, let the 2y treasury trade at 100-09/100-092, with PV01 of $185.10 per $1M face. Also assume that PV01 of 2y swap is $189 per $1M notional. A *spread* inquiry goes as follows: "My client wants to receive in $100M 2y spreads. Where is your bid?" Dealer response: "2y spreads are 55-55.5, this is a good client, I'll bid/pay 55.1!" If the trade is done, one agrees on the price of the treasury, let's say 100-08+, compute the yield (3.85501%) and compute the swap rate 4.40601%(= 3.85501% + 55.1bp). One then calculates the PV01-equivalent amount of treasuries: $100M × 189/185.10 = $102.107M face. The trade ticket will state that the client sold $102.107M face of 2y treasury at the clean price of 100-08+, and simultaneously the client is receiving 4.40601% in $100M 2y swaps.

Note that since the dealer is being provided with the treasury hedge, he does not have duration risk, and the exact price of the passed-on treasuries is not as critical as when trading rates. However, he does have spread risk, expressed as *Spread-PV01*: $100M 2y-spread risk, or $18,900 (2y) Spread PV01.

Interpolated Spreads

For swap maturities where an equivalent-maturity Current Treasury does not exist, one uses an *interpolated* treasury yield, and quotes swap spread relative to this interpolated yield. For example, a quoted 7y swap-spread market of 67-67.5 bp is relative to $3/5y_5 + 2/5y_{10}$ where y_5, y_{10} are the yields of the current 5y, 10y treasuries (CT5, CT10).

Let's assume that the CT5 is trading at 100-242/100-24+ (4.07835%-4.07659%) with a PV01 of $444.90 per $1M face. Also, let CT10 trade at 102-19/102-19+ (4.42050%-4.41855%) with a PV01 of $801.30 per $1M face. Finally, let the PV01 of a 7y par swap be $589.70 per $1M notional.

A dealer will compute the 7y interpolated treasury yield market as 4.21337%-4.21521%. With 7y spreads trading at 67-67.5 bp, his market when trading rates would be 4.88337%-4.89021%. If receiving in $100M 7y rates, he will receive 4.89021% = 3/5 × 4.07835% + 2/5 × 4.42050% + 67.5 *bp* = 4.21521% + 67.5 *bp*. In order to hedge himself, he will then compute how much 5y and 10y treasuries he needs to sell: $79.528M = $100M × 3/5 × 589.70/444.90 of CT5 at 100-242, and $29.437M = $100M × 2/5 × 589.70/810.30 of CT10 at 102-19.

If receiving in spreads, the dealer will quote 67.5 bp as his offer. When the spread trade is done, one then fixes the 5y and 10y treasury prices that will be sold to the client as the hedge, and computes the interpolated yield from these prices. Let's assume we use the offers: 100-24+ (4.07659% yield) for CT5, and 102-19+ (4.41855% yield) for CT10. The interpolated yield is then 4.21337% = 3/5 × 4.07659% + 2/5 × 4.41855%, and the dealer will be receiving in 4.88837% = 4.21337% + 67.5 bp in $100M 7y swaps. Simultaneously, he sells $79.528M CT5 at 100-24+ and $29.437M CT10 at 102-19+ to the client.

Swap Curve Trading

Similar to the treasury curve, one can express views or hedge exposure to the slope (longer rate - shorter rate) of the swap curve via *curve* trades. For 2 given swap maturities, one can put on a steepener by *buying* the curve, that is, receiving in the shorter-maturity swap and paying in the longer-maturity, with the notional of each swap chosen so that each swap has the same PV01. Similarly, one can put on a flattener by selling the curve: paying in the shorter-maturity and receiving in PV01-equivalent amount of the longer swap. For example, one can buy the 2's/10's swap curve by receiving in $100M 2y swap and paying in $24.54M (= $100M × 7.62/1.87) 10y swaps, where PV01(2y) = 1.87, PV01(10y) = 7.62 cents. In this trade, one is immune to parallel moves in the swap curve, but is carrying $18,700-per-01 2's/10's *curve risk*. For each 1 bp steepening/flattening of the 2's/10's curve, one makes/loses $18,700.

One can also trade curves forward. A forward swap curve steepener trade consists of receiving in shorter-maturity *forward* swap while paying in PV01-equivalent longer forward swap. For example a 1y-forward 2's/10's steepener consists of receiving in a 2y swap, 1y forward, while paying in a PV01-equivalent 10y swap, 1y forward.

SWAP SPREADS

In the USD swap market, swap traders are primarily trading swap spreads, and hedge most of their duration risk, either with other swaps or with U.S. treasuries. As such, they are mostly focused on swap spreads, and manage that risk. To understand swap spreads, one has to remember that they primarily represent the average *credit spread* of the Libor Panel—consisting of the banks polled by BBA to determine its estimate of Libor—generally thought to be equivalent to AA-, versus U.S. government credit. While many explanations have been offered as to what drives swap spreads, they all come back to relative supply/demand of bank versus government credit. For example, in the early 1990s government-sponsored agencies like Fannie-Mae, Freddie-Mac, would hedge the duration mismatch in their mortgage portfolios with U.S. treasuries, resulting in tightening swap spreads. When later in the decade, they switched to use swaps, swap spreads in general widened. Similarly, in a steep curve environment, corporates will swap their fixed-rate debt (either existing or new issue) by receiving in swaps to take advantage of lower short-term funding costs. This increased demand for receiving in swaps results in tightening swap spreads. Another supply/demand driver occurs when the government is running a deficit and issuing more debt via U.S. treasuries: this results in the tightening of swap spreads. On the flip side, during periods of economic turmoil and flight-to-safety, there is high demand for U.S. treasuries, resulting in widening swap spreads. As noted, all of these drivers boil down to relative supply/demand.

Another way to understand swap spreads is as the financing spread between U.S. treasuries versus swaps, that is, Libor versus repo. The 2y swap spread is the market's expectation of the average UST repo versus Libor rates for the next 2 years. This is the basic understanding of quoted swap spreads, sometimes called *headline spreads* as they are the difference in the yields of the current treasuries versus par-swap rates. As a given current treasury, say CT10, is issued quarterly, it will remain *current* for 3 months, while the 10-year par-swap rate is for a swap that matures in exactly 10 years from trade date, headline swap spreads suffer from calendar roll-down and abrupt shift on auction dates.

Matched-Maturity Spread

A similar measure of swap spreads is the *Matched-Maturity* (sometimes called *Yield-Yield*) swap spreads, which measure the yield of a given treasury security to the par-swap rate of a swap maturing on the same date as the given treasury. When one buys/sells a matched-maturity spread, one buys/sell a given treasury and pays/receives in PV01-equivalent amount of a swap with the same maturity date. Therefore it is 2 trades, done as a package. When dealing with short-term treasuries, say treasury bills or treasuries less than 2 years remaining maturity, instead of swaps, one can buy/sell a strip of ED futures versus selling/buying the treasury. This yield spread is referred to as the *Treasury-ED (TED) spread*, expressed usually as the semi-annual yield of both (Treasury, ED) components.

Asset-Swap Spread

Another way of trading swap spreads is via *asset-swaps* where the swap fixed leg's payment and dates are required to match exactly those of a given bond, and an *asset-swap spread* is added to the Libor leg of the swap, with either the notional of the floating leg matching the principal amount of the bond, *par-par* asset swap, or the initial dirty price of the bond, *Market Value* asset swap. In either case, the *asset-swap spread* is primarily the difference between the funding level for the treasury, that is, its repo rate, versus Libor until the maturity of swap/bond.

For example, if on trade date 2-Oct-2007, the U.S. CT2 with coupon rate $C = 4\%$, maturity 30-Sep-2009 is trading at clean price of $P = 100 - 02+$, $y = 3.95866\%$, with gross price of 100.11091% for settlement date 3-Oct-2007, the cash flows of $100M CT2 on a asset swap are as follows:

1. On 3-Oct-2007, the buyer buys $100M CT2 from seller for either $100M in Par-Par, or $100,110,910 in Market-Value asset swap.
2. The buyer passes on all received payments of the bond. On every coupon date, 31-Mar-2008, 30-Sep-2008, 31-Mar-2009, 30-Sep-2009, the buyer pays the received coupon ($2M = $100M \times 0.04/2$) to the seller (receiver in swap), and also the principal $100M at maturity.
3. For each quarterly calculation period until maturity, the buyer receives "3m-Libor minus Spread" on $100M notional for par-par, or $100,110,910 notional for market-value, with Libor fixed at beginning of each calculation period and paid at end.
4. At maturity, the buyer receives the notional of the Libor leg: $100M for Par-Par, or $100,110,910 for Market-Value in exchange for passing the bond principal payment ($100M).

Note that in a par-par asset swap, the seller has to initially deliver the bond for par, so she is making a loan of $110,910 to the buyer, while in a market-value asset swap, the seller's loan ($110,910) is shifted from up-front to the maturity date of the swap. In either case, the asset swap spread is solved for such that the PV of all these cash flows—including the up-front or back-end loan—is zero when discounted off the swap discount curve.

For the duration of the swap, a leveraged investor has to finance $100M CT2 at the prevailing overnight or term repo rate (plus variation margin) versus receiving Libor-Spread. Therefore, an asset swap's ongoing payment are Libor-Spread versus repo. Said in another way, a leveraged buyer has locked in Libor-Repo spread at the asset swap level, and benefits if the realized spread payments turn out to be higher during the life of the swap.

Zero-Coupon Swap Spreads

The purest expression of swap spreads is the swap rate for a *zero-coupon swap* versus the yield of a similar-maturity zero-coupon treasury bond, as each instrument has a single cash flow, and hence their yield spread is just a measure of credit quality for the maturity point. A *Zero-Coupon Swap* consists of a fixed and a floating leg, with both legs having a single (net) payment at maturity. The floating leg is usually based on the benchmark swap index, Libor-3m for USD, and the final payment is based on the compounded interest of current and future Libor settings:

$$N_0 \times [(1 + L_{3m}(0)/4) \times (1 + L_{3m}(3m)) \times \cdots \times (1 + L_{3m}(T - 3m)/4) - 1]$$

where T is the maturity of the swap, and N_0 is the initial notional of the swap. Similarly, the fixed leg's single payment is based on the compounded interest based on the quoted zero-coupon rate. For example, the fixed payment of an N-year swap with semi-annual zero-coupon rate of Z is

$$N_0 \times \left[(1 + Z/2)^{2N} - 1\right]$$

In practice, one has to specify the initial notional (N_0) or final notional (N_{Final}) of the swap, related by

$$N_0 \times (1 + Z/2)^{2N} = N_{Final}$$

The fixed leg's single payment is then $N_{Final} - N_0$ and is called the fixed payment, paid at swap maturity (T).

Note that as long as our financing cost equals Libor-3m, then the present value of the floating leg is

$$N_0 - PV(N_0 \text{ Paid at T})$$

In this case, since the par zero-Coupon rate is quoted so that the value of the swap at inception is zero, it is simply a way of expressing the Libor discount factor for T:

$$PV(Float\ Leg) = PV(Fixed\ Leg)$$

$$\Rightarrow N_0 = PV(N_{Final} \text{ paid at T}) = N_{Final} \times D(T)$$

$$\Rightarrow \frac{1}{(1 + Z/2)^{2N}} = D(T)$$

Z-Spread

Finally, another measure of swap spreads is the *zero rate spread*, most often called *z-spread*. The idea is to apply a parallel shift to the Libor discount curve so that the market (dirty) price of the bond is recovered if all the remaining cash flows are discounted using this shifted curve. The size of the required parallel shift applied to the zero rates is the z-spread. Note that to be precise, one has to pin down the quote convention of the zero rates (compounding frequency, if any, and treatment of fractional years), so there is no universal z-spread. Moreover, while popular with quants, z-spreads are not traded: they are merely a (and yet another) measure of swap spreads, and often provide pretty much the same information or cheap/rich signals as other (traded) spreads (matched-maturity, asset swap).

Swap Spread Curve

A graphical representation of any of the above spreads (headline, matched-maturity, asset swap, z, zero-coupon) versus maturity is referred to as the *swap spread curve*, or simply the spread curve. One can express views or hedge exposures to different points of the spread curve. When engaging in 2 simultaneous *spread trades* of different maturities, one is said to be trading *spread of spreads* or alternatively since each spread trade consists of two trades, one cash (treasury), and one swap, it is also referred to as a *box trade*. For example, when taking views on the slope of spread curve, say between 2y point and 5y point, buying a "2's-5's spread of spreads" means buying the 5y spreads (buying 5y cash, paying in 5y swaps), and selling the 2y spread (selling 2y cash, receiving in 2y swaps), thereby profiting from steepening of spread curve between the 2-year and 5-year maturities. The amount of treasuries (and hence swaps) on each leg is adjusted so that each will have the same spread PV01. In this way, the trade is immune to parallel moves in the spread curve.

Spread-Locks

A future headline swap spread can be locked via spread-lock trades, which come in 2 varieties: *discrete-setting* (also called European) spread-lock, or *rolling* spread-lock. In a discrete-setting spread-lock agreement for the N-year spread, the N-year headline swap spread is locked at a fixed level K for a future date, and at expiry, one enters into a N-year spread trade. If long a spread-lock, one pays in N-year swap with fixed rate set to expiry date's par-swap rate S (as published by ISDAFIX 11:00 a.m. New York) and buying PV01-equivalent amount of US CT[N] at a yield of $S - K$, that is buying the headline spread at K. If one is short the spread-lock, then one receives in swaps at S and sells PV01-equivalent amount of CT[N] at $S - K$ yield. Instead of physical settlement, one could instead opt for cash-settlement with cash value set to the difference between the N-year headline spread (as published by ISDAFIX 11:00 a.m. New York) versus the locked spread K, multiplied by PV01 of an N-year swap.

A rolling spread-lock is the periodic fixing and payments of the ISDAFIX headline spread versus the locked rate, accrued for the length of each calculation period. For example, in a 1-year quarterly rolling 10y spread-lock struck at K, there are 4 periodic payments of

$$(S(T_i) - K) \times \alpha(T_i, T_{i+1})$$

per unit notional for each calculation period $[T_i, T_{i+1}]$, where $\alpha(T_i, T_{i+1})$ is the accrual fraction according to some day-count (typically 30/360) with payment at T_{i+1}.

Spread-locks are typically quoted as a spread to the current headline spread.

RISK, PV01, GAMMA LADDER

As opposed to bonds where we are dealing with a single yield-to-maturity, in swap-land we are dealing with a series of interest rates that are aggregated to construct a discount factor curve. This discount factor curve is then used to discount swap cash flows and calculate par-swap rates and forward rates. Therefore the value of a swap depends on all the input instruments used to construct the discount factor curve.

In order to compute the sensitivity of a swap-related instrument to changes in interest rates, 2 procedures are commonly used:

1. Parallel PV01: Bump up all input rates (cash, futures, par-swaps) by 1 bp, and revalue the instrument. The change in the value of the swap is called parallel PV01 (also called delta). A variation is to compensate for different input quote conventions (Act/360 for simple cash, futures rates; SA 30/360 for swaps), and either convert all quotes to a single convention, or reconstruct a new discount factor curve by bumping all the implied zero rates.
2. Partial PV01: For each input instrument, bump up its rate by 1 bp while holding all other inputs constant, and revalue the instrument. This gives rise to a series of sensitivities—one for each input—called bucket or partial PV01/Delta. The sum of partial PV01s should be close to parallel PV01, the difference due to instrument's convexity and higher order effects.

Admittedly, interest rates do not move in either fashion: it is rare that only one rate changes while the others do not. Also, even when they move together, interest rates do not move by the same amount: short-term rates (say 2y) typically move more than longer (say 30y) rates. In order to hedge under a real-life rate movement scenario, we can compute the change in value due to a curve shift scenario. The assumed scenario is usually derived from a statistical analysis of historical curve movements using methods such as principal component analysis (PCA).

Armed with Partial PV01s, and the PV01 of each input instrument, we can then compute the amount of each input instrument needed to hedge. An example is shown in Table 3.2.

As alluded to before, the choice of curve build method greatly affects the prescribed hedge. For example, when hedging a $100M 5.5-year receiver swap, the log-linear interpolation method, while discontinuous in forward rates, prescribes paying in $48.8M 5y swaps, and $51.2M 6y swaps. This is intuitive, and close to what a trader expects. On the other hand, using cubic splines results in a smooth forward curve, but the prescribed hedge for a 5.5-year receiver swap is to receive in $18.6M 2y swap, pay in $21M 3y swap, receive in $39.7M 4y swap, pay in $93.6M 5y swap, and pay in $32.7M 6y swap! This tradeoff between smoothness in forward rates versus reasonable (local) hedge behavior affects any curve build method, and needs to be considered when choosing one.

Convexity, Gamma Ladder

Swap and option traders are not only interested in the parallel/partial deltas, but also how their deltas change when the market moves, that is, convexity which in swap-land is also referred to as *gamma*. When the market moves, a completely hedged book can gain/lose duration, and needs to be rebalanced. Often when there is a large market movement (market gap), there is not enough time to recompute partial deltas for a large book. In order to be prepared for such movements, traders precompute parallel and partial deltas for a variety of scenarios (typically a series of parallel shifts) to come up with a *gamma ladder*. This allows them to quickly rebalance their books under fast market conditions.

Reset Risk, IMM Swaps

Another risk that swap traders pay attention to is exposure of the floating leg to upcoming Libor fixings. Swap curves are usually constructed out of O/N, 1m, 2m, 3m, money-market futures, and par-swap quotes, and the bucketed risk to these rates are calculated. However, for the very front end, say the first 3 months, the difference between derived forward-3m rates versus their actual fixings, called *reset risk*, has to be monitored and hedged. The hedging is usually done via FRAs that start on the same date as the upcoming resets, and interdealer brokers routinely quote a strip of daily FRAs for, say, any day from today to 3 months from now.

If the reset dates coincided with those of ED futures, loosely called IMM dates, then one could use ED futures to mitigate reset risk. Indeed, there is a

TABLE 3.2 Parallel and Partial PV01s for a $100M 5.5y Swap

				Log-Linear		Cubic Spline	
		Rate	PV01 $/$M-Face	PV01 ($)	Needed Hedge ($M)	PV01 ($)	Needed Hedge ($M)
Cash Rate	O/N	5.33011%		−1		−398	
	T/N	5.33011%		−1		457	
	1m	5.32025%	8	−7		−185	
	3m	5.34003%	25	16		−41	
ED Rate	Sep 07	5.33250%	25	−29	−1.2	−286	−11.4
	Dec 07	5.25250%	25	−1	0.0	−285	−11.4
	Mar 08	5.13650%	25	−1	0.0	−254	−10.2
	Jun 08	5.04950%	25	14	0.6	−290	−11.6
	Sep 08	5.02250%	25		0.0	−190	−7.6
	Dec 08	5.03550%	25	−1	0.0	−421	−16.8
Swap Rate	2y	5.26402%	187	−1	0.0	3,488	18.6
	3y	5.29601%	274	−2	0.0	−5,747	−21.0
	4y	5.34502%	356	−3	0.0	14,147	39.7
	5y	5.40001%	434	−21,181	−48.8	−40,582	−93.6
	6y	5.44904%	507	−25,939	−51.2	−16,596	−32.7
	7y	5.49401%	576				
	8y	5.53401%	642				
	9y	5.57103%	704				
	10y	5.60402%	762				
	12y	5.65604%	868				
	15y	5.70701%	1,006				
	20y	5.75452%	1,188				
	30y	5.79801%	1,423				
	40y	5.79791%	1,554				
	Sum of Partial PV01 ($)			−47,137		−47,183	
	Parallel PV01 ($)			−47,123		−47,178	

variant of swaps, called *IMM swaps*, whose reset dates by design fall exactly on IMM dates. For IMM swaps, the fixed leg's calculation periods are also required to fall on IMM dates. For example, 1-year USD IMM swap starting on March-2009 has 4 quarterly calculation periods book marked by [18-Mar-2009, 17-Jun-2009, 16-Sep-2009, 16-Dec-2009, 15-Mar-2010], and 2 semiannual calculation periods book marked by [18-Mar-2009, 16-Sep-2009, 15-Mar-2010]. Note that each calculation period starts/ends on 3rd Wednesday of each quarter end (IMM date), with reset date 2 London days prior to it.

CALENDAR RULES, DATE MINUTIAE

When trading swaps and their derivatives, they are generally quoted and traded based on *terms*, for example, a "2-year" swap, since the specification of all the relevant dates is cumbersome and time-consuming. Each swap market has a series of standard conventions used as default to generate most of the relevant dates (see Table 3.3). Therefore, only the most salient terms of a swap are communicated at trade time, and any remaining date ambiguity is generally resolved at the trade confirmation level, and if not captured at that stage, ultimately resolved (usually not amicably!) on payment dates. Note that each day of missed interest for a typical level of interest rates, say 5%, will cost 1.3889 cents, or $13,889.89 for a $100M swap, a typical size. A missed day here, and a missed day there, and pretty soon....

Calculation Periods, Roll Conventions

Each swap leg is based on a series of contiguous calculation periods, book marked by the effective and the maturity dates. For each typical calculation period, there are 4 salient dates. *Calculation start/end dates*: the first/last day for the calculation period where interest *accrues*. These dates do not need to be, but often are, *adjusted* to be good business days; *payment date*: the date where the interest payment is made, which needs to be a good business day; *index reset date*: for floating payments, the date where the index, say 3m-Libor, is observed/reset.

All of the above dates are usually adjusted or *rolled* to be good business days according to some specified banking center(s), for example, New York and London for USD swaps. The two prevalent *roll conventions* are *following* and *modified following*. In the Following roll convention, if the date falls on a holiday, it is rolled to the next good (nonholiday) business day. In the modified following (MF) roll convention, a holiday date is adjusted to the next good business day, unless it rolls into the next month, in which

TABLE 3.3 Typical Swap Conventions

Currency	Fixed Leg Freq/Basis	Float Leg Freq/Basis	Roll Cals	Float Index	Spot Date
USD	SA, 30/360	Q, A/360	MF NY+LON	USD 3m Libor	2d LON, Adjusted Foll NY+LON
EUR EUR 1y	A, 30/360	SA, A/360 Q, A/360	MF, Target	EUR 6m Libor Eur 3m Libor	2d Target
JPY	SA, A/365	SA, A/360	MF, Tokyo	JPY 6m Libor	2d TOK
CAD CAD 1y	SA, A/365 A, A/365	Q, A/365	MF, Toronto	CAD 3m CDOR	Same Day
		Floating Leg, compounded Q at CDOR Flat, Paid SA (A for 1y)			
GBP GBP 1y	SA, A/365 Q, Act/365	SA, A/365 Q, A/365	MF, London	GBP 6m Libor GBP 3m Libor	Same Day
AUD AUD 1y, 2y, 3y	SA, A/365 Q, A/365	Q, A/365	MF, Sydney	AUD 3m Bill	Same Day
CHF	A, 30/360	S, A/360	MF, Zurich	AUD 3m Bill	2d ZUR

case, the date is instead adjusted *backwards* to the last good business day. Similarly a previous and modified previous roll convention can be defined, but these are rarely used in practice.

To highlight the date issues, assume that it is Wednesday 27-Feb-2008, and we have just traded a *standard* 1-year USD swap. By standard, we mean the following default (see Table 3.3) attributes of USD swaps:

Fixed Leg: Semiannual, 30/360, Modified Following (MF), New York and London

Floating Leg: Quarterly reset and payment, Act/360, MF, New York and London, based on 3-month Libor (quoted Act/360, MF, London)

The above convention is sometimes abbreviated to Semi-Bond vs 3's, which denotes semiannual, 30/360 (sometimes referred to as "Bond") convention for the fixed leg, versus 3-month Libor.

Effective, Maturity Dates

The first step is to resolve the effective and maturity dates of the swap, as these control the total number of interest-accrual days for each leg. Unless otherwise specified, swaps are spot-starting, so the Effective date is the same as the *spot date*. The spot date, or the default settlement date is market-specific: for USD market, it is 2 London business days after the trade date, adjusted forward if necessary to be a good NY+LON business day. In our example, the trade date is Wed 27-Feb-2008, and the spot date and hence the effective date is Fri, 29-Feb-2008 (2008 is a leap year). Maturity date is "1-year" after the effective date, which gets us to Sat, 28-Feb-2009. Since USD swaps are adjusted MFOL, this means that the adjusted maturity date is Fri, 27-Feb-2009. So we have a swap from 29-Feb-2008 to 27-Feb-2009.

Fixed Leg's Calculation Dates

The fixed leg of USD swaps is paid semiannually, so we need to break the swap term into two calculation periods, [29-Feb-2008, X], [X, 27-Feb-2009]. To determine the X, we have to first generate the date, and then adjust it according to the specified rule, MF—if "unadjusted" was specified, then we would leave it be even if it is a holiday.

The choice for the unadjusted intermediate date X can be:

Option 1. "*28-th rolls*" 6 months prior to *unadjusted* maturity date, Sat, 28-Feb-2009. This is the most common choice, where the intermediate unadjusted dates are generated *backwards* starting from unadjusted maturity date, and specified to fall on a particular day of the month ("roll day = 28th", or "28-th rolls"). In this case, the unadjusted intermediate date is Thu 28-Aug-2008, which is a good New York and London business day, so we do not need to adjust it.

Option 2. "*Month-end rolls*" 6 months prior to *unadjusted* maturity date, Sat, 28-Feb-2009. Since the unadjusted maturity date falls on the last day of the month, another option is to require X to also fall on the last day of the month, 6 months prior to it. In this case, the unadjusted intermediate date becomes Sun 31-Aug-2008, which gets adjusted (modified following) to Fri 29-Aug-2008.

Option 3. "*29-th rolls*" 6 months after the effective date, leading to Fri 29-Aug-2008, which is a good New York and London business day. This is rarely used in practice.

Option 4. 6 months prior to the *adjusted* Maturity Date, Fri, 27-Feb-2009. This choice is rare, but if chosen it leads to Wed 27-Aug-2008, a good New York and London business day, and can be specified as "27-th rolls."

Floating Leg's Calculation Dates

The floating leg of USD swaps is based on the 3-month Libor index, and is reset, accrued Act/360, and paid quarterly, so we need to generate 3 new quarterly intermediate dates between the effective and maturity dates: [29-Feb-2008, X_1], [X_1, X_2], [X_2,X_3],[X_3, 27-Feb-2009]. A new wrinkle that arises is whether these dates are generated recursively, or with respect to the effective/maturity dates. For example, assume that we are generating the dates backwards starting from the maturity date. Having generated the intermediate date 3 months prior to the maturity date, X_3, do we use X_3 to generate a date 3 months prior to it, X_2, or do we generate a date 6 months prior to the maturity date? The latter choice is the most common. A similar approach applies if generating dates forward from the effective date.

Similar to the preceding discussion for fixed leg, there are different choices on generating the calculation dates. We consider only Options 1 and 2, which are the most common:

> *Option 1. "28-th rolls"* Generate dates backwards with reference to the unadjusted maturity date. The unadjusted intermediate dates following 28-th rolls are Wed 28-May-2008, Thu 28-Aug-2008, Fri 28-Nov-2008, which all happen to be good New York and London business days. If not, they would have to be adjusted MF, New York and London.

> *Option 2. "Month-End rolls"* The unadjusted dates are required to fall on the last day of each month: Sat 31-May-2008, Sun 31-Aug-2008, Sun 30-Nov-2008, which are then adjusted MF to Fri 30-May-2008, Fri 29-Aug-2008, Fri 28-Nov-2008.

Payment Dates

Having generated the calculation periods, the next step is to generate the payment dates corresponding to each calculation period Since calculation dates are usually adjusted to be good business days, payment dates equate the calculation end date for each period (as long as the payment/calcuation periodicity and holiday calendars match), however for unadjusted calculation periods, the calculation end date (if a holiday) needs to be adjusted to be a good business day so that payments can actually be made and settled.

Index Dates: Reset, Start, End

Finally, for each calculation period of the floating leg, the rate reset date for the floating index needs to be generated. For USD swaps, the index is

3m-Libor and is observed/reset 2 London days prior to the beginning of each calculation period. On each calculation period's index reset date, the market rate for a 3-month Libor deposit starting on the calculation start date, as published by BBA, is observed. These start/end dates of this underlying deposit are sometimes called rate effective/maturity dates or index start/end dates. While by construction, the rate effective date coincides with calculation start date, the rate end date does not necessarily coincide with the calculation end date, and these dates can be off by a few days. This is due to the way the swap calculation periods are generated (multiple months from the anchored unadjusted maturity date) and then rolled (MF, New York, and London) versus how the rate end date is generated (3 months after the calculation/rate start date) and rolled (MF, London only). Another way that this mismatch can arise is for IMM Swaps, where calculation periods are not 3 months apart, but cover inter-IMM intervals—sometimes called *IMM gaps*—that is, they run through 3rd Wednesdays of each quarter-end, and usually have 13 weeks (91 days), but occasionally 14 weeks (98 days). This date mismatch—while small, a few days for regular swaps, but as long as 6 days for IMM swaps—somewhat invalidates the perfect replication needed to establish the value of a floating leg as $D(Effective\ Date) - D(Maturity\ Date)$, but is usually ignored in practice, or compensated for via a *delay-of-payment convexity adjustment*.

Day Count Basis

The actual cash flows of the swap for each calculation period consist of the interest rate—either fixed rate or the floating index—accrued for the length of the calculation period according to the specified day-count basis, and paid on the corresponding payment date. For a given calculation period, the day-count basis specifies the length of year for which the interest accrues. The most common type of bases are 30/360 (or any of its variants), Act/365, Act/360, and to a much lesser degree, Act/Act which is different and not to be confused with the Act/Act convention used to calculate accrued interest for bonds. The value of a swap is the PV of these cash flows, FV'ed to the *settlement date*—sometimes called the *as-of date*—which usually corresponds to the spot date.

Calculating the day-count fraction for Act/360 or Act/365 is simple. Count the actual number of calendar days in the calculation period, and divide by 360 or 365. The Act/Act ISDA method, while not common, is not the same as act/act method used to calculate the accrued interest for bonds. The latter is called Act/Act ISMA (now ICMA), or act/act bond convention, and is defined as the actual number of days for the partial coupon period divided by the "number of days in the full calculation period multiplied by the number of coupons per year." The act/act ISDA method (also called act/act swap, or act/act historical) on the other hand, is calculated as the sum of the number of days falling in a non-leap-year divided by 365, plus number of accrual days falling in a leap-year divided by 366.

The 30/360 basis is based on each year having 12 30-day months, and is computed as $360(y_2 - y_1) + 12(m_2 - m_1) + (d_2 - d_1)$ divided by 360 for calculation period $[y_1/m_1/d_1, y_2/m_2/d_2]$. While this might seem a straightforward process, it turns out to introduce nuances when month-ends are considered, and has led to different variants to tackle them. All variants use the above formula, but require first adjusting the original dates as follows:

> 30/360 ISDA, bond basis, 30/360: If $d_2 = 31$ and $d_1 = 30, 31$, change d_2 to 30. If $d_1 = 31$, change d_1 to 30.
>
> 30E/360 ICMA (formerly ISMA), Eurobond basis: If $d_{1,2} = 31$, change $d_{1,2}$ to 30.
>
> 30E/360 ISDA: If d_1 is last day of month, change d_1 to 30. If $d_2 = 31$, change d_2 to 30. If d_2 is not the maturity date and is last day of Feb, change d_2 to 30.

There do exist other variants: SIA 30/360, SIFMA (formerly PSA, BMA) 30/360, 30E + 360, German 30/360, but these are not that common for swaps.

Worked-Out Example

The cash flows for a *standard* 1y USD swap with 28-th rolls traded on Wed 27-Oct-2008 are presented in Tables 3.4 and 3.5. Note that if the fixed leg's basis was 30E/360 ISDA instead of 30/360, the first calculation period (29-Feb-08 to 28-Aug-08) would have 178 days rather than 179, and would result in a different par-swap rate or swap value.

TABLE 3.4   Fixed Leg for 1y USD Swap

Calc Start Date	Calc End Date	Acc Days (30/360)	Accrual Fraction	Payment Date
29-Feb-08	28-Aug-08	179	0.497222	28-Aug-08
28-Aug-08	27-Feb-09	179	0.497222	27-Feb-09

TABLE 3.5 Floating Leg of a 1y USD Swap

Rate Reset Date	Calc Start Date	Calc End Date	Acc Days (Act/360)	Accrual Fraction	Payment Date
27-Feb-08	29-Feb-08	28-May-08	89	0.24722	28-May-08
26-May-08	28-May-08	28-Aug-08	92	0.25556	28-Aug-08
26-Aug-08	28-Aug-08	28-Nov-08	92	0.25556	28-Nov-08
26-Nov-08	28-Nov-09	27-Feb-09	91	0.25278	27-Feb-09

CHAPTER 4

Separating Forward Curve from Discount Curve

The previous two chapters presented the standard treatment of building swap curves from traded instruments. Alongside plain-vanilla swaps, there is another class of floating-for-floating swaps, referred to as *money-market basis swaps* or simply *basis swaps*, where both legs of the swap are floating, but based on different short term (money-market) interest-rate indices.

Pricing and risk management of basis swaps is more nuanced than plain-vanillas. For one reason, the primary risk captured by them is the credit risk between the indices, say Government (Fed-Funds) versus Bank (Libor) credit. They also at times represent supply-demand dynamics of one index versus another one, independent of the inherent credit risk in each index. In order to provide a consistent framework to price them, one has to step back from the previous setup, where a single discount factor curve captured both discounting and calculation of forward rates, as basis swaps provide independent information about the forward/locking curve of an index, separate from the discount (funding) curve.

FORWARD CURVES FOR ASSETS

We have so far presented forward prices and rates in specialized instances. It will help to step back, and provide a generic definition of a forward contract. At a given time t, the value of an asset A for *spot* (cash) delivery is obviously $A(t)$. However, if we need the asset only at some future time $T > t$, then we can enter into a *forward* contract. Such a forward contract for some specified delivery price, K, has a value today. From a buyer's point of view, if K is too large, then the forward contract is an agreement to buy an asset in the future at an inflated price, and hence has negative value. Similarly, if K is too small, then one is buying an asset in the future on the cheap, and the value of the forward contract is positive. The delivery price K that would make the contract have zero value today is called the *forward price* of the asset, and is denoted by $F_A(t, T)$, $T \geq t$.

Notice that there are two dates here: trading date t, and forward delivery date $T > t$. On any given trading date t, we can graph $F_A(t, \cdot)$ as a function of forward dates T, and come up with *forward curve* of the asset at t. Obviously, if $T = t$, then we have the spot/cash price of the asset: $F_A(t, t) = A(t)$. We can think of the forward curve as the *indifference* curve of the asset: Given all the information today, we are indifferent between paying $A(t)$ for the asset today, or agreeing to pay $F_A(t, T)$ at some future delivery date T.

For a fixed forward delivery date T, the forward price at any trading day $t \leq T$ will fluctuate depending on market conditions. At the delivery date, of course, the forward price will coincide with the spot price: $A(T) = F(T, T)$. Since the forward price fluctuates at any trading day, the value of a given (seasoned) forward contract with a fixed delivery price K will also fluctuate. For example, assume it is January 1, and an asset is trading at 100, and its forward value for delivery on March 31 is 101. We might enter into this contract at 101 with no exchange of money (just a handshake). For the next 3 months, the value of this contract will fluctuate, depending on each day's market perception of the March-31 (forward) delivery price of the asset. At the maturity of the contract, if the spot price of the asset is higher than 101, then the contract has positive value, since it enables a long to gain the asset for lower than its market value. Similarly, if the spot price is lower than 101, then the contract has negative value, since it obligates the long to buy an asset for higher than its market value. Depending on the contract, one can either cash-settle, or take/make physical delivery of the asset at the *agreed* rather than the actual spot price.

One might think that determining the T-forward value would involve forecasting of the T-realized price of the asset. However, a simple *cash-and-carry* argument shows that we can determine the forward value of an asset without resorting to forecasting at the inception of the contract, t, he has to deliver the asset at time T in exchange for the (to be determined) forward value $K = F_A(t, T)$. He can conceptually buy that asset today t at $A(t)$ by taking a loan—potentially collateralized by the asset—with maturity T and hold on to the asset till maturity. At maturity, he will deliver the asset, receive the K (agreed upon at time t and fixed thereafter), and repay the $A(t)$ loan plus the interest. As long as K equals the loan and interest, he will have no risk. So the forward price, K, must equal loan plus its interest. If the asset can only be carried via an uncollateralized risk-free loan, then the forward prices can be related to risk-free interest rates or, equivalently, their implied discount factors:

$$F_A(t, T) = A(t)/D(t, T)$$

A similar expression can be derived for collateralized loans: for treasury bonds one should use their financing (repo) rate to arrive at the discount factor.

In general, the cash-and-carry argument shows that the forward value of an asset is the spot value *plus* the cost of carrying the asset *minus* any income that accrues to the holder of the asset, properly future valued to the forward date. For example, the forward gross value of a bond is its spot gross value plus the repo (carry cost) minus the future value of any intermediate coupon income. For dividend-paying stocks with known discrete dividends we need to subtract the future-value of the dividends from the carrying cost.

IMPLIED FORWARD RATES

When talking about forward rates, we need to distinguish between two ways that they can arise. If the underlying forward contract is an actual forward loan, requiring actual movement of cash, then the agreed-upon forward rate must express one's indifference between spot and forward-start loans. The underlying asset, the loan, can be considered as a package of two simple cash flows: unit currency at inception and unit plus interest at maturity. As discount factors are today's prices of future moneys, if available, they completely characterize each of these cash flows: To replicate a forward loan $[T, T + \Delta T]$ at a given loan lock rate K, one needs:

$$D(T) - (1 + K\Delta T)D(T + \Delta T)$$

today, and the implied forward rate is the loan lock rate K that makes today's value of this loan 0:

$$K = f([T, T + \Delta T]) = [D(T)/D(T + \Delta T) - 1]/\Delta T$$

As such, it is just a derived (implied) rate from an already known discount factor curve.

The second way that forward rates arise is as a contract based on only the interest component of a *hypothetical* loan, with the future interest rate locked at some level K. For example, a USD FRA—equivalent to a single-period forward swap—is simply the interest component of a nominal loan at the future setting of the specified index, $r_{\Delta T}(T)$ (read Libor-3m), versus that of a locked (fixed) level K:

$$[r_{\Delta T}(T) - K)] \times \Delta T$$

paid at $T + \Delta T$, with K chosen so that this contract has zero value today. We previously argued that as long as we can invest future moneys at the same index, that is, our funding is based on $r_{\Delta T}$, we can replicate the unknown future cash flow by owning/owing unit currency at start/end of the loan. Hence the value of floating payment paid at $T + \Delta T$ equals

$$PV[r_{\Delta T}(T) \times \Delta T \text{ paid at } T + \Delta T] = D(T) - D(T + \Delta T)$$
$$= f([T, T + \Delta T]) \times \Delta T \times D(T + \Delta T)$$

which means that the rate K of a zero-cost FRA is the same as the implied forward rate. Therefore, if we already have our funding/discount curve, we can use it to calculate forward locking rates for the index. Alternatively, and more commonly, given a series of forward locking rates for our funding index, we can extract our funding/discount curve. For example, if we fund ourselves at some index X periodically, our funding/discount curve becomes:

$$D_X(T_{n+1}) = 1 \times \frac{1}{1 + K_X([T_0, T_1])\Delta T_0} \times \cdots \times \frac{1}{1 + K_X([T_n, T_{n+1}])\Delta T_n}$$

where $K_X([T_i, T_{i+1}])$ is the locking (FRA) rate for the forward period $[T_i, T_{i+1}]$ with $0 = T_0 < T_1 < \ldots$, and $\Delta T_n = T_{n+1} - T_n$.

FLOAT/FLOAT SWAPS

The above relationship between discount/funding curve, and forward lock rates is no longer valid for rate-lock agreements based on indexes different than our funding index. For example, if one funds at Libor-3m, and is asked to quote a rate-lock agreement where the floating index is another index X, say commercial paper (CP), then having money at the beginning of the hypothetical forward loan period is not sufficient to get to the desired final amount (initial + CP-based interest) as one cannot invest the funds at CP. As such, there is no arbitrage argument that will provide the fair locking level for X.

Still, one can focus on the *expected* difference between the index $X(T)$ and the lockable funding index $r(T)$. The payment of an FRA based on an index X is $X(T) - K_X$ properly accrued for the duration of the hypothetical loan, ΔT, and paid at $T + \Delta T$. This can be reexpressed as:

$$[X(T) - K_X] \times \Delta T = [(X(T) - r(T)) - K_{X-r}] \times \Delta T + (r(T) - K_r) \times \Delta T$$

where $K_X = K_{X-r} + K_r$. To determine the K_X that will make the value of this rate-lock agreement zero, since we fund ourselves at r, we know how to calculate K_r so that the value of the second term becomes zero. Therefore, we just need to focus on selecting K_{X-r}, that is, the locking level for our *basis risk*: the exposure to the difference between X and our funding index, r.

Basis swaps are locking levels for forward basis risks, and their market quotes are based on expected future difference (spread) between the indexes. These market consensus levels are primarily based on market's forecast of future credit spreads—usually projected forward from their historical levels—modulated by supply-demand dynamics. For example, the difference between Fed-Funds rate versus Libor is primarily U.S. Government credit versus banking credit. In times of good financial health for banking, this spread runs around 15 bp, and as such will be the expected spread as captured in Fed-Fund-Libor basis swaps. In times of turmoil, however, it can easily blow out.

USD Basis Swaps

The following are typical basis swaps traded in USD:

Fed-Funds versus 3M-Libor: Weighted arithmetic average of overnight Fed-Funds effective rate plus spread versus 3m-Libor, both legs paid Q, Act/360.

Prime versus 3M-Libor: Weighted average of daily resets of prime rates taken from the Fed statistical release H.15 minus spread versus 3m-Libor, both legs paid Q, Act/360.

Commercial-Paper (CP) versus 3M-Libor: Unweighted monthly average of daily resets of 1-month CP rate taken from the Fed statistical release H.15, converted from discount basis to Act/360, compounded monthly at CP flat, minus spread versus 3m-Libor, both legs paid Q, Act/360.

T-Bills versus 3M-Libor: Average of the bond-equivalent yield of the weekly auction average of the 3-month U.S. T-Bills taken from the Fed statistical release H.15 plus spread versus 3m-Libor, both legs paid Q, Act/360.

Basis swap based on constant-maturity-treasury (CMT) indexes published in H.15 used to be quoted, but these are now backed out from CMS swap level and spread-locks, although care has to be taken to adjust for the difference between a CMT index versus the U.S. current (CT) yields.

Table 4.1 shows sample quote sheets for a few of these swaps.

TABLE 4.1 Sample Mid-Market USD Basis Swap Quotes

Maturity	Fed-Fund	CP	Prime	T-Bills
6m	15	7	−280	20
1y	17	8	−275	22
2y	20	9	−270	25
5y	22	10	−265	30
10y	25	15	−260	32

Extracting Forward Rate Lock Curves

As seen from Table 4.1, each market quote for a basis swap refers to the *average* locking level for the basis risk for the relevant period. For example, the 1-year T-Bill/Libor basis swap quote of 22 bp refers to 4 quarterly resets of T-Bill index versus Libor-3m. In order to extract the individual locking level for each locking date (today, 3m, 6m, 9m), a de-averaging (bootstrap) method is needed. A simple way to proceed is to start from the spot level of the spread, say for Libor-3m versus T-Bills, and assume that the locking level for this spread is piecewise linear between quoted maturities. The end point of each linear segment is adjusted so that when we extract the locking spread level—and hence the locking level for the index—as the projected index, the basis swap for that maturity prices to zero at the quoted spread. The discounting of projected cash flows for both indices are off of our already extracted discount curve. This gives us a bootstrapped forward spread curve.

A consistent framework for capturing, pricing, and risk management of plain-vanilla *and* basis swaps emerges as follows:

1. Decide on our benchmark funding index L, say Libor-3m for a U.S. broker/dealer.
2. Using rate-lock instruments (FRAs, ED futures, par-swap rates) keyed to our funding index, via bootstrapping or other methods, *simultaneously* extract the locking curve for our index, $f_L(T)$, and our funding curve, $D_L(T)$.
3. For any other index X, extract its locking curve $f_X(T)$ so that the market basis swaps price to 0. To price the basis swap, we use $f_X(T)$ and $f_L(T)$ curves to replace future (unknown) floating resets with their locking rates, and discount the cash flows on both legs using our funding curve $D_L(T)$. Alternatively and equivalently, one can extract and use the forward spread curve, $f_{X-L}(T) = f_X(T) - f_L(T)$.
4. Having extracted the locking curve, $f_X(T)$, extract the funding/discount curve $D_X(T)$ for an X-funded entity.

TABLE 4.2 Sample Mid-Market USD Libor/Libor Basis Swap Quotes

Maturity	1m vs. 3m	1m vs. 6m	3m vs. 6m
3m	36		
6m	28	77	49
1y	19	49	30
2y	12	30	18
5y	4	11	7
10y	0	2	2
30y	−4	−3	1

LIBOR/LIBOR BASIS SWAPS

In addition to basis swaps based on different indexes, there exist basis swaps between Libors of different maturities. For example, in USD, there is market for pairs of 1m, 3m, and 6m Libor, referred to as *Libor/Libor* basis swaps. A sample quote screen appears in Table 4.2.

It might seem strange that these swaps exist, since by prior arbitrage arguments, the compounded shorter-term rate must equal the longer rate, and the arbitrage-free spread should be zero. For example, the periodic payoff of a 3's/6's with a spread of s for each calculation period $[T, T + 6m]$ is the net payment at $T + 6m$ of

$$[(1 + L_{3m}(T)/4)(1 + L_{3m}(T + 3m)/4) + s/2] - 1$$

versus

$$(1 + L_{6m}(T)/2) - 1$$

or equivalently

$$\left[\frac{L_{3m}(T)}{4} \left(1 + \frac{L_{3m}(T + 3m)}{4} \right) + \frac{L_{3m}(T + 3m)}{4} + s/2 \right] - \frac{L_{6m}(T)}{2}$$

Prior arbitrage arguments suggest that the spread s above should be zero. However, we need to remember that our arbitrage arguments only hold for *risk-free* interest rates. If there is no potential for counterparty default, then any deviation of quoted forward rates from their arbitrage-free values can be arbitraged by entering into offsetting loans. For example, let us assume that there are risk-free interest rates quoted by default-free banks for 3m and 6m at $r_{3m}(0), r_{6m}(0)$. What should the 3x6 FRA rate be? If there is no potential for the banks to default, then one can buy a 3x6 FRA struck at X, borrow at $r_{3m}(0)$ for the first 3 months, pay the principal and interest $((1 + r_{3m}(0)/4))$ in 3m, with the principal and interest financed by a new loan at the prevalent 3m rate, $r_{3m}(3m)$. In 6 months, one needs to pay

$$(1 + r_{3m}(0)/4) \times (1 + r_{3m}(3m)/4)$$

while one receives

$$(r_{3m}(3m) - X)/4$$

as the reinvested payoff of the FRA, and also receives $1 + r_{6m}(0)/2$ as the 6m loan matures. Since it cost us nothing to enter these transactions, no-arbitrage requires the final moneys in 6m be the same and X to satisfy:

$$(1 + r_{3m}(0)/4) \times (1 + X/4) = 1 + r_{6m}/2$$

Since there is no net exchange of cash until maturity, the above relationship—being just a mathematical identity—must still hold even if all transactions were with a single *risky* bank. However, if we are borrowing, lending, and buying FRAs from different risky banks, it could happen that we lend money to a bank that subsequently defaults, while our other counterparties remain solvent, and we have to pay them. If we are dealing with counterparties of the same credit worthiness, the riskiest transaction is the longest loan as it has the longest default exposure window. Therefore, whoever is going to lend for 6m will quote/require a rate higher than what is implied by shorter-term (3m-rate, 3x6 FRA) rates.

$$(1 + r_{3m}(0)/4) \times (1 + X/4) - 1 + (r_{6m} + \text{Spread})/2$$

This is the main reason that two successive 3m FRAs do not equate to a 6m FRA even after adjusting for compounding, and why Libor-6m versus Libor-3m trades at a (usually) positive spread. In practice, this credit spread is further adjusted for liquidity of one tenor versus another tenor—which can make the spreads trade negative—and in consideration of particulars of Libor-fixing (BBA's polling and averaging of bank's *estimate* of what 3m interbank lending rates are).

To properly handle these basis swaps, we have to decide what our funding index is, say Libor-3m, and treat the other Libors (1m, 6m) just like other basis swaps, that is, extract a rate-lock curve for them so that the Libor-Libor basis swaps at market spreads price back to 0.

OVERNIGHT INDEXED SWAPS (OIS)

While most plain-vanilla swaps are indexed to unsecured interbank (Libor) rates with tenor of 3m or 6m, there is another variety of swaps indexed to overnight rates. The index is usually based on the policy rate of central banks for each currency, and are based on actual traded deposits. For example, in USD, the benchmark is daily Fed-Fund effective rate, which is a volume-weighted average of rates on Fed-Fund trades arranged by major brokers, and calculated and published next day by the Federal Reserve.

An *overnight indexed swap (OIS)* is a fixed-for-floating swap where the floating leg is based on an overnight index. The floating payment is typically the daily compounded interest at each overnight rate (weekends/holidays use previous business day's fixing) over the calculation period,

$$[1 + \alpha_1 \times r_1] \times [1 + \alpha_2 \times r_2] \times \cdots \times [1 + \alpha_N \times r_N] - 1$$

where α_i is the length of each *compounding day* according to some day-count basis (for example, $\alpha_i = 1/360$ or $3/360$ for Fridays in USD), while the fixed payment is the fixed rate accrued for the same calculation period, resulting in a single net cash flow for each calculation period. OIS swaps of maturity less than 1-year have one calculation period, while longer-term swaps are broken into annual calculation periods. Below is a list of OIS swaps and their benchmark index for different currencies:

USD: FFER (Fed-Funds effective rate) as calculated by the New York Fed, Act/360.

EUR: EONIA (Euro overnight index average), the effective overnight rate computed as a weighted average of all overnight unsecured lending transactions in the interbank market, calculated by European Central Bank (ECB) and published by the European Bank Federation, Act/360.

GBP: SONIA (Sterling overnight index average), the weighted average rate of all unsecured overnight cash transactions brokered in London by the Wholesale Markets Brokers' Association (WMBA). SONIA closely follows the Bank of England's (BOE) policy rate, Act/365.

JPY: TONAR (Tokyo overnight average rate), based on uncollateralized overnight average call rates for lending among financial institutions, published by the Bank of Japan (BOJ). BOJ affects TONAR using open market operations to keep it in line with its policy rate (called *Mutan*), Act/365.

CAD: CORRA (Canadian overnight repo rate average) released by the Bank of Canada, Act/365.

OIS versus Libor Discounting

With the recent market turmoil affecting banks, and concern over reliability of Libor as a benchmark index, there has been an increased focus on OIS swaps, as these are keyed to actual traded effective policy rates by central banks. Another reason for renewed focus is that most swaps are traded under the Credit Support Annex (CSA) to the ISDA Master Agreement, which requires counterparties to post collateral as the mark-to-market value of the swap changes. Of special attention is the interest rate paid on posted collateral: Most CSAs specify overnight effective rates (for example, Fed-Funds effective rate for USD) to be paid on the posted collateral (cash or cash-equivalent like government securities). This means that the actual funding cost for a swap is not Libor, but the overnight effective rate. As such, one should use OIS swaps to extract the funding/discount curve for swaps and their derivatives, and use this OIS discount curve to extract rate lock (projection) curves for other indexes.

While this idea is gaining traction and acceptance among market participants, the market practice is to still use Libor rather than OIS discounting when creating projection curves out of quoted market swaps. At the same time—*and inconsistently*—when offering unwind prices for existing/seasoned swaps with large mark-to-market value, the actual funding curve is conveniently remembered/invoked, usually (and not surprisingly) by the benefiting party!

As OIS swaps gain more liquidity and are traded for longer terms—there are currently liquid points for at most a few years—a more consistent framework for building Libor curves and pricing swaps should emerge. Until then, most at-market swaps would be priced and discounted off of the Libor curve, while off-market swaps with large mark-to-market value would use OIS or similar discount curves.

Interest-Rate
Flow Options

Derivatives Pricing: Risk-Neutral Valuation

While derivatives (forwards, options) have been around for a long time, and many attempts were made to value them, the first successful pricing formula was derived by Fisher Black, Myron Scholes, and Robert Merton.[1] The resulting formula is the celebrated Black-Scholes-Merton Formula, and was derived via an application of stochastic calculus by setting up and solving a partial differential equation relating the price of a derivative to the underlying. While the techniques used are rather daunting, the basic idea is simple and powerful: You can replicate an option payoff by taking a position in the underlying asset and financing this position. Therefore the value of an option is the value of its replicating portfolio. The only nuance is that the portfolio is not static, and needs to be dynamically rebalanced (delta-hedged) in response to changes in the underlying.

The original derivation of Black-Scholes-Merton Formula and its variants (Black's Formula) somewhat obscured this dynamic. In a 1979 paper,[2] Cox, Ross, and Rubenstein (CRR) distilled the replication argument to a simple binomial tree model, and showed that the Black-Scholes-Merton Formula can be obtained as the number of time steps in the tree tends to infinity. This constructive algorithm did away with the stochastic calculus machinery and highlighted the dynamic replicating portfolio.

Extensions of the CRR binomial tree model to more general settings were swift. While the original CRR paper was for single tradeable assets (stocks, FX, commodities) under deterministic interest rates, Harrison and Kreps[3] (in discrete-time setting) followed by Harrison and Pliska[4] (continuous-time) generalized the CRR insights to cover multiple assets. Since interest rate options depend on multiple underlyings (zero coupon bonds, or discount factors as their prices), this allowed for a consistent framework for their pricing and risk management. Moreover, Harrison and colleagues' papers formalized and generalized the principles in CRR, and showed the price of an option—which is the price of its dynamically replicated portfolio—can also be obtained by taking expected discounted value of the option payoff in a risk-neutral world. This valuation framework has become known as *Risk-Neutral Valuation*, and has introduced terms as martingales, numeraires, market completeness, change-of-measure, ... into option pricing. Their result can be tersely summarized as follows: In an arbitrage-free market, there exists an equivalent market measure where assets' prices relative to some numeraire are martingales. If the market is complete, this martingale measure is unique, and option prices are expected relative (to the numeraire) prices! While a mouthful, we will show that each component of this statement has a direct counterpart in CRR's simple binomial model.

The works of Harrison et al. were further extended by Geman and colleagues[5] who highlighted the flexibility in choosing the numeraire. This gave rise to a slew of new insights and extensions, the most famous being risk-neutral valuation under *forward measures*, and the ability to interchange discounting and taking expectation for interest-rate options. This interchange ability somewhat validated the long-term market practice of misapplying Black's formula for interest-rate options.

EUROPEAN-STYLE CONTINGENT CLAIMS

Given an underlying asset, derivatives or contingent claims are contracts with specified payoffs based on the value of the underlying. The simplest contingent claim—after a forward contract—is a *European-style* exercise option that has a specified payoff at a single exercise time t_e in the future. For example, a *call*, $C(t)$, with strike K on an asset $A(t)$ has the following payoff: $C(t_e) = \max(0, A(t_e) - K)$, while a *put*, $P(t)$, has payoff $P(t_e) = \max(0, K - A(t_e))$. While the value of the contingent claim is known at expiration, the goal of *contingent-claim pricing* is to determine its value prior to expiry.

Risk-neutral valuation is the modern framework for contingent claim valuation. As most of the core concepts of risk-neutral valuation have a direct counterpart in the CRR binomial model, we will present their model with a slight adaptation to allow for nondeterministic (random) interest rates.

ONE-STEP BINOMIAL MODEL

Given today's $t = t_0$ price of an underlying asset $A(t)$, consider a European-style contingent claim $C(t)$ with a single expiration time t_e in the future. Assume that the underlying asset has no cash flows over the period $[t_0, t_e]$,

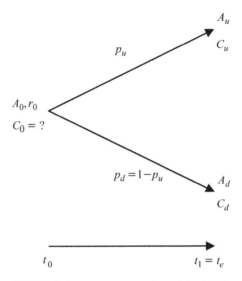

FIGURE 5.1 A One-Step Binomial Model

and let us consider the simplest case where the underlying asset at expiration can only take on two values A_u, A_d, as shown in Figure 5.1. Let C_u and C_d denote the corresponding then-*known* values of the contingent claim in each state at expiration.

Our goal is to construct a portfolio today $(t = t_0)$ so that its value at expiration, t_e, replicates the value of the contingent claim. Therefore if we are the seller of the option, we can replicate the option's contingent cash flows at expiration via this *replicating portfolio*. The fair price of the option today, C_0, would be the cost of setting up the portfolio.

Our portfolio consists of taking a position in the asset, Δ units of it, by financing it via a risk-free loan of size L at the prevalent risk-free rate r until expiration date t_e, so the value of the loan at expiration would be $L(1 + r \times (t_e - t_0)) = L/D(t_0, t_e)$ regardless of the state of the world.

At expiry, t_e, if we are in A_u state of the world, we want this portfolio to be worth C_u:

$$\Delta \times A_u + L/D(t_0, t_e) = C_u$$

Similarly, if we are in A_d state of the world, we want the portfolio to be worth C_d:

$$\Delta \times A_d + L/D(t_0, t_e) = C_d$$

We have two equations and two unknowns (Δ, L). Solving for these, we get:

$$\Delta = \frac{C_u - C_d}{A_u - A_d}$$

$$L = D(t_0, t_e) \left(C_u - \frac{C_u - C_d}{A_u - A_d} A_u \right)$$

Therefore, today's value of the contingent claim is:

$$C_0 = \Delta \times A_0 + L$$
$$= \frac{C_u - C_d}{A_u - A_d} A_0 + D(t_0, t_e) \left(C_u - \frac{C_u - C_d}{A_u - A_d} A_u \right)$$

The seller of the option can charge C_0 as above, make a loan of size L as above, and use these proceeds to buy Δ units of the asset at spot price A_0. At expiration, in either state of the world, A_u or A_d, the value of his holdings (Δ units of the asset) exactly offsets his liabilities: repayment of loan plus interest, and cash-settlement value of the option (C_u or C_d).

Note that in the preceding setup, we did not have to consider the probability of either state happening! As long as A_u, A_d can happen and are the only two possibilities, we are golden!

A bit of algebra allows us to rewrite the formula for C_0 as follows:

$$C_0 = D(t_0, t_e)[p_u C_u + (1 - p_u)C_d]$$

where

$$p_u = \frac{A_0 / D(t_0, t_e) - A_d}{A_u - A_d}$$

No Arbitrage

Lack of arbitrage is equivalent to p_u being a *probability*,

$$0 \leq p_u \leq 1$$

Consider the case $p_u > 1$, which means that $A(0)/D(t_0, t_e) > A_u > A_d$. We can sell the asset short today, and lend the proceeds, A_0, until expiration. At expiration, we receive $A_0/D(t_0, t_e)$, and need to pay either A_u or A_d to cover our short. Regardless, we have made money with no risk!

Similarly, if $p_u < 0$, then $A_0/D(t_0, t_e) < A_d < A_u$. In this case, we take a loan of A_0 to buy the asset today. At expiration, we owe $A_0/D(t_0, t_e)$ while we own an asset that is worth A_d or A_u. Regardless, we can sell the asset and pay off the loan for positive profit and no risk! Therefore, if there is no arbitrage in the above simple economy, p_u can be considered as a probability, and today's value of the option is simply the expected discounted value of the option payoff under this probability.

Risk-Neutrality

We obtained C_0 by constructing a portfolio that replicates the option payoff, regardless of the probability of each state. We then showed that we can get the same value by taking the expected value under a probability p_u. Other than a mathematical identity—p_u is the probability that gets you the correct option value, as long as you know the option value!—is there another way of interpreting p_u? The answer is in the affirmative: p_u is the probability that a *risk-neutral* investor would apply to the above setting.

Most people are *risk-averse*: between a guaranteed return and a risky investment with identical *expected* returns, they would opt for the former. That is why risky investments (stocks, real-estate, ...) need to have higher-than-average expected returns. Otherwise, one could simply put one's money in the bank and have the same return with no volatility.

On the other hand, most of us have bought a lottery ticket or played in casinos, *investments* whose expected gain is less than what we paid for. These types of investing are examples of *risk-taking*, where although risky, we are batting for the fences.

In between, there is an investment behavior that considers any investments with the same expected return as equivalent, and does not require a risk premium for risky bets. Consider such an investor given a choice between two investments: (1) invest A_0 at the bank, and get $A_0/D(t_0, t_e)$ at t_e, or (2) buy an asset at A_0 and either get A_u or A_d at t_e. For a risk-neutral investor, these two investments would be equivalent if

$$p_u A_u + (1 - p_u)A_d = A_0/D(t_0, t_e)$$

or equivalently, when

$$p_u = \frac{A_0/D(t_0, t_e) - A_d}{A_u - A_d}$$

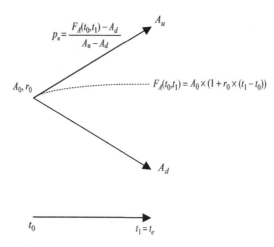

FIGURE 5.2 No-Arbitrage Requirement

Therefore, rather than setting up a replicating portfolio and computing its value today, we can simply take the expected discounted value of the option payoff using *risk-neutral probabilities*.

Relationship to Forwards

Recall that for an asset with no interim cash flows, its forward price on t_0 for t_e-delivery, $F_A(t_0, t_e)$, equals $A(t_0)/D(t_0, t_e)$. Therefore, a geometric way to interpret lack of arbitrage is that *future states must bracket forward prices*, that is, lack of arbitrage is equivalent to

$$A_d \leq F_A(t_0, t_e) \leq A_u)$$

(see Figure 5.2).

Similarly, we observe that in our simple risk-neutral world, *one-step expected future prices must equal forward prices*:

$$E_{t_0}[A(t_e)] = F_A(t_0, t_e)$$

FROM ONE TIME-STEP TO TWO

The two-state setup is obviously too simplistic. Assets can take a variety of values at expiration. However, using the previous setup as a building block,

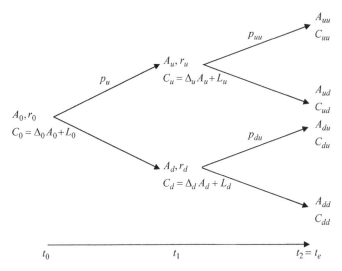

FIGURE 5.3 A Two-Step Binomial Model

we can arrive at more complex cases. The trick is to subdivide the time from now till expiration into multiple intervals, and for each state in each interval, generate two new arbitrage-free future states. With enough subdivisions, we can arrive at a richer and more real-life terminal distribution for the asset.

Consider the two-step model shown in Figure 5.3. If we have moved to the *up* state (A_u, r_u) by time t_1, we have:

$$C_u = \Delta_u \times A_u + L_u$$

$$\Delta_u = \frac{C_{uu} - C_{ud}}{A_{uu} - A_{ud}}$$

$$L_u = D(t_1, t_2, u)\left(C_{uu} - \frac{C_{uu} - C_{ud}}{A_{uu} - A_{ud}} A_{uu}\right)$$

where $D(t_1, t_2, u)$ is derived from the financing rate r_u of the asset in the up-state for $[t_1, t_2]$:

$$D(t_1, t_2, u) = \frac{1}{1 + r_u \times (t_2 - t_1)}$$

We can get the same value via risk-neutral probabilities:

$$C_u = D(t_1, t_2, u) \left[p_{uu} C_{uu} + (1 - p_{uu}) C_{ud} \right]$$

$$p_{uu} = \frac{A_u / D(t_1, t_2, u) - A_{ud}}{A_{uu} - A_{ud}}$$

Similar equations hold if we have moved to the *down* state (A_d, r_d) by time t_1:

$$C_d = \Delta_d \times A_d + L_d$$

$$\Delta_d = \frac{C_{du} - C_{dd}}{A_{du} - A_{dd}}$$

$$L_d = D(t_1, t_2, d) \left(C_{du} - \frac{C_{du} - C_{dd}}{A_{du} - A_{dd}} A_{du} \right)$$

or expressed via risk-neutral probabilities:

$$C_d = D(t_1, t_2, d) \left[p_{du} C_{du} + (1 - p_{du}) C_{dd} \right]$$

$$p_{du} = \frac{A_d / D(t_1, t_2, d) - A_{dd}}{A_{du} - A_{dd}}$$

where

$$D(t_1, t_2, d) = \frac{1}{1 + r_d \times (t_2 - t_1)}$$

Having obtained C_u, C_d at time t_1, we are back in familiar territory, and can solve for C_0:

$$C_0 = \Delta_0 A_0 + L_0$$

$$\Delta_0 = \frac{C_u - C_d}{A_u - A_d}$$

$$L_0 = D(t_0, t_1) \left(C_u - \frac{C_u - C_d}{A_u - A_d} A_u \right)$$

or equivalently,

$$C_0 = D(t_0, t_1) \left[p_u C_u + (1 - p_u) C_d \right]$$

$$p_u = \frac{A_0 / D(t_0, t_1) - A_d}{A_u - A_d}$$

where

$$D(t_0, t_1) = \frac{1}{1 + r_0 \times (t_1 - t_0)}$$

Rewriting the above equations, we have that risk-neutral probabilities must satisfy:

$$A_u = D(t_1, t_2, u)[p_{uu} A_{uu} + p_{ud} A_{ud}]$$
$$A_d = D(t_1, t_2, d)[p_{du} A_{du} + p_{dd} A_{dd}]$$
$$A_0 = D(t_0, t_1)[p_u A_u + p_d A_d]$$
$$= p_u p_{uu} D(t_0, t_1) D(t_1, t_2, u) A_{uu}$$
$$+ p_u p_{ud} D(t_0, t_1) D(t_1, t_2, u) A_{ud}$$
$$+ p_d p_{du} D(t_0, t_1) D(t_1, t_2, d) A_{du}$$
$$+ p_u p_{dd} D(t_0, t_1) D(t_1, t_2, d) A_{dd}$$

The above equations are written in short hand as:

$$A(t_1, \omega) = E_{t_1}[D(t_1, t_2, \omega) A(t_2, \omega)]$$
$$A(t_0) = E_{t_0}[D(t_0, t_1, \omega) D(t_1, t_2, \omega) A(t_2, \omega)]$$

where ω denotes the generic random future path (uu, ud, du, dd).

Once we have computed risk-neutral probabilities satisfying the preceding, today's and future's price of any contingent claim is

$$C(t_1, \omega) = E_{t_1}[D(t_1, t_2, \omega) C(t_2, \omega)]$$
$$C(t_0) = E_{t_0}[D(t_0, t_1, \omega) D(t_1, t_2, \omega) C(t_2, \omega)]$$

Notice the similarity in the form of these equations for the underlying asset and contingent claims. As the asset itself can be considered as a trivial contingent claim—a claim whose payoff equals the underlying asset, $C(t, \omega) = A(t, \omega)$—the equations for the contingent claim are all we need to both characterize risk-neutral probabilities, and to value *all* contingent claims.

Path Discounting

Note that the preceding terms $D(t_1, t_2, \omega)$ are state-dependent, and reflect the short-term financing rates (expressed as discount factors) in each state:

$$D(t_1, t_2, \omega) = \frac{1}{1 + r(t_1, \omega) \times (t_2 - t_1)}$$

This means that each final payoff $C(t_2, \omega)$ has to get discounted back to today along the path of short-term financing rates (or discount factors) that lead to that final state. This is referred to as *stochastic discounting* or *path discounting*. We arrive at the core idea of risk-neutral valuation: *The value of any contingent claim at any time, state, (t, ω), is the risk-neutral expectation of its stochastically discounted future cash flows.*

Self-Financing, Dynamic Hedging

As we subdivide the time to expiration into finer partitions, we have to ensure that the original portfolio can be dynamically managed to replicate the option value. At each state, we can change the amount of asset we hold by securing requisite funds at the prevailing financing rates. As we do this dynamic rebalancing (changing Δs), we have to ensure that the value of the portfolio entering into each state equals the value of the portfolio leaving the state, that is, the replicating portfolio should be *self-financing*.

Consider the *up* state (A_u, r_u). As we enter it, we hold a portfolio that consists of Δ_0 units of the asset (now worth A_u at t_1), and a loan of size L_0 plus its interest (worth $L_0/D(t_0, t_1)$ at time t_1). Therefore the value of the portfolio value is:

$$C_u = \Delta_0 A_u + L_0/D(t_0, t_1)$$

On the other hand, $C_u = \Delta_u A_u + L_u$, since (Δ_u, L_u) is the required portfolio to replicate the option payoffs (C_{uu}, C_{ud}) at the next time step t_2. Therefore, we need to change our holding of the asset from Δ_0 to Δ_u only by changing the size of our loan from $L_0/D(t_0, t_1)$ to L_u, that is, the change in the underlying holding should only be financed by the loan:

$$(\Delta_u - \Delta_0) A_u = L_u - L_0/D(t_0, t_1)$$

ensuring that the portfolio is *self-financing*.

Example in Two-Period Setting

To make the previous ideas clear, we consider a 2-month call option on $100M 2-year 5% semi-annual bond struck at par ($K = 100\%$), where the time to expiration has been broken into two 1-month periods, Figure 5.4. The seller of the option can replicate the option cash flows as follows:

(A_0, r_0) - Receive the option premium $0.945M today, borrow (in repo) $53.527M at 1-month repo rate of 4%, and use the proceeds, $54.472M (= $0.945M + $53.527M), to buy $54.472M face of the bond trading at full price of 100%. In 1 month, he will owe (repo) financing of $53.705M (= $53.527M × (1 + 0.04/12)), and will own $54.472M face of the bond.

(A_u, r_u) - If we end up in the (101%, 3.75%)-state, the incoming value of our replicating portfolio is $1.312M = $54.472M × 101% − $54.472M. To replicate the option payoffs for the next period, we need to adjust our holding of the bond and the (repo) loan to (Δ_u, L_u) = (100%, −$99.688M), that is, we buy an additional $45.528M face of the bond at full price of 101% and

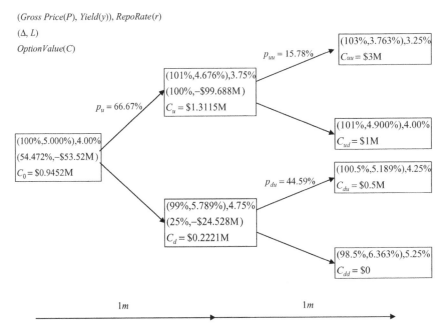

(Gross Price(P), Yield(y)), RepoRate(r)

(Δ, L)

OptionValue(C)

$P_{uu} = 15.78\%$

(103%,3.763%),3.25%
$C_{uu} = \$3M$

(101%,4.676%),3.75%
(100%,−$99.688M)
$C_u = \$1.3115M$

$p_u = 66.67\%$

(101%,4.900%),4.00%
$C_{ud} = \$1M$

(100%,5.000%),4.00%
(54.472%,−$53.52M)
$C_0 = \$0.9452M$

(100.5%,5.189%),4.25%
$P_{du} = 44.59\%$
$C_{du} = \$0.5M$

(99%,5.789%),4.75%
(25%,−$24.528M)
$C_d = \$0.2221M$

(98.5%,6.363%),5.25%
$C_{dd} = \$0$

1m   1m

FIGURE 5.4 Example of Option Pricing in a Two-Period Setting

finance $99.688M at 1-month repo rate of 3.75% to owe $100M = $99.688M × (1 + 3.75%/12) while owning $100M face of the bond in 1 month. In either future state, (A_{uu}, A_{ud}), the value of our bond ($103M, $101M), minus the financing cost $100M, is exactly what we owe the option buyer: $3M, or $1M. Notice that while we rebalanced the portfolio, the outgoing value $1.312M (= $100M × 101% − $99.688M) is the same as incoming value, that is, the portfolio is self-financing.

(A_d, r_d) - If instead, we end up in the (99%, 4.75%)-state, we need to reduce our bond position to Δ_d = $25M face, and change the repo borrowing to L_d = −$24.528M. Regardless of what happens 1 month later, the option seller will owe the (repo) financing of $24.625M (= $24.528M × (1 + 0.0475/12)), and own $25M face of the bond. If we end up in A_{du} = 100.5%, the option will be exercised for cash value of $0.5M, while we can sell the bond for $25.125M (= $25M × 100.5%), and pay $24.625M for financing, a wash. If instead, we end up in A_{dd} = 98.5% state, the option will not get exercised. The seller liquidates his $25M face of bond trading at 98.5% for $24.625M (= $25M × 98.5%), and uses these proceeds to settle exactly the financing cost ($24.625M). Again note that the incoming value, $0.222M (= $54.472M × 99% − $54.472M) is the same as outgoing portfolio value $0.222M (= $25M × 99% − $24.528M).

FROM TWO TIME-STEPS TO . . .

We can continue to subdivide the interval $[t_0, t_e]$ into smaller short intervals. Let $\{t_i\}_{i=0}^{N}$ be partition of $[t_0, t_e]$ into N intervals, with $0 = t_0 < t_1 < \cdots < t_N = t_e$, and let $r_i(\omega)$ denote the financing rate at t_i for $[t_i, t_{i+1}]$, along ω, the random future state/path of the world. Then sitting at today $t = 0$, we only know r_0, and if interest rates are nondeterministic, $r_1(\omega), r_2(\omega), \ldots, r_{N-1}(\omega)$ are all random. The generalized version of risk-neutral formula becomes

$$C(t_0, \omega) = E_{t_0}\left[\frac{1}{1 + r_0(\omega)dt_0} \times \cdots \times \frac{1}{1 + r_{N-1}(\omega)dt_{N-1}} C(t_N, \omega) \right]$$

$$C(t_0, \omega) = E_{t_0}\left[D(t_0, t_1, \omega) \times \cdots \times D(t_{N-1}, t_N, \omega) \times C(t_N, \omega) \right]$$

where

$$D(t_i, t_{i+1}, \omega) = \frac{1}{1 + r_i(\omega)dt_i} \qquad dt_i = t_{i+1} - t_i$$

Hence, each random payoff at expiration, $C(t_N, \omega)$, has to get discounted along the series of random short-term financing rates that lead to that state of the world. Once we collect all these random payoffs and their corresponding random PVs, we can average over all possible states ω to arrive at today's value.

RELATIVE PRICES

Focusing on the term multiplying the final payoff, we observe that the term

$$D(t_0, t_1, \omega) \times \cdots D(t_{N-1}, t_N, \omega)$$

can be interpreted as the stochastic discount factor over the interval $[t_0, t_N]$, while its inverse, $M(t_0, t_N, \omega)$, is the *stochastic future value*:

$$M(t_0, t_N, \omega) = \frac{1}{D(t_0, t_1, \omega) \times \cdots D(t_{N-1}, t_N, \omega)}$$
$$= [1 + r_0(\omega)dt_0][1 + r_1(\omega)dt_1] \ldots [1 + r_{N-1}(\omega)dt_{N-1}]$$

As $M(t_0, t_N, \omega)$ is simply the value of unit currency reinvested at successive short term rates $r_i(\omega)$, it is usually called the *money-market account*. Since $M(t_0, t_0, \omega) = 1$, the risk-neutral formula can be rewritten as:

$$\frac{C(t_0, \omega)}{M(t_0, t_0, \omega)} = E_{t_0}\left[\frac{C(t_N, \omega)}{M(t_0, t_N, \omega)}\right]$$

Expressed this way, we observe that the risk-neutral formula is just a simple condition on *relative prices*, that is, the value of any contingent claim relative to the money-market account, $C(t, \omega)/M(t_0, t, \omega)$.

No Expected Change in Relative Prices

In terms of relative prices, a characterization of risk-neutral probabilities is that at any point of time t_0, the expected future relative prices, $E_{t_0}[C(t_N)/M(t_0, t_N)]$, are the same as the current relative prices, $C(t_0)/M(t_0, t_0)$. *Relative prices have no expected profit/loss in a risk-neutral world.*

This characterization evokes fair games from probability theory. For example, if we continually toss a fair coin with payoff of ± 1 if heads/tails, then at any point, our expected future stake is whatever our current stake is, since the expected gain from each coin toss is 0. In probability theory, this is called the *martingale* property. In general, martingales are an abstraction of fair games, that is, processes that have zero expected change. In this language, *relative prices are martingales under risk-neutral probabilities.*

RISK-NEUTRAL VALUATION: ALL RELATIVE PRICES MUST BE MARTINGALES

We now have all the concepts for risk-neutral valuation. While the above discussion has been focused on a single risky asset, the arguments can be generalized to multiple risky assets, as established in papers by Harrison et al., and we refer the interested reader to them. We will be content with the following variant of their results: *In a risk-neutral setting with multiple risky assets, all relative prices relative to the money-market account must be martingales.* The *all* in the previous statement includes both the underlyings *and* contingent claims on them.

Focusing on the underlying tradeable assets in fixed income, that is, zero-coupon bonds, and their prices expressed as discount factors, since a t_e-expiry zero-coupon bond has unit value at t_e, the risk-neutral probabilities must satisfy

$$\frac{D(t_0, t_e, \omega)}{M(t_0, t_0)} = E_{t_0}\left[\frac{D(t_e, t_e, \omega)}{M(t_0, t_e, \omega)}\right]$$

$$\Rightarrow D(t_0, t_e, \omega) = E_{t_0}\left[\frac{1}{M(t_0, t_e, \omega)}\right]$$

With this setup, risk-neutral valuation reduces to ensuring that the above is satisfied for all $t_e \geq t_0 \geq 0$, and valuing contingent claims via:

$$C(t_0) = E_{t_0}\left[\frac{C(t_e, \omega)}{M(t_0, t_e, \omega)}\right]$$

Continuous-Time

By letting the number of time intervals N go to infinity, we arrive at the continuous-time version of risk-neutral formula. We let $M(t, \omega)$ denote the money-market account:

$$M(t, \omega) = e^{\int_0^t r(u, \omega) du}$$

started today $(t = 0)$ with unit currency: $M(0) = 1$, where $r(u, \omega)$ denotes the instantaneous financing rate over $[u, u + du]$ along the future random path ω. The martingale condition becomes

$$(0 \leq t \leq T) \qquad \frac{C(t, \omega)}{M(t, \omega)} = E_t \left[\frac{C(T, \omega)}{M(T, \omega)} \right]$$

for all futures dates t and maturities T, including any particular expiry $T = t_e$. This can also be expressed as

$$(0 \leq t \leq T) \qquad C(t, \omega) = E_t[e^{-\int_t^T r(u,\omega)du} C(T, \omega)]$$

The above applies to all contingent claims. In particular, since discount factors at any time t are prices of unit currency at future dates $T \geq t$, we have

$$(0 \leq t \leq T) \qquad D(t, T, \omega) = E_t[e^{-\int_t^T r(u,\omega)du}]$$

and today's $(t = 0)$ discount factors must satisfy

$$(0 \leq T) \qquad D(0, T, \omega) = E_0[e^{-\int_o^T r(u,\omega)du}]$$

INTEREST-RATE OPTIONS ARE INHERENTLY DIFFICULT TO VALUE

Notice that as we were laying out scenarios for the future states of the world, for each state we had to specify both the underlying tradeable asset value *and* the short-term financing rates in that same state, that is, we had to consider the *co-evolution* of financing rates and the underlying tradeable asset. For example, for the 2-month bond call option, at each state we had to consider the bond price/yield *and* the repo rate. If instead we were looking to price an option on a swap, we would have to consider the underlying (forward) swap value and the financing (Libor) rate. As the value of a swap depends on the discount factor curve at each state, we would have to consider the evolution of the whole discount factor curve, a multidimensional problem. Of course, we can collapse all the information from the discount curve to the relevant underlying instrument (swap rate, swap value, bond price/yield), but still we would have to co-evolve this information with the financing rates.

This is in sharp contrast to pricing options on single stocks, FX, commodities, where the underlying is a single asset (1-dimensional), and since most of the risk is in the underlying, interest rates are conveniently assumed to be deterministic. For deterministic (nonrandom) interest rates, the stochastic discount factor can be replaced by its nonstochastic counterpart:

$$1/M(t_e, \omega) = e^{-\int_0^{t_e} r(u,\omega)du} = D(0, t_e)$$

In this case, the discount factor can be taken outside the expectation, simplifying risk-neutral formula to:

$$C(0) = E_0[e^{-\int_0^{t_e} r(u,\omega)} C(t_e, \omega)]$$
$$= D(0, t_e) \times E_0[C(t_e, \omega)]$$

For deterministic interest rates, contingent claim valuation then reduces to computing *discounted expected payoffs*, an easier feat than calculating *expected discounted payoffs,* which would require co-evolution of assets and interest rates. As we will in later chapters, by assuming certain terminal distributions (Normal, Log-Normal) for the underlying asset, we can get closed-form formulae (Black) for simple European options such as calls, puts, digitals. Due to their relatively simple structure and ease of quoting— much like flat yield-to-maturity for quoting bonds—these Black formulae and their variants are commonly used even for interest-rate options, despite the inconsistency of simultaneously assuming deterministic discounting *and* nondeterministic interest rates at expiration.

FROM BINOMIAL MODEL TO EQUIVALENT MARTINGALE MEASURES

We stated, "In an arbitrage-free market, there exists an equivalent measure where assets' prices relative to some numeraire are martingales. If the market is complete, this martingale measure is unique, and option prices are expected relative (to the numeraire) prices."

Let us try to see if we can now parse the above and see their primordial counterparts in our simple CRR binomial model:

"Arbitrage-Free": We showed that lack of arbitrage is equivalent to p_u being a probability, $0 \le p_u \le 1$.

"Equivalent": The asset possibility-space A_u, A_d was fixed. We ignored the real probabilities, and focused on new (risk-neutral) probabilities. Note that we can only do this as long as we are interested in pricing contingent claims. The risk-neutral probabilities are not true-world probabilities, and should not be used to forecast future expected outcomes (although many people do!).

"Complete": The assumption that option payoffs can be replicated via underlyings.

"Unique": We set up two equations and two unknowns, and we could solve for Δ, L. If we had more unknowns than equations, the solution would be indeterminate, and hence not unique.

"Numeraire": The *currency* relative to which asset prices are expressed. We selected the rolled-over money-market account, $M(0, t, \omega)$, as our choice of numeraire.

"Relative prices are martingales": $E_t[C(T, \omega)/M(T, \omega)] = C(t)/M(t)$. This compact formula completely characterizes the risk-neutral probabilities, relating them to the assumed underlying asset value evolution, and also is the pricing operator for contingent claims.

Indeed, the two-step binomial model captures all the key ingredients of option pricing, and is all one really needs to understand the concept of risk-neutral valuation.

A final note is that the *money-market account* choice of numeraire, although common, is not required, and any positive-valued process can serve as the numeraire. For interest rate options, we chose the money-market account as this is the most common and intuitive numeraire. Chapter 11 picks up the discussion on the choice of other numeraires.

CHAPTER 6

Black's World

The Black-Scholes-Merton formula, and its Black variant for futures was historically derived for non-interest-rate-related underlying assets (equities, FX, commodities), and under the assumption that interest rates are nonrandom. When interest rate options (cap/floors, swaptions) were introduced, traders co-opted these formulas and applied them to interest rates. While everyone recognized that the formulae need to be adjusted since interest rates are not traded assets, and *are* random, nevertheless, in the absence of any other simple alternatives, Black's formula became (and still continues to be) the standard option pricing formula for interest-rate flow products.

Therefore, we will suspend disbelief for a while and derive the Black-Scholes-Merton formula in a world where interest rates are deterministic, and then turn around and apply these to interest rate options!

Before we get there, however, a bit of probability review is in order.

A LITTLE BIT OF RANDOMNESS

A random variable (r.v.) X is said to have a *Normal* distribution with mean μ and standard deviation σ, if the probability that it lies in some region $[x, x + dx]$ is approximately

$$\frac{1}{\sqrt{2\pi\sigma^2}} e - \frac{(x-\mu)^2}{2\sigma^2} dx$$

We will use the shorthand $X \sim N(\mu, \sigma^2)$. More precisely, the *cumulative distribution function* (CDF) of an $N(\mu, \sigma^2)$ random variable X is

$$F_X(x) \equiv P[X \le x] = \int_{-\infty}^{x} \frac{1}{\sqrt{2\pi\sigma^2}} e^{-\frac{(z-\mu)^2}{2\sigma^2}} dz$$

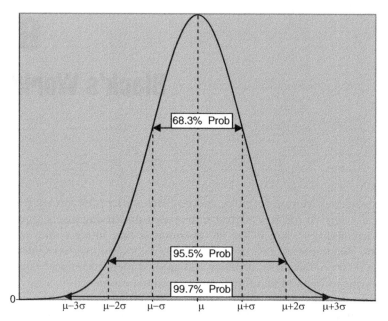

FIGURE 6.1 Distribution Function of a Normal $N(\mu, \sigma^2)$ Random Variable

and its *density function* (DF) is

$$f_X(x) \equiv \frac{d}{dx} F(x) = \frac{1}{\sqrt{2\pi\sigma^2}} e - \frac{(x-\mu)^2}{2\sigma^2}$$

The density $f_X(\cdot)$ looks like a bell-shaped curve, centered around the mean μ, and symmetric around it. The fatness of the bell is directly proportional to the standard deviation σ, Figure 6.1.

The Normal distribution is a *stable* distribution, that is, closed under scaling and shifting: If $X \sim N(\mu, \sigma^2)$, then any linear function $Y = aX + b$ is also Normally distributed and $Y \sim N(\mu + a, b^2\sigma^2)$. That is why we can always start with a *Standard Normal*, $N(0, 1)$, and get another Normal r.v. with any desired mean and variance:

$$N(\mu, \sigma^2) \sim \mu + \sigma N(0, 1)$$

The CDF of a standard normal, $N(x) \equiv P[N(0, 1) \leq x]$ is widely available in tabulated form, or from numerical recipes with varying degree of precision.

$N(\cdot)$ is symmetric: $N(x) = N(-x)$, and satisfies

$$P[N(0, 1) \geq x] = 1 - P[N(0, 1) \leq -x] = 1 - N(-x)$$

Moreover,

$$P[N(\mu, \sigma^2) \leq x] = P[\mu + \sigma N(0, 1) \leq x]$$
$$= P\left[N(0, 1) \leq \frac{x - \mu}{\sigma}\right]$$
$$= N\left(\frac{x - \mu}{\sigma}\right)$$

Expected Values, Moments

The *mean* or *expected value* of a random variable X with density $f_X(\cdot)$ is defined as:

$$E[X] \equiv \int x f_X(x) dx$$

For an $N(0, 1)$ r.v., $E[X] = 0$ and since Expectation is a linear operator

$$E[N(\mu, \sigma^2)] = E[\mu + \sigma N(0, 1)]$$
$$= \mu + \sigma E[N(0, 1)]$$
$$= \mu$$

The *variance* or the second *central moment* of a random variable is defined as

$$Var(X) \equiv E(X - EX)^2 = E[X^2] - (EX)^2$$

and its square root is called the *standard deviation*. For an $N(\mu, \sigma^2)$ r.v., its variance is σ^2, and its standard deviation is σ.

In general, for any function $g(\cdot)$ of an r.v. X, its mean is defined as

$$E[g(X)] \equiv \int g(x) f_X(x) dx$$

Finally, two r.v.'s X, Y are said to be *independent*, if

$$E[f(X) \times g(Y)] = E[f(X)] \times E[g(Y)]$$

for any arbitrary functions f, g. For independent r.v.'s, their variances add up:

$$Var(X + Y) = Var(X) + Var(Y)$$

The *covariance* of two r.v.'s X, Y is defined as

$$Cov(X, Y) = E[(X - EX)(Y - EY)]$$

while the *correlation* is the covariance normalized by the standard deviations:

$$\rho = Corr(X, Y) = \frac{E[(X - EX)(Y - EY)]}{\sqrt{Var(X)}\sqrt{Var(Y)}}$$

Independence is a stronger condition than uncorrelatedness ($\rho = 0$), although for jointly Normal r.v.'s, they coincide.

Log-Normal Distribution

A random variable Y is said to have a *Log-Normal* distribution, $Y \sim LN(\mu, \sigma^2)$, if its *natural* log is an $N(\mu, \sigma^2)$ r.v., or in other words, $Y \sim e^{N(\mu,\sigma^2)}$. Its CDF is

$$\begin{aligned} F_Y(y) &= P[LN(\mu, \sigma^2) \leq y] \\ &= P[N(\mu, \sigma^2) \leq \ln(y)] \\ &= P[\mu + \sigma N(0, 1) \leq \ln(y)] \\ &= N\left(\frac{\ln(y) - \mu}{\sigma}\right) \end{aligned}$$

and its density function (DF) can be obtained as

$$\begin{aligned} f_Y(y) &= \frac{d}{dy} P[LN(\mu, \sigma^2) \leq y] \\ &= \frac{d}{dy} P[N(\mu, \sigma^2) \leq \ln(y)] \\ &= \frac{d}{dy} F_X(\ln(y)) \\ &= \frac{1}{y} f_X(\ln(y)) \\ &= \frac{1}{y\sqrt{2\pi\sigma^2}} e^{-\frac{(\ln(y) - \mu)^2}{2\sigma^2}} \end{aligned}$$

where F_X and f_X denote the CDF and DF of an $N(\mu, \sigma^2)$ r.v.

TABLE 6.1 Properties of Normal and Log-Normal Random Variables

	Normal $N(\mu, \sigma^2)$	Log-Normal $LN(\mu, \sigma^2)$
Density Function	$\frac{1}{\sqrt{2\pi\sigma^2}}e^{-\frac{(x-\mu)^2}{2\sigma^2}}$	$\frac{1}{\sqrt{2\pi\sigma^2}x}e^{-\frac{(\ln(x)-\mu)^2}{2\sigma^2}}$
Mean	μ	$e^{\mu+\sigma^2/2}$
Variance	σ^2	$e^{2\mu+\sigma^2}(e^{\sigma^2}-1)$
Mode	μ	$e^{\mu-\sigma^2}$

A $LN(\mu, \sigma^2)$ r.v. can only take positive values, and its mean is

$$E[LN(\mu, \sigma^2)] = e^{\mu+\sigma^2/2}$$

Note that for a Log-Normal $LN(\mu, \sigma^2)$ r.v., the parameters $\mu, \sigma^2)$ are *not* its mean and variance. A Log-Normal $LN(\ln(\mu^2/\sqrt{\mu^2+\sigma^2}), \ln(1+\mu^2\sigma^2))$ r.v. will have mean μ and variance σ^2, and can be compared to a Normal $N(\mu, \sigma^2)$ r.v., as shown in Figure 6.2.

Central Limit Theorem

Why is the Normal distribution so important? For one thing, it is analytically tractable, and many functionals of it can be evaluated in closed form. More important, it is the limiting distribution of many sequences of r.v.s. Specifically, let X_i be independent, identically distributed r.v.'s with mean μ and variance σ^2 with some distribution. Then

$$\lim_{n\to\infty} \frac{1}{\sqrt{n}} \sum_{i=1}^{n} \frac{X_i - \mu}{\sigma} \sim N(0, 1)$$

This is one version of the *Central Limit Theorem*, which essentially states the distribution of an average tends to be Normal, even when the distribution from which the average is computed is decidedly not Normal.

Random Walk → Brownian Motion

An example of Central Limit Theorem is the random walk. Imagine a particle starting at some origin 0, and for each interval Δt takes a positive or negative step of size Δx with equal probability of $1/2$. On average, the particle is not moving since at each point, the expected movement is zero.

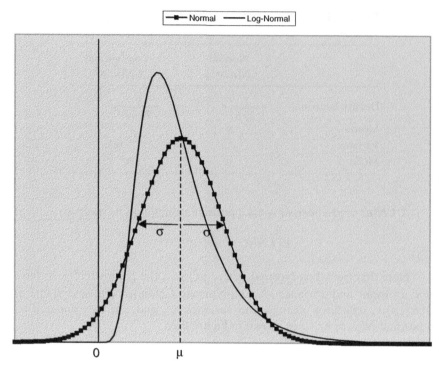

FIGURE 6.2 Comparison of Normal versus Log-Normal Distribution Functions with Same Mean, Variance (μ, σ^2)

However our uncertainty (read variance) about its location increases over time. While initially we were quite certain that it is within a small distance of the origin, over time it will have had more chances to drift away, and we need to assign higher probabilities of further distances from the origin.

If we let the time interval and step size go to zero, while maintaining $\Delta x = \sigma \sqrt{\Delta t}$ for some average step size per unit time σ, we arrive at *Brownian motion* with diffusion coefficient σ. When $\sigma = 1$, the Brownian motion is called a *standard Brownian motion*.

Brownian motion is a deep mathematical subject and has many properties: Markov, Martingale, Independent Increments, everywhere continuous, but nowhere differentiable, ... It has been said that one is not a great probabilist unless one proves a yet new property of the Brownian motion.

For our purposes, we will just use the fact that the increments of a Brownian motion $B(t)$ are independent and Normal:

$$(t_1 < t_2 < t_3) \qquad B(t_2) - B(t_1) \sim N(0, \sigma^2(t_2 - t_1))$$

and $B(t_3) - B(t_2)$ is independent of $B(t_2) - B(t_1)$. Due to the additive property of Normal distributions, this means that the distribution function of a Brownian motion is Normal: $B(t) \sim N(B(0), \sigma^2 t)$.

We have so far focused on Brownian motion with no drift. If instead, $B(t) \sim N(B(0) + \mu t, \sigma^2 t)$, then $B(t)$ is called a Brownian motion with *drift* μ. It can be thought of as the limit of a random walk with a constant drift μ.

MODELING ASSET CHANGES

Normal distributions, random walks, and Brownian motions are commonly used to model the underlying asset value at option expiration. The focus is on the change in asset value from today until the expiration, with the change expressed either in *percentage/proportional* or *absolute* terms. Specifically, starting with asset value today, $A(t_0)$, a European-style option depends on the unknown/random asset value at expiration, $A(t_e, \omega)$.

Proportional Change

One way to model the asset at expiration is to consider its changes over time via:

$$A(t_e, \omega) = A(t_0)e^{r([t_0, t_e], \omega) \times (t_e - t_0)}$$

where $r([t_0, t_e], \omega)$ is the random *return* over investment period $[t_0, t_e]$ for the generic unknown future state of the world ω:

$$r([t_0, t_e], \omega) = \frac{1}{t_e - t_0} \ln \frac{A(t_e, \omega)}{A(t_0)}$$

This measure is also referred to as proportional return, percentage return, or log return. Its standard deviation is referred to as percentage, proportional, or log volatility, or just *volatility*:

$$\sigma = \sqrt{Var \left[\frac{1}{t_e - t_0} \ln \frac{A(t_e, \omega)}{A(t_0)} \right]}$$

Assuming that the percentage return is Normal

$$r([t_0, t_e], \omega) \sim N(\mu \times (t_e - t_0), \sigma^2 \times (t_e - t_0))$$

implies that the asset value at expiration will be Log-Normal:

$$A(t_e)/A(t_0) \sim LN(\mu \times (t_e - t_0), \sigma^2 \times (t_e - t_0))$$

This Log-Normal distribution is somewhat close to the empirical distributions observed for equities—although the empirical/realized distributions tend to have fatter tails than Log-Normal—and is commonly used for equity/FX/commodity options. The original Black-Scholes-Merton formula was derived assuming this dynamic for the evolution of asset prices, written in differential shorthand as

$$\frac{dA(t, \omega)}{A(t, \omega)} = \mu dt + \sigma dB(t, \omega)$$

with the interpretation that over a small period dt, the proportional/percentage change, dA/A, has a known drift μ, and a random component modeled as increments of a Brownian motion with diffusion coefficient σ.

Absolute Change

Another way to model changes is to focus on the absolute change, $A(t_e, \omega) - A(t_0)$, and to model this random change as a Normal r.v.

$$A(t_e) - A(t_0) \sim N(\mu \times (t_e - t_0), \sigma_N^2 \times (t_e - t_0))$$

Under this model, the underlying can take on negative values at expiration, and while inappropriate for equities/FX/commodities, it turns out to be the lesser of the two evils for interest rates, and has become the dominant base-case model for interest rate derivatives. The differential shorthand for the Normal dynamic is

$$dA(t, \omega) = \mu dt + \sigma_N dB(t, \omega)$$

where σ_N is referred to as the absolute or *Normal volatility*.

BLACK-SCHOLES-MERTON/BLACK FORMULAE

We are now ready to derive the Black-Scholes-Merton formula. We will assume that interest rates are deterministic, and consider an asset $A(\cdot)$ with no interim cash flows whose *return*, $\ln A(t)/A(0)$, can be modeled as the limit of a random walk with drift, that is, a Brownian motion. We have

$$(t \geq 0) \quad \ln \frac{A(t)}{A(0)} \sim N(\mu t, \sigma^2 t)$$

Fixing our attention on the expiration date t_e, according to the Risk-Neutral Formula for deterministic interest rates, we must have

$$A(0) = D(0, t_e) E_0[A(t_e)]$$

or equivalently,

$$E_0[A(t_e)] = F_A(0, t_e)$$

where $F = F_A(0, t_e)$ is the forward value of the asset for t_e-delivery. Now since $A(t_e)/A(0)$ is $LN(\mu t_e, \sigma^2 t_e)$, we must also have

$$E_0[A(t_e)] = A(0)e^{\mu t_e + 1/2\sigma^2 t_e}$$

Therefore, under the risk-neutral probabilities, μ must satisfy:

$$e^{\mu t_e} = \frac{1}{D(0, t_e)} e^{-1/2\sigma^2 t_e}$$

which implies

$$A(t_e)/F_A(0, t_e) \sim LN(-1/2\sigma^2 t_e, \sigma^2 t_e)$$

As can be seen, risk neutrality forces the drift μ to be implied by choice of volatility, and in a risk-neutral world, the drift is not an independent parameter. We have seen this before in our binomial model, where we replaced actual probabilities with risk-neutral probabilities once we laid out the possible outcomes. The volatility parameter has the same role in this version as it lays out the possibility space, while μ has to get adjusted so that we are operating in a risk-neutral world. This elimination of μ is referred to as *drift correction* or *change of measure*.

For a call option with strike K, the payoff at expiration is $C(t_e) = \max(0, A(t_e) - K)$. According to Risk-Neutral Formula when interest rates are deterministic, its value today is $C(0) = D(0, t_e)E_0[\max(0, A(t_e) - K)]$.

Letting $F = F_A(0, t_e)$ for notational ease, we have:

$$
\begin{aligned}
C(0) &= D(0, t_e) E_0[\max(0, A(t_e) - K)] \\
&= D(0, t_e) \times F \times E_0\left[\max\left(0, \frac{A(t_e)}{F} - \frac{K}{F}\right)\right] \\
&= D(0, t_e) \times F \times \int_{-\infty}^{\infty} \max\left(0, x - \frac{K}{F}\right) f_X(x) dx \\
&= D(0, t_e) \times F \times \int_{K/F}^{\infty} \left(x - \frac{K}{F}\right) f_X(x) dx \\
&= D(0, t_e) \times F \times \int_{K/F}^{\infty} x f_X(x) dx - D(0, t_e) \times K \times \int_{K/F}^{\infty} f_X(x) dx
\end{aligned}
$$

where $f_X(\cdot)$ is the distribution function of $A(t_e)/F \sim LN(-1/2\sigma^2 t_e, \sigma^2 t_e)$:

$$
f_X(x) = \frac{1}{\sqrt{2\pi\sigma^2 t_e} x} e^{-\dfrac{(\ln x + 1/2\sigma^2 t_e)^2}{2\sigma^2 t_e}}
$$

The integral in the second term is simply the area under the distribution function of a $LN(-1/2\sigma^2 t_e, \sigma^2 t_e)$ r.v., which is just the probability of falling in that region:

$$
\begin{aligned}
\int_{K/F}^{\infty} f_X(x) dx &= P[LN(-1/2\sigma^2 t_e, \sigma^2 t_e) \geq K/F] \\
&= P[N(-1/2\sigma^2 t_e, \sigma^2 t_e) \geq \ln K/F] \\
&= N\left(\frac{\ln F/K}{\sigma\sqrt{t_e}} - 1/2\sigma\sqrt{t_e}\right)
\end{aligned}
$$

In order to compute the first term, we do a change of variable:

$$
z = \frac{\ln x + 1/2\sigma^2 t_e}{\sigma\sqrt{t_e}}
$$

hence,

$$
dx = \sigma\sqrt{t_e} e^{\sigma\sqrt{t_e} z - 1/2\sigma^2 t_e} dz
$$

and

$$\int_{K/F}^{\infty} x f_X(x) dx = \int_{K/F}^{\infty} \frac{1}{\sqrt{2\pi\sigma^2 t_e}} e^{-\frac{(\ln x + 1/2\sigma^2 t_e)^2}{2\sigma^2 t_e}} dx$$

$$= \int_{\frac{\ln K/F}{\sigma\sqrt{t_e}}+1/2\sigma\sqrt{t_e}}^{\infty} \frac{1}{\sqrt{2\pi}} e^{-\frac{(z-\sigma\sqrt{t_e})^2}{2}} dz$$

$$= P\left[N(\sigma\sqrt{t_e}, 1) > \frac{\ln K/F}{\sigma\sqrt{t_e}} + 1/2\sigma\sqrt{t_e} \right]$$

$$= P\left[N(0, 1) > \frac{\ln K/F}{\sigma\sqrt{t_e}} - 1/2\sigma\sqrt{t_e} \right]$$

$$= N\left(\frac{\ln F/K}{\sigma\sqrt{t_e}} + 1/2\sigma\sqrt{t_e} \right)$$

Putting it all together, we have the celebrated Black-Scholes formula for calls:

$$C(0) = D(0, t_e) \times [F_A(0, t_e) N(d_1) - K N(d_2)]$$

$$d_{1,2} = \frac{\ln(F_A(0, t_e)/K)}{\sigma\sqrt{t_e}} \pm \frac{1}{2}\sigma\sqrt{t_e}$$

Put-Call Parity

Rather than going through the previous procedure to derive the value of a put, we would appeal to another argument. Consider two portfolios:

1. A t_e-expiry call option with strike K, and cash holding equal to the present value of K, that is, $K D(0, t_e)$.
2. A t_e-expiry put option with strike K, and the underlying asset, $A(0)$.

If the underlying asset has no interim cash flows until t_e, then the two portfolios will have the same value, $\max(A(t_e), K)$, at expiration t_e. Therefore, they must have the same value today $(t = 0)$, and we must have:

$$P(0) + A(0) = C(0) + K D(0, t_e)$$

This identity is called *put-call parity*, and holds for European-style options on underlyings with no interim cash flows. Using Black-Scholes-Merton call formula, we get

$$P(0) = C(0) + KD(0, t_e) - A(0)$$
$$= D(0, t_e)[C(0)/D(0, t_e) + K - F_A(0, t_e)]$$
$$= D(0, t_e)[F_A(0, t_e)N(d_1) - KN(d_2) + K - F_A(0,e)]$$
$$= D(0, t_e)[K(1 - N(d_2)) - F_A(0, t_e)(1 - N(d_1))]$$
$$= D(0, t_e)[KN(-d_2) - F_A(0, t_e)N(-d_1)]$$

In particular, when the strike equals the *at-the-money-forward (ATMF)* value of the asset, $K = F_A(0, t_e)$, then the call and put prices coincide: $P(0) = C(0)$.

Black's Formula

Continuing with the assumption that interest rates are deterministic, consider the T-forward value of an asset with no interim cash flows. In this case, $F_A(t, T) = A(t)/D(t, T)$, and an option on the forward can be related to the option on the underlying. For example, a t_e-expiration call on the T-forward with strike K can be valued as

$$D(0, t_e)E_0[\max(0, F_A(t_e, T) - K)] = D(0, t_e)E_0\left[\max\left(0, \frac{A(t_e)}{D(t_e, T)} - K\right)\right]$$
$$= \frac{D(0, t_e)}{D(t_e, T)}E_0[\max(0, A(t_e) - KD(t_e, T))]$$
$$= \frac{D(0, t_e)}{D(t_e, T)}[F_A(0, t_e)N(d_1) - KD(t_e, T)N(d_2)]$$
$$= D(0, t_e) \times [F_A(0, T)N(d_1) - KN(d_2)]$$

where

$$d_{1,2} = \frac{\ln(F_A(0, T)/K)}{\sigma\sqrt{t_e}} \pm 1/2\sigma\sqrt{t_e}$$

since $D(0, t_e)D(t_e, T) = D(0, T)$ where interest rates are deterministic.

If the settlement date of the forward contract coincides with the option expiration, that is, $t_e = T$, then the above equation reduces to the Black-Scholes formula expressed in terms of t_e-forwards.

While derived using different methods, this formula, derived by Black,[1] is the most commonly used (and abused) formula to price interest rate derivatives.

Black's Normal Call/Put Formulae

The Black formulae were derived by assuming that asset *returns* have a Normal Distribution. This would imply that future asset prices are Log-Normally distributed.

Alternatively, one can assume that the future underlyings themselves, rather than their returns, are Normally distributed. While unrealistic for equities, and semirealistic for interest rates, it focuses the attention on *absolute changes* in the underlying rather than *percent changes*. This seems to be a better way to think about interest rates, as they themselves are related to asset returns. Moreover, similar to the Log-Normal case, one can derive analytical formulas for calls and puts.

For the Normal model, we will assume that

$$(t \geq 0) \qquad A(t) - A(0) \sim N(\mu t, \sigma_N^2 t)$$

Risk neutrality implies that

$$(t \geq 0) \qquad A(t) \sim N(F_A(0, t), \sigma_N^2 t)$$

For a t_e-expiry call option with strike K, we have:

$$
\begin{aligned}
C(0) &= D(0, t_e) E_0[\max(0, A(t_e) - K)] \\
&= D(0, t_e) \int_{-\infty}^{\infty} \max(0, x - K) f_X(x) dx \\
&= D(0, t_e) \int_{K}^{\infty} (x - K) f_X(x) dx \\
&= D(0, t_e) \left[\int_{K}^{\infty} (x - F_A(0, t_e)) f_X(x) dx + (F_A(0, t_e) - K) \int_{K}^{\infty} f_X(x) dx \right]
\end{aligned}
$$

where $f_X(\cdot)$ is the DF of $A(t_e)$:

$$f_X(x) = \frac{1}{\sqrt{2\pi \sigma_N^2 t_e}} e^{-\frac{(x - F_A(0, t_e))^2}{2\sigma_N^2 t_e}}$$

The integral in the second term is simply the area under the DF of a $N(F_A(0, t_e), \sigma_N^2 t_e)$ r.v., which is just the probability of falling in that region:

$$\int_K^\infty f_X(x)dx = P[N(F_A(0, t_e), \sigma_N^2 t_e) \geq K]$$

$$= P[F_A(0, t_e) + \sigma_N\sqrt{t_e}N(0, 1) \geq K]$$

$$= P\left[N(0, 1) \geq \frac{K - F_A(0, t_e)}{\sigma_N\sqrt{t_e}}\right]$$

$$= N\left(\frac{F_A(0, t_e) - K}{\sigma_N\sqrt{t_e}}\right)$$

The first integral can be reduced:

$$\int_K^\infty (x - F_A(0, t_e)) f_X(x)dx = \frac{-\sigma_N\sqrt{t_e}}{\sqrt{2\pi}} \int_K^\infty \frac{d}{dx}\left(e^{-\frac{(x-F_A(0,t_e))^2}{2\sigma_N^2 t_e}}\right)dx$$

$$= \frac{1}{\sqrt{2\pi}}\sigma_N\sqrt{t_e}e^{-\frac{(F_A(0,t_e)-K)^2}{2\sigma_N^2 t_e}}$$

Therefore,

$$C(0) = D(0, t_e)\sigma_N\sqrt{t_e}\left[N'(d) + dN(d)\right] \qquad d = \frac{F_A(0, t_e) - K}{\sigma_N\sqrt{t_e}}$$

Note that d (actually $-d$) is a measure of the *moneyness* of the option as it expresses the distance between the forward versus the strike, $F_A - K$, expressed in units of standard deviation, $\sigma_N\sqrt{t_e}$. A similar interpretation can be given to d_1 for Log-Normal dynamics.

By put-call parity, the value of a put, $P(0)$, becomes

$$P(0) = C(0) + (K - F_A(0, t_e))D(0, t_e)$$

$$= D(0, t_e)\left[\sigma_N\sqrt{t_e}\left(N'(d) + dN(d)\right) + (K - F_A(0, t_e))\right]$$

$$= D(0, t_e)\sigma_N\sqrt{t_e}\left[N'(d) + dN(d) - d\right]$$

$$= D(0, t_e)\sigma_N\sqrt{t_e}\left[N'(d) - dN(-d)\right]$$

Similar to the Log-Normal case when interest rates are deterministic, options on forwards with delivery date T later than expiration date t_e

using Normal dynamics can be valued using above formulae with $F_A(0, t_e)$ replaced $F_A(0, T)$.

Implied Volatilities

In practice, one has to back out the implied volatility from the quoted market prices of options. When using Log-Normal formulae, one arrives at the *implied* Log-Normal volatility, or log-vol, while Normal formulae give implied normal volatility, sometimes called *basis-point volatility* (BPVol), or normalized, normal volatility.

For interest rate options, ATMF ($K = F$) straddle prices are typically quoted. Since for ATMF options, call and put prices are equal, a straddle price is simply twice the call: $S(0) = C(0) + P(0) = 2C(0)$. Since $K = F$, $d_{1,2} = \pm 1/2\sigma\sqrt{t_e}$, and

$$S(0) = 2F\left[N\left(\frac{\sigma\sqrt{t_e}}{2}\right) - N\left(-\frac{\sigma\sqrt{t_e}}{2}\right)\right]$$

for Log-Normal dynamics, while $d = 0$, and

$$S(0) = 2\sigma_N\sqrt{t_e}N'(0)$$

for Normal dynamics. Therefore,

$$F\left[N\left(\frac{\sigma\sqrt{t_e}}{2}\right) - N\left(-\frac{\sigma\sqrt{t_e}}{2}\right)\right] = \sigma_N\sqrt{t_e}N'(0)$$

By using a Taylor series approximation around 0, we have

$$N\left(\frac{\sigma\sqrt{t_e}}{2}\right) - N\left(-\frac{\sigma\sqrt{t_e}}{2}\right) \approx N'(0)\sigma\sqrt{t_e}$$

which results in the following approximation for converting between ATMF Normal and Log-Normal implied vols:

$$\sigma_N \approx \sigma \times F$$

A similar expression can be derived to relate the implied Normal and Log-Normal vols for different strikes:

$$\sigma_N(K) \approx \sigma(K) \times \sqrt{FK}$$

reducing to the preceding when $K = F$.

GREEKS

Recall that Black's formulae were obtained as special instances of risk-neutral valuation under the assumed dynamics for proportional or absolute returns. We should not forget that risk-neutral valuation gives the same value as a self-financing replicating portfolio. The question arises as to what happened to the replicating portfolio, and how do we replicate an option's payoff? The answer lies in the *Greeks*.

Recall that in our binomial setting, the replicating portfolio was Δ units of the underlying asset financed via a risk-free loan. The Δ amount had to be (dynamically) changed in response to market movements. In the simple 1-step binomial model, we computed

$$\Delta = \frac{C_u - C_d}{A_u - A_d}$$

which can be interpreted as the sensitivity of the option price with respect to the underlying asset.

In the limit, $\Delta \to \frac{\partial C}{\partial F}$, and the replicating portfolio consists of $\frac{\partial C}{\partial F}$ units of a forward contract on the asset. This is called the *delta* of the option. The delta is a number between 0 and 1, and expresses how much of the forward asset is needed to replicate the option payoff. For Log-Normal dynamics, it is measured as $N(d_1)$, while for Normal it is $N(d)$.

As we saw in the 2-step binomial model, the delta changes. The rate of change of delta with respect to the underlying is called *gamma* and is defined as $\frac{\partial^2 C}{\partial F^2}$. Gamma measures the curvature of the option payoff, and is also called the *convexity*.

The intrinsic value of an option is its value at expiration, and the time value of an option is the difference between the option value and its intrinsic value. Time value tends to 0 as one gets closer to expiration. *Theta* or time-decay is defined as the rate of change of option value due to time $\frac{\partial C}{\partial t_e}$. An option holder typically loses time value as one gets closer to expiry.

Finally, the sensitivity of an option with respect to volatility $\frac{\partial C}{\partial \sigma}$ is called *Vega*.

Black-Scholes PDE

The original Black-Scholes-Merton formula was derived by considering the inter relationship of gamma, theta, delta, of a generic contingent claim $C(t, A(t))$ in relationship to the underlying $A(t)$, expressed as a partial differential equation (PDE). While this PDE approach and the associated numerical algorithms are used for single-dimensional underlyings (equities, FX, . . .), it is less common for interest rate derivatives. We will simply state the *Black-Scholes-Merton PDE*, and refer the interested reader to other sources for this approach. Under deterministic interest rates, for underlyings with no interim cash flows evolving according to

$$dA(t, \omega) = \mu(t, \omega)dt + \sigma(t, \omega)dB(t, \omega)$$

the Black-Scholes PDE for any European-style contingent claim $C(t, A(t, \omega))$ must satisfy:

$$\frac{\partial C}{\partial t}(t) + r(t)A(t)\frac{\partial C}{\partial A}(t) + \frac{1}{2}\frac{\partial^2 C}{\partial A^2}(t)\sigma^2(t) = r(t)C(t, A(t))$$

where $r(t)$ is the instantaneous risk-free financing rate. The PDE applies to any contingent claim. In particular, for a t_e-expiry call with strike K, we have $C(t_e) = \max(0, A(t_e) - K)$, and with this terminal condition, the PDE can be solved backwards to arrive at $C(0)$:

$$C(0) = e^{-\int_0^{t_e} r(t)dt}[F_A(0, t_e)N(d_1) - KN(d_2)]$$

Gamma versus Theta

As seen in Figure 6.3, the Black's call value is a convex function of the underlying, and its delta changes when the underlying moves. The dynamic rebalancing of the replicating portfolio is primarily the result of this convexity, and it confers a systematic edge to the replicating portfolio. Loosely said, a delta-hedged replicating portfolio consisting of a financed position of $\frac{\partial C}{\partial F}$ units of the underlying will need to get rebalanced as forwards move. For the option holder, be it call or put, it requires reducing/increasing the position if the underlying appreciates/depreciates, that is, the option holder will have to buy-low, sell-high to replicate the option payoff! The amount of this excess P&L of a delta-hedged option is predominantly $1/2 \times$ Gamma $\times (\Delta F)^2$, similar to the convexity P&L of a duration-neutral portfolio of bonds.

A delta-hedged long option position experiences 2 dominant P&Ls: it loses time value every day, and it gains a gamma P&L as the position is rebalanced (delta has changed). Note that the gamma P&L is incurred whether the asset moves up or down. This is shown in Figure 6.3 for a call option.

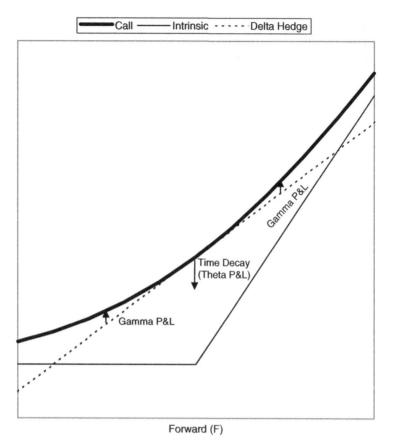

FIGURE 6.3 Gamma P&L versus Time Decay for a European Call Option

The typical (expected) movement of the forward asset over a short interval time dt is prescribed by volatility as $dF \approx \sigma F \sqrt{dt}$ or $dF \approx \sigma_N \sqrt{dt}$. Hence for a delta-hedged option, we have:

$$\frac{\partial C}{\partial t_e} dt_e + \frac{1}{2} \frac{\partial^2 C}{\partial F^2} \sigma^2 F^2 dt_e = 0$$

or

$$\frac{\partial C}{\partial t_e} dt_e + \frac{1}{2} \frac{\partial^2 C}{\partial F^2} \sigma_N^2 dt_e = 0$$

Black's formula is the correct computation of the expected value of the sum of these P&L's over the life of the option.

TABLE 6.2 Black Log-Normal Greeks

	Call	Put	ATMF Straddle
Premium	$F\,N(d_1) - K\,N(d_2)$	$K\,N(-d_2) - F\,N(-d_1)$	$2F(N(\sigma\sqrt{t}/2) - N(-\sigma\sqrt{t}/2))$
Delta $\left(\frac{\partial}{\partial F}\right)$	$N(d_1)$	$N(d_1) - 1$	$2N(\sigma\sqrt{t}/2) - 1$
Gamma $\left(\frac{\partial^2}{\partial F^2}\right)$	$\dfrac{N'(d_1)}{F\sigma\sqrt{t}}$	$\dfrac{N'(d_1)}{F\sigma\sqrt{t}}$	$2\dfrac{N'(\sigma\sqrt{t}/2)}{F\sigma\sqrt{t}}$
Vega $\left(\frac{\partial}{\partial\sigma}\right)$	$F\sqrt{t}N'(d_1)$	$F\sqrt{t}N'(d_1)$	$2F\sqrt{t}N'(\sigma\sqrt{t}/2)$

Cheat Sheet

The following tables summarize various Black formulae and their Greeks, although in practice Greeks are usually computed numerically (bump-and-revalue). All of these are for European options *without the discounting from payment date to today*. Recall that

$$d_{1,2} = \frac{\ln(F/K)}{\sigma\sqrt{t}} \pm \frac{1}{2}\sigma\sqrt{t} \qquad d = \frac{F - K}{\sigma_N\sqrt{t}}$$

$$N(d) = \int_{-\infty}^{d} \frac{1}{\sqrt{2\pi}}e^{-x^2/2}dx \qquad N'(x) = \frac{1}{\sqrt{2\pi}}e^{-x^2/2}$$

TABLE 6.3 Black Normal Greeks

	Call	Put	ATMF Straddle
Premium	$\sigma_N\sqrt{t}\,[N'(d) + dN(d)]$	$\sigma_N\sqrt{t}\,[N'(d) - dN(-d)]$	$\dfrac{2}{\sqrt{2\pi}}\sigma_N\sqrt{t}$
Delta $\left(\frac{\partial}{\partial F}\right)$	$N(d)$	$N(d) - 1$	0
Gamma $\left(\frac{\partial^2}{\partial F^2}\right)$	$\dfrac{N'(d)}{\sigma_N\sqrt{t}}$	$\dfrac{N'(d)}{\sigma_N\sqrt{t}}$	$\dfrac{2}{\sqrt{2\pi}}\dfrac{1}{\sigma_N\sqrt{t}}$
BPVega $\left(\frac{\partial}{\partial\sigma_N}\right)$	$\sqrt{t}N'(d)$	$\sqrt{t}N'(d)$	$\dfrac{2}{\sqrt{2\pi}}\sqrt{t}$
Theta $\left(\frac{\partial}{\partial t}\right)$	$\dfrac{\sigma_N}{2\sqrt{t}}N'(d)$	$\dfrac{\sigma_N}{2\sqrt{t}}N'(d)$	$\dfrac{1}{\sqrt{2\pi}}\dfrac{\sigma_N}{\sqrt{t}}$

DIGITALS

In deriving Black's formula, we had to evaluate the integral

$$\int_{K/F}^{\infty} f_X(x)dx = P[A(t_e)/F > K/F]$$
$$= P[A(t_e) > K]$$
$$= N(d_2)$$

where f_X denotes the distribution function of $LN((r - \sigma^2/2)t_e, \sigma^2 t_e)$ r.v. Therefore, $N(d_2)$ can be interpreted as the risk-neutral *probability that the call finishes in-the-money*, and can also be used to evaluate *digitals*. A digital call option $C(t_e)$ has unit payoff if the asset $A(t_e)$ at expiration t_e is above the strike K:

$$DigiCall(t_e) = \begin{cases} 1 & \text{if } A(t_e) > K \\ 0 & \text{otherwise} \end{cases}$$

To evaluate a t_e-expiry/t_p-pay digi-call on an asset when interest rates are deterministic, we calculate

$$DigiCall(0) = D(0, t_p)E_0[C(t_e)]$$
$$= D(0, t_p)E_0[C(t_e)]$$
$$= D(0, t_p)P[A(t_e) > K]$$
$$= D(0, t_p)N(d_2)$$

Valuation of digi-puts is similar, since $DigiPut(t_e) = 1 - DigiCall(t_e)$, hence

$$DigiPut(0) = D(0, t_p)(1 - N(d_2)) = D(0, t_p)N(-d_2)$$

giving us

$$DigiCall/Put(0) = D(0, t_p)N(\pm d_2) \qquad d_2 = \frac{\ln(F_A(0, t_e)/K)}{\sigma\sqrt{t_e}} - \sigma\sqrt{t_e}/2$$

for Log-Normal dynamics. For Normal dynamics, the value of t_e-expiry/t_p-pay digital is

$$DigiCall/Put(0) = D(0, t_p)N(\pm d) \qquad d = \frac{F_A(0, t_e) - K}{\sigma_N\sqrt{t_e}}$$

TABLE 6.4 Black Log-Normal Formulae for Digitals

	Digi-Call	Digi-Put
Premium	$N(d_2)$	$N(-d_2)$
Delta	$\dfrac{1}{F\sigma\sqrt{t}}N'(d_2)$	$\dfrac{-1}{F\sigma\sqrt{t}}N'(d_2)$

CALL IS ALL YOU NEED

One can continue along the above lines to derive analytical formulae for European style options with more complicated payoffs. In practice, however, the call and digi-call formulae are all one really needs to evaluate European-style options. Indeed, a functional analysis result states that functions with call or digi-call payoffs form a *total basis* for continuous functions, which means that any real-world option payoff is economically equal to—or can be approximated arbitrarily closely—via a portfolio of calls and/or digi-calls. Hence calls and digi-calls serve as the salient *building blocks* of European-style options.

The following is a list of some common European-style (single-exercise) payoffs encountered in practice:

1. Straddle: A put and call with same strike K
2. Strangle: A put and call with different strikes (K_1, K_2)
3. Collar: Being long a collar is being long a K_2-call, and short a K_1-put with $K_1 < K_2$. The strikes K_1, K_2 are usually chosen around the forward rates, so that the package is worth 0, that is, a costless-collar.
4. Risk-Reversal: Long a call at $ATMF + d$ and short a put at $ATMF - d$ is called a $2d$-total-width (or d on each side) risk-reversal. Under Normal dynamics with no skews, a risk-reversal should be worth zero. Traders track the price of various-width risk-reversals to discover the implied skews in the market.

TABLE 6.5 Black Normal Formulae for Digitals

	Dig-Call	Digi-Put
Premium	$N(d)$	$N(-d)$
Delta	$\dfrac{1}{\sigma_N\sqrt{t}}N'(d)$	$-\dfrac{1}{\sigma_N\sqrt{t}}N'(d)$
Gamma	$-\dfrac{d}{\sigma_N^2 t}N'(d)$	$\dfrac{d}{\sigma_N^2 t}N'(d)$

5. Call/Put Spread - Being long a call-spread is being long a K_1-call, and short a K_2-call, with $K_1 < K_2$.

6. Ratio - Most common is a 1x2 (1 by 2) ratio. Being long a 1x2 call ratio means being long one K_1-call, and short two K_2-calls. Some traders track the implied market skews by setting $K_1 = ATMF$, $K_2 = K_1 + d$, and solving for d that would make the ratio costless, the higher the call-skew, the higher the solved d.

7. Fly - Being long a call-fly is being long one K_1-call, short 2 K_2-calls, and long one K_3-calls, with $K_1 < K_2 < K_3$, and $K_2 - K_1 = K_3 - K_2$. This is usually used to pin down and express strong views on the setting of Libor at expiration, leading to *pin risk* for the option seller.

8. Digitals - Digi-calls, Digi-puts. Due to their high gamma, these are usually sold as a conservative (from seller's point of view) call or put spreads, with the strikes chosen to be 10-20 basis point apart (called the "width of the ramp").

9. Knock-in Caplet/Floorlet - A K_1-strike call with K_2-knock-in ($K_1 < K_2$) has the same payoff as a K_1-call, but only if the underlying is above K_2 at expiration. The payoff is zero if the underlying is below K_2 at expiration. This can easily be priced as a K_2-call plus a K_2-Digi-Call with payoff $K_2 - K_1$. A periodic knock-in cap/floor is a portfolio of different expiry Knock-in caplets/floorlets.

These are shown in Figure 6.4. All of the above products can be priced via Black's Normal/Log-Normal formulae, as the payoffs are simple portfolios of different-strike calls/puts and digi-calls/puts.

Market-Implied Risk-Neutral Distribution

Under assumed simple dynamics (Normal/Log-Normal), we can derive formulae for various payoffs. In practice, it is observed that neither dynamic recovers market-quoted option prices for all strikes, and for each strike, one has to adjust the implied volatility driving the dynamics. This variation of volatility versus strike is referred to as the *volatility smile/skew*. The existence of smiles/skews begs the question as to whether there is a true market-implied distribution that will recover all option prices. It turns out that one could potentially recover all market quoted option prices if one had access to price of calls for *all* strikes.

Recall that in the Black-Scholes setting, today's price of a K-strike call is

$$C(K) = D(0, t_p)E_0[\max(0, C(t_e) - K)]$$

$$= D(0, t_p) \int \max(0, x - K) f_X(x)dx$$

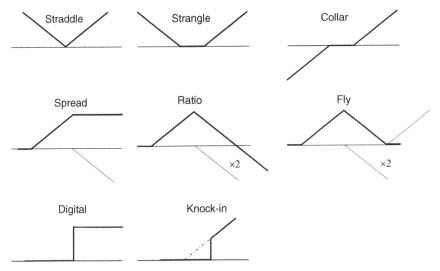

FIGURE 6.4 Common European-Style Payoffs

where f_X is the assumed distribution function of the asset at expiration. This distribution function can be recovered as the second derivative of $C(K)$ with respect to the strike K:

$$\frac{1}{D(0, t_p)} \frac{\partial^2}{\partial K^2} C(K) = \frac{\partial^2}{\partial K^2} \int \max(0, x - K) f_X(x) dx$$

$$= \int \frac{\partial^2}{\partial K^2} \max(0, x - K) f_X(x) dx$$

$$= \int \delta(x - K) f_X(x) dx$$

$$= f_X(K)$$

where $\delta(x)$ is the delta function (derivative of a step function) commonly used in engineering and physics, and satisfies the following *convolution integral* property:

$$g(K) = \int \delta(x - K) g(x) dx$$

for any function g.

CALENDAR/BUSINESS DAYS, EVENT VOLS

Black's formulae only depend on average volatility. Indeed, these formulae were derived by assuming that the underlying asset or its return follows a Brownian motion with constant diffusion parameter (σ, σ_N), leading to either a Log-Normal or Normal distribution at expiry. The various formulae are simply the evaluation of the payoff integral under this terminal distribution. The main driver of these formulae is the terminal variance $\sigma^2 t_e$. If instead we let the driver be a Brownian motion with a time-varying but deterministic diffusion function, $\sigma(t)$, because of the additive property of Normal r.v.'s—the infinitesimal building-blocks of Brownian motions—the terminal distribution is still Normal/Log-Normal, with terminal variance:

$$\int_0^{t_e} \sigma^2(t)dt$$

Defining the *average volatility*, sometimes called *root-mean-square (RMS) vol*, or *integrated vol*, as

$$\overline{\sigma} = \sqrt{\frac{1}{t_e} \int_0^{t_e} \sigma^2(t)dt}$$

all previous formulae hold with σ, σ_N replaced by their *averages*: $\overline{\sigma}, \overline{\sigma_N}$.

This observation allows one to fine-tune the timing of volatility, controlling for days where there is anticipated above-average uncertainty/volatility (major economic releases, central bank rate announcement), and days with below-average market volatility (weekend, holidays, ...). This *event-vol* volatility is essential and critical for pricing and risk management of short-dated options.

In practice, a daily resolution with constant volatility for each day is usually adopted. This allows for easy implementation and calculation of the integrals, as they become sums:

$$\int_0^{t_e} \sigma^2(t)dt = \frac{1}{365} \sum_{i=1}^{N} \sigma_i^2$$

where N is the number of days to expiry t_e, and σ_i denotes the annualized volatility for i-th day.

A common practice is to assume that there is no volatility $\sigma_i = 0$ on weekends/holidays, and that volatility is constant for other business days until the expiry under consideration. In this case, the market-quoted calendar-day-based volatility σ will get converted to business-day volatility σ_B as follows:

$$C\sigma^2 = B\sigma_B^2 \Rightarrow \sigma_B = \sqrt{\frac{C}{B}}\sigma$$

where B, C refer to the number of Business, Calendar days till expiry. The computed σ_B (multiplied by the appropriate number of *business* days) can then be used for pricing shorter-dated options.

A related concept is the notion of *daily vol*, interpreted as the average daily movement for a delta-hedged option to break-even. Volatilities are quoted in annualized terms, so for a constant Normal volatility σ_N over a 1-year period with B business days, the final variance is

$$\sum_{i=1}^{365} \frac{\sigma_N^2}{365} = \sum_{i=1}^{B} (\text{Daily-Vol})^2 = B \times (\text{Daily-Vol})^2$$

implying

$$\text{Daily-Vol} = \frac{\sigma_N}{\sqrt{B}} \approx \frac{\sigma_N}{16}$$

since it is usually assumed that a typical calendar year has $B = 252$ (52 weeks × 5–8 holidays) business days, although other numbers ($256 = 16^2$, $250, \ldots$) are also used. For example, a swaption trading at an implied vol of 100bp/annum, $\sigma_N = 1\%$, implies an *average* move of $6.3 = 100/\sqrt{252}$ bp's 1 day until expiry.

Since an ATMF straddle undiscounted price is $\frac{2}{\sqrt{2\pi}}\sigma_N\sqrt{t_e}$, knowledge of the price of a 1-day expiry option allows us to quickly backout the implied daily move:

$$\text{1-day Straddle Price} = \frac{2}{\sqrt{2\pi}} \text{ Daily Vol} \approx 0.8 \text{ Daily Vol}$$

These options are sometimes quoted in the form of *forward option agreement* (FOA), where the strike is set in the morning of an event-full day (major announcements, releases), and settle at day-end. The time until the expiry (afternoon of strike-setting date) is usually small (at most a week or 2), and that's why we can ignore the discounting.

CHAPTER 7

European-Style
Interest-Rate Derivatives

Recall that the correct price (coming from a self-financing replicating portfolio) for European-style interest rate options is the risk-neutral expectation of the stochastically discounted option payoff:

$$C(t_0) = E_0[e^{-\int_{t_0}^{t_e} r(u,\omega)du} C(t_e, \omega)]$$

where in a risk-neutral world, prices of underlying assets (zero-coupon bonds) must satisfy

$$E_0[e^{-\int_{t_0}^{t_e} r(u,\omega)du}] = D(t_0, t_e)$$

While the preceding is the right framework for pricing interest rate options, market practice is to try to use Black's Formula as much as possible, resorting to the above framework only when it cannot be co-opted in any reasonable shape or form!

The common misapplication is to approximate

$$E_0[e^{-\int_0^{t_e} r(u,\omega)du} C(t_e, \omega)] \approx E_0[e^{-\int_0^{t_e} r(u,\omega)du}] E_0[C(t_e, \omega)]$$

$$= D(0, t_e) E_0[C(t_e, \omega)]$$

and to further assume that rates are tradeable assets, and evaluate $E_0[C(t_e, \omega)]$ by using Black's Formula with forward rates rather than forward asset values. Chapter 11 shows how using Black's formula as used in practice can be justified using the forward measure lens, but for this chapter, we will simply illustrate the market practice for common products.

MARKET PRACTICE

Market practice is to use Black's Formulae for pricing and hedging flow products despite the theoretical inconsistency of treating discounting as deterministic, while interest rates as random. For most market practitioners, Black's formula is mostly a quoting mechanism, and also a *guide* on calculating deltas needed to replicate the option payoff under the *assumed* (often too simplistic) dynamics. Just like bonds, ultimately all interest-rate options trade on price. And just like bonds where implied yields are calculated, implied vols are calculated to help assess the fairness of the quoted option prices.

Extracting implied vols is more involved than extracting yields via the commonly accepted simple price-yield formula. For rate options, we first need to build a Libor discount factor curve, calculate the relevant forward rate(s), and discount factors to the payment dates, and then apply Black's formula in conjunction with these to back out the implied vol. The calculated implied vol is then not only a function of the quoted price, but also of how the Libor curve is constructed. Every trading shop on the street has their own curve building mechanism, with enough minor variations and nuances so that starting from the same option price, each will get a similar—but not exactly identical—implied vol.

For interest rate options, since At-The-Money-Forward (ATMF) straddles have little duration risk, and are predominantly a function of the volatility, ATMF straddle prices are actively quoted and traded. Option traders are in the business of taking and managing volatility risk, not duration or spread risk, as each option desk will try to maintain a delta-neutral position and takes only volatility risk. By monitoring and trading ATMF straddles, they are then trading volatility itself.

Initially, Black's Log-Normal formulae were co-opted for interest rate products. In recent years, however, most traders have switched to the Normal dynamics as the base case, and brokers quite often quote Normal vols alongside prices in preference to Log-Normal vols.

INTEREST-RATE OPTION TRADES

As with any other derivative, interest-rate options can be used as a hedging or speculation tool.

Hedging, Protection

Mortgage servicing companies often buy swaptions to hedge the negative convexity of their servicing portfolios. Insurance companies typically buy cap/floors to hedge their guaranteed-payoff annuity products.

Speculation, Penny Options, Lottery Tickets

Hedge funds typically utilize interest-rate options to express a view on the terminal setting of interest rates at expiration. Rather than entering into a forward agreement, they usually buy cheap out-of-the-money options to cap the down-side (premium paid) while benefitting handsomely if their view is borne out. These buyers do not hedge the interest-rate options, except sometimes under a favorable outcome before expiration to lock in profit, or by rolling the strike.

Gamma Trading, Realized versus Implied Vol

The dominant P&L of short-dated (6m and under) options when delta-hedged is due to their gamma. If the actual realized volatility turns out to be higher/lower than the implied volatility (paid/received through the up-front premium), then delta-hedging can be a source of profit for long/short position in an option.

Vega Trading, Supply/Demand

For longer-dated options (1y and longer expiries), the dominant P&L is due to changes in implied volatility, that is, their vega. These changes in implied vols are primarily due to supply and demand of volatility. For example, a large hedging program by a servicing company can drive up volatilities in one sector, while the hedging needs of exotics desks can pressure a specific sector of the volatility surface. An astute anticipation of these flows allows one to take a position—usually via straddles in order to minimize delta-hedging needs—in vega pieces, and then unwinding the position for profit/loss after a favorable/unfavorable outcome. As these trades can span a few months for the flows to be realized, one needs to consider the volatility carry (loss of time-value) and roll-down (slope of the volatility surface along expiry).

CAPLETS/FLOORLETS: OPTIONS ON FORWARD RATES

A caplet/floorlet is a European option on a rate, typically the benchmark interest rate, say 3m Libor. A typical caplet/floorlet on 3m Libor is based on a single calculation period: $[t_e, t_e + 3m]$. At expiration t_e the market rate is compared to the strike K, and the option payoff is accrued for the duration of the calculation period, and paid at the end of the calculation period $t_e + 3m$. For example, a 6m-expiry caplet on 3m Libor has the following payoff 9m from today:

$$\max(0, L_{3m}(6m) - 0.05) \times \alpha(te, t_e + 3m)$$

per unit notional, where α is the accrual fraction.

Market practice is to use Black's formula (Log-Normal or Normal versions) to price options on futures. For a given calculation period $[T_1, T_2]$, the risk-neutral formula for a caplet on a rate R is approximated as:

$$C(0) = E_0\left[e^{-\int_0^{T_2} r(u,\omega)du} \max(0, R(T_1, \omega) - K)\right] \times \alpha(T_1, T_2)$$

$$\approx D(0, T_2)E\left[\max(0, R(T_1, \omega) - K)\right] \times \alpha(T_1, T_2)$$

and further assuming that a forward *rate* is a tradeable asset, hence the appropriate (Log-Normal or Normal) Black's call formula is used to evaluate the $E[.]$ term. Similarly, for floorlets, the payoff $E[\max(0, K - R(T_1, \omega))]$ is evaluated using Black's put formula.

Example 1. A 6-month 5.5% caplet on 3m Libor is quoted as 5 cents ($500 for $1M notional) when $D(0, 6m) = 0.975$, $D(0, 9m) = 0.9625$. In this case, the calculation period is $[6m, 9m]$, and we observe 3m-Libor in 6m, compare it with the strike 5.5%, and on payment date (9m from today), the payoff is $\max(0, L_{3m}(6m) - 0.05) \times 1/4$, where 1/4 is the length of the calculation period in years (we are ignoring day-counts here). For instance, if 3m-Libor in 6m is 5.25%, then there is no payoff in 9m, while if it is 5.70%, the payoff per unit notional is 4 cents: $0.04\% = 0.0020\%/4$ in 9m.

In order to analyze this price, we can use Black's formula, say Normal version, to back out the implied vol of the quoted price. We compute the 6m-forward 3m-Libor:

$$F = (D(0, 6m)/D(0, 9m) - 1)/0.25 = 5.19481\%$$

and with $K = 5.5\%$, $t_e = 0.5$, and the implied Normal Vol must be backed out of

$$0.0005 = E[\max(0, L_{3m}(6m) - 5.5\%)] \times 0.25 \times D(0, 9m)$$

$$= \sigma_N\sqrt{t_e}[N'(d) + dN(d)] \times 0.25 \times 0.9625$$

where

$$d = \frac{F - K}{\sigma_N\sqrt{t_e}} = \frac{5.19481\% - 5.5\%}{\sigma_N\sqrt{0.5}}$$

Trial and error gives us $\sigma_N = 1.20\%$ or 120 bp/year. Depending on our view of volatility of interest rates for the next 6m, the "5-cent" price might be cheap, fair, or rich.

Example 2. From the previous example, having backed out the implied vol $\sigma_N = 1.20\%$, we can compute the value of a 6-month 5.5% *floorlet* on 3m-Libor. We compute

$$\text{Floorlet} = E[\max(0, 5.5\% - L_{3m}(6m))] \times 0.25 \times D(0, 9m)$$

$$= \sigma_N \sqrt{t_e}[N'(d) - dN(-d)] \times 0.25 \times 0.9625$$

$$= 0.1234\%$$

or 12.34 cents. Note that put-call parity is satisfied:

$$\max(0, F - K) - \max(0, K - F) = F - K$$

or

$$\text{Caplet} - \text{Floorlet} = (F - K) \times 0.25 \times D(0, 9m)$$

Caps/Floors

A cap/floor is simply a portfolio of caplets/floorlets, all having the same strike. For example, a 2y 5% quarterly cap on 3m Libor is a collection of 8 caplets based on 8 calculation periods: $[0, 3m], [3m, 6m], \ldots, [21m, 2y]$, where each caplet's strike is 5%. Each caplet/floorlet is valued using Black's formula using its own (depending on its expiration date) volatility, and the value of the cap/floor is simply the sum of all these values.

An $m \times n$ (pronounced m by n) *forward cap/floor* is a cap/floor starting m years from today, and maturing n years from today. So a 1x2 cap is a 1y cap, starting in 1y; a 3x5 cap is a 2y cap, starting in 3y.

In practice, only prices of a few caps/floors are actively quoted in the form of *cap-floor straddles*. Typical maturities are 1y, 1x2, 2x3, 3x5, 5x7, 7x10 for USD cap/floors. For example a 1x2 USD "cap-floor straddle" quoted as 25 cents denotes a price of $250,000 for a package consisting of one $100M 1x2 quarterly cap (4 caplets) and one $100M 1x2 quarterly floor (4 floorlets). The common strike for all caplets/floorlets is chosen so that all caplet+floorlets pairs (one pair for each expiration) are close to ATMF.

A final note is that for spot-start caps/floors, the first caplet/floorlet is ignored, so a 1y quarterly cap is really a 3mx1y cap, and actually has 3 caplets: $[3m, 6m], [6m, 9m], [9m, 1y]$. A forward quarterly cap, say 1x2, has 4 caplets.

Options on Euro-Dollar Futures

Options on Euro-dollar futures trade at the Chicago Mercantile Exchange (CME), and they are quoted in Euro-dollar ticks ($25 per contract). Options on Euro-dollar futures are treated as caplets/floorlets, using Black's formula to evaluate them.

Example 3. Assume the first ED contract expires in 60 days, and is trading at 95.10. Also assume that $D(0, 60d) = 0.97$. (Euro-dollar options cash-settle on expiration date, not 3m later.) A 95.50 call (called a "55" call) is trading at 5 ticks, so $125 per contract. Although all ED prices and strikes are quoted in price, we are always thinking of the implied rate/strike, so we compute the forward rate $F = (100 - 95.10)/100 = 4.90\%$, and the strike $K = (100 - 95.50)/100 = 4.5\%$. Also a call on the price is a floor on the implied rate, so to analyze a ED call, we have to use Black's put formula. The implied Normal vol σ_N must be backed out from the following:

$$\$125 = 0.97 \times \$1M \times \sigma_N\sqrt{60/365}\left[N'(d) - dN(-d)\right] \times (90/360)$$

where

$$d = \frac{4.95\% - 4.5\%}{\sigma_N\sqrt{60/365}}$$

Trial and error gives us $\sigma_N = 1.15\%$ or 115 bp's/annum.

Buying a naked (unhedged) 60-day ED 95.50 call is a bet that rates will fall through 4.50% in 60 days. If at expiration, 3m Libor sets at 4.25% (so ED settles at 95.75), then we have made 25 ticks, so $625 per option contract, a 5-to-1 return.

Caplet Curve = ED Options+Cap/Floors

Options on the first few ED contracts are fairly liquid, and can be used to back out the implied volatilities of 3m-Libor rates for the relevant expirations. Since a dealer cap/floor book consists of many expiration dates, with each expiry having its own volatility, a *caplet curve* is needed to mark this book. The caplet curve is a graph of implied-vols of options on the benchmark floating index versus expiration.

For USD, the instruments used to construct this curve are ATMF options (or strikes as close to forwards as possible) on ED1, ED2,..., and a series of cap/floor straddles: 1x2, 2x3, 3x5, 5x7, 7x10. Since each cap/floor

TABLE 7.1 A 1x2 5.5% Cap

Calc Period	Forward Rate	Normal Vol	$N(d)$	DF(PayDate)	Expected Cash Flow	Caplet Price
(1y,1y3m)	5%	1.00%	0.30854	0.939413	0.1978%	0.1858%
(1y3m,1y6m)	5.25%	1.10%	0.41946	0.927743	0.3757%	0.3486%
(1y6m,1y9m)	5.5%	1.20%	0.50000	0.916219	0.5863%	0.5372%
(1y9m,2y)	5.75%	1.30%	0.55779	0.904837	0.8183%	0.7404%
					Total	1.812%

straddle consists of multi-expiration caplet+floorlet pairs, with each expiration requiring its own volatility, a bootstrap+interpolation routine is typically used to back out the implied vol for each expiration. A common procedure is to use implied vols from ED futures options for the first few expiries, and use the following parametric shape for the rest of the curve:

$$\sigma_{Caplet}(T) = \alpha_1 + \alpha_2 \times T \times e^{-\alpha_3 T}$$

Example 4. Let a USD 1x2 cap with strike 5% be shown in Table 7.1. The value of the cap 1.812% is the sum of the values of the four quarterly caplets. We can also back out the common Normal vol (116.3 bp/annum) that applied to all caplets would recover the same price.

EUROPEAN-STYLE SWAPTIONS

An m-year into n-year receiver/payer swaption with strike K is an m-year European option to receive/pay the fixed rate K in an n-year swap. Let us focus on a *right-to-pay* (RTP) or *payer* swaption. At the option expiry, only if the n-year par swap rate $S(t_e)$ is above the strike K, then it is advantageous to exercise the option and pay K (below market). Otherwise, if $S(t_e) < K$, the option holder will not exercise the option, as it is cheaper to pay $S(t_e)$ as a market swap rather than the higher rate K.

Considering when $S(t_e) > K$, the option will get exercised and the option owner will *pay K* for the next n years. He could also (conceptually) *receive* fixed in a par swap (worth 0), that is, receiving $S(t_e)$ and pay floating for n-years. Netting these two swaps, the floating legs cancel out, and effectively one is paying K and receiving $S(t_e)$ for the next n-years. Since this is just a series of known cash flows at expiration, one could cash-settle by receiving the PV of these cash flows. Assuming that the underlying swap is semiannual, let $\{T_1, \ldots, T_{2n}\}$ be the payment dates for the fixed leg of the swap. The economic value of the payer swaption at expiration t_e then is

$$\max(0, S(t_e, \omega) - K) \frac{1}{2} \sum_{i=1}^{2n} D(t_e, T_i, \omega)$$

where $D(t_e, \cdot, \omega)$ is the random discount-factor curve at t_e.

Notice that the sum term is simply the value of a semiannual annuity with unit payoff at expiration. Let us denote this factor by $A(t_e, \omega)$:

$$A(t_e, \{T_1, \ldots, T_{2n}\}, \omega) = \frac{1}{2} \sum_{i=1}^{2n} D(t_e, T_i, \omega)$$

According to risk-neutral valuation, today's price of this option is simply the expected stochastically discounted value of the above payoff. This is approximated as follows:

$$P(0) = E\left[e^{-\int_0^{t_e} r(u,\omega)du} \max(0, S(t_e, \omega) - K) A(t_e, \ldots, \omega) \right]$$

$$\approx E\left[e^{-\int_0^{t_e} r(u,\omega)du} A(t_e, \ldots, \omega) \right] E[\max(0, S(t_e, \omega) - K)]$$

$$= \left(\frac{1}{2} \sum_{i=1}^{2n} E\left[e^{-\int_0^{t_e} r(u,\omega)du} D(t_e, T_i, \omega) \right] \right) E[\max(0, S(t_e, \omega) - K)]$$

$$= \left(\frac{1}{2} \sum_{i=1}^{2n} D(0, T_i) \right) E[\max(0, S(t_e, \omega) - K)]$$

$$= A(0, \{T_1, \ldots, T_{2n}\}, \omega) E[\max(0, S(t_e, \omega) - K)]$$

and further assuming that swap *rates* are tradeable assets, hence the last term is evaluated using Black's call formula. Similarly, the formula for a receiver swaption is

$$R(0) = E\left[e^{-\int_0^{t_e} r(u,\omega)du} \max(0, K - S(t_e, \omega)) A(t_e, \{T_1, \ldots, T_{2n}\}, \omega) \right]$$

$$\approx A(0, \{T_1, \ldots, T_{2n}\}, \omega) E[\max(0, K - S(t_e, \omega))]$$

where the last term is evaluated using Black's put formula using forward swap rates.

Example 5. Let the following discount factors be given: $D(0, 1y) = 0.95$, $D(0, 1.5y) = 0.925$, $D(0, 2y) = 0.90$, $D(0, 2.5y) = 0.875$, $D(0, 3y) = 0.85$, and let the implied log vol of a 1y into 2y swaption ATMF swaption be quoted as 18.5%. In order to price a $100M 1y into 2y ATMF right-to-pay (RTP, Payer) swaption, we first need to calculate the 2y-par swap rate, 1y forward:

$$F = \frac{D(0, 1y) - D(0, 3y)}{1/2[D(0, 1.5y) + D(0, 2y) + D(0, 2.5y) + D(0, 3y)]} = 5.63380\%$$

Since the swaption is ATMF, the strike K equals the forward: $K = F = 5.63380\%$. The time to expiration t_e is 1y, $t_e = 1.0$, and $\sigma = 0.185$. Using Black's Log-Normal call formula, we form:

$$d_{1,2} = \frac{\ln(F/K)}{\sigma\sqrt{t_e}} \pm \frac{1}{2}\sigma\sqrt{t_e}$$

$$= \frac{\ln(0.056338/0.056338)}{0.185\sqrt{1.0}} \pm \frac{1}{2}(0.185)\sqrt{1.0}$$

$$= \pm 0.0925$$

Using Black's call formula,

$$E[\max(0, S(t_e, \omega) - K)] = F N(d_1) - K N(d_2)$$

$$= 0.056338 N(0.0925) - 0.056338 N(-0.0925)$$

$$= 0.004152068$$

Finally, the price of an ATMF payer RTP swaption is obtained as 73.7 cents:

$$P(0) = 1/2 [D(0, 1.5y) + D(0, 2y) + D(0, 2.5y) + D(0, 3y)]$$

$$\times E[\max(0, S(t_e, \omega) - K)]$$

$$= 1/2 [0.925 + 0.90 + 0.875 + 0.85] \times (0.004152068)$$

$$= 0.737\%$$

Example 6. Using the same discount factors as in the previous example, let us consider a right-to-receive (RTR, receiver) 1y-into-2y swaption with strike 25 bp lower than ATMF rate. This is called "25-low 1-into-2 receiver." Let the Normal Vol be quoted as 110 bp/annum. In this case, the strike

$K = 5.38380\% = F - 0.0025$, and $\sigma_N = 0.0110$. Since this is a receiver, we have to use Black's put formula under Normal distribution.

$$d = \frac{F - K}{\sigma_N \sqrt{t_e}}$$
$$= \frac{0.056338 - 0.053838}{0.0110\sqrt{1.0}}$$
$$= 0.227273$$

and

$$E[\max(0, K - S(t_e, \omega))] = \sigma_N \sqrt{t_e}\left[N'(d) - dN(-d)\right]$$
$$= 0.0110\sqrt{1.0}\left[\frac{1}{\sqrt{2\pi}}e^{-0.227273^2/2} - (0.227273)N(-0.227273)\right]$$
$$= 0.003595728$$

Finally, the price of 25-low receiver swaption is obtained as 63.82 cents:

$$P(0) = 1/2\left[D(0, 1.5y) + D(0, 2y) + D(0, 2.5y) + D(0, 3y)\right]$$
$$\times E[\max(0, K - S(t_e, \omega))]$$
$$= 1/2\left[0.925 + 0.90 + 0.875 + 0.85\right] \times (0.003595728)$$
$$= 0.6382\%$$

Swaptions in Practice

Interdealer brokers maintain ATMF straddle prices for various expirations and maturities, and communicate bids/offer prices for specific straddles between dealers. They also maintain a general swaption price grid for all expiries and maturities in electronic format (broker screens), and update them periodically during the day, and send a final settlement grid at end of day. Alongside the price, they might also quote the implied Log-Normal or Normal vol, but that is mostly for informational purposes, as at the end of the day, price is king (see Tables 7.2 through 7.4). So a 1m-into-2y swaption straddle is trading at 29 cents ($290,000 per $100M notional), and this price is equivalent to Black Log-Normal vol of 13.0%, or Black Normal vol of 68.3 bp/annum.

When trading ATMF straddles, a price is agreed on, and the next step is to agree on the forward swap rate. Due to their curve differences, each side might set the ATMF rate at slightly different values. However, since

TABLE 7.2 A Swaption Straddle Price Grid (cents)

					Underlying Swap Term				
		1y	2y	3y	4y	5y	7y	10y	15y	30y
"Gamma" Expiries	1m	9	29	43	60	78	103	134	175	242
	3m	22	57	87	115	144	188	245	324	446
	6m	34	80	123	162	199	262	339	443	608
"Vega" Expiries	1y	60	119	174	227	276	363	469	608	837
	2y	86	169	246	318	385	502	645	833	1,124
	3y	103	201	291	376	454	594	760	975	1,316
	5y	120	232	337	434	524	680	876	1,118	1,500
	7y	124	238	347	448	542	704	897	1,136	1,497
	10y	120	230	333	428	516	669	855	1,075	1,401

TABLE 7.3 Implied Black Log-Normal Vols (%)

	1y	2y	3y	4y	5y	7y	10y	15y	30y
1m	8.1	13.0	13.3	14.1	14.9	14.5	14.0	13.7	13.1
3m	10.8	14.8	15.2	15.3	15.5	15.0	14.5	14.3	13.7
6m	12.5	14.8	15.4	15.4	15.4	15.0	14.4	14.0	13.4
1y	15.9	15.9	15.7	15.6	15.4	15.0	14.4	14.0	13.4
2y	16.5	16.4	16.1	15.9	15.7	15.2	14.6	14.2	13.4
3y	16.6	16.4	16.1	15.9	15.7	15.3	14.7	14.2	13.5
5y	16.0	15.8	15.7	15.5	15.3	14.9	14.5	14.0	13.3
7y	15.4	15.1	15.0	14.9	14.8	14.5	14.0	13.5	12.6
10y	14.5	14.3	14.2	14.1	14.0	13.7	13.3	12.7	11.8

TABLE 7.4 Implied Black Normal Vols (bp)

	1y	2y	3y	4y	5y	7y	10y	15y	30y
1m	43.2	68.3	70.4	75.5	80.5	79.9	78.7	77.8	75.8
3m	57.0	77.6	80.4	81.9	83.8	82.5	81.4	81.1	79.0
6m	65.0	77.4	81.6	82.6	83.5	82.8	81.1	79.8	77.4
1y	81.9	83.6	83.9	84.4	84.3	83.5	81.6	79.9	77.7
2y	88.5	89.2	88.6	88.4	88.0	86.4	84.1	82.1	78.3
3y	91.6	91.4	90.7	90.2	89.7	88.4	85.8	83.3	79.3
5y	92.2	91.4	91.3	90.6	89.9	88.0	86.1	83.2	78.6
7y	90.7	89.4	89.2	88.8	88.4	86.8	84.0	80.5	74.6
10y	87.1	86.0	85.5	84.9	84.4	82.6	80.2	76.2	69.7

straddles will have little PV01, both sides agree on a rate (perhaps aided by the broker). Here is a typical transaction: ... "Okay, I just bought $100M 1y-into-2y ATMF straddles for 124 cents ($1,240,000). I see the forward rate as 5.256%, is that where you see it, too?" "I see it as 5.242%. Let's set it in the middle: 5.249%. Works for you?" "Okay. Done." The reason that both parties amicably agree is that straddles have little PV01: The buyer who agreed to pay 124 cents for a straddle struck at 5.256% (his forward rate), would pay almost the same amount if the market moved and the ATMF rate became 5.242% (seller's forward rate). The seller sees the situation in the same way, so they both easily agree to meet in the middle.

If instead of straddles, a receiver or payer swaption is traded, one needs to specify whether the hedge/delta is exchanged or not. The standard hedge, regardless of the option strike, consists of a delta-weighted amount of a forward swap (struck at the forward swap rate, so with 0 value).

If the trade is with the delta/hedge, then one first sets the option price, and the forward rate and the size of the hedge are agreed upon later. In this case, similar to trading straddles, since the PV01 of the combined position (option+hedge) are small, minor rate or delta differences as seen by different sides are amicably settled. A typical transaction might go as follows: ... "Okay. I bought $100M 25-high 3m-into-10y payers for 110 bp ($1,100,000). I see the forward rate at 5.10% and the delta as 42%. Agreed?" "Agreed on rate, I am using a blah-blah model, and see the delta as 39%. How about 40%?" "Okay. I pay 110 bp for $100M 3m-into-10y payer struck at 5.35% (25 bp higher than forward). I will also receive in $40M 3m-into-10y forward swap with fixed rate at 5.10%. Thanks."

If the trade is done without the delta/hedge, then a sufficient extra (hedging) premium is built into the option price to cover the subsequent hedging bid/offer cost. The natural preference of an option trader is to transact options with delta, thereby just trading volatility.

For swaption expiries and maturities that do not fall on the grid, one typically uses linear interpolation in square root of time-to-expiry on the expiry axis, and linear interpolation on the maturity axis.

Swaption Settlement

At expiration, swaptions can be either physical or cash-settled. For physical settlement, the owner of an in-the-money receiver/payer swaption will enter into a plain-vanilla swap where she will receive/pay the strike as the fixed rate. Physical settlement is the preferred method for swaptions that are sufficiently (say more than 10 bp) in the money, even if the originally agreed-upon settlement method is cash.

Cash settlement involves determining the market par-swap rate at expiration time, and then agreeing upon the value of a swap with fixed rate equal to the strike instead of the par-swap rate. As we saw before, the economic value of an in-the-money swaption struck at K when par-swap rate is S is an annuity of $S - K$ bp's for RTP ($K - S$ for RTR) for the length of the swap. Therefore, both parties must agree upon the *size* ($|S - K|$) and the *present-value* of this annuity.

Since the strike K is by contract, the swaption counterparties first have to agree on the par-swap rate S at expiration time. This can be by mutual agreement, or polling dealers, or some other method as specified in the option confirm. For generic USD swaptions, the standard is to use the 11:00 a.m. ISDA fixing of swap rates. Once the size of the annuity ($|S - K|$) is known, the counterparties have to then agree on its PV.

There are two methods to calculate the PV of the annuity. The first method (the standard for USD swaptions) is to use a discount factor curve to PV the annuity. For example for an n-year swap with m coupons per year, with payment dates $\{T_1, \ldots, T_{nm}\}$, each party needs to compute:

$$|S - K| \times \frac{1}{m} \sum_{i=1}^{nm} D(T_i)$$

As each counterparty can have a different discount curve (even using the same rate S as the n-year par-swap rate), a bit of horse trading precedes an amicable cash settlement of the swaption. This method does not have a standard name, and can be referred to as "cash-settlement off the curve" or cash-settlement "USD-style."

The second cash-settlement method is to PV the annuity using the annuity formula from bonds, using the agreed-upon swap rate as the *yield*. This method is the standard for European currencies, and is referred to as "cash-settlement via annuity (or IRR) method." For an n-year swap with m coupons per year, the payoff is

$$|S - K| \times \frac{1}{m} \sum_{i=1}^{nm} \frac{1}{(1 + S/m)^i} = \frac{|S - K|}{S} \left(1 - \frac{1}{(1 + S/m)^{nm}} \right)$$

Swaption Vols for Nonstandard Swaps

Occasionally, one needs to provide a swaption price for a swap with a nonstandard frequency or day-count on the fixed leg. For example, in USD, 1y swaps are quoted SA, 30/360, but one is sometimes asked to price an option on a 1y swap quotes Quarterly, Act/360. The daycount difference can be managed by assuming that 30/360 is equivalent to Act/365, and by multiplying the vol of the standard (30/360) swap by 360/365. This is justified by considering the relationship between a simple rate quoted Act/365 ($R_{Act/365}$) versus quoted Act/360 ($R_{Act/360}$), via their common discount factors for the start T_s and end dates T_e of the rates:

$$R_{Act/365} = \frac{D(T_s)/D(T_e) - 1}{(T_e - T_s)/365}$$

$$R_{Act/360} = \frac{D(T_s)/D(T_e) - 1}{(T_e - T_s)/360}$$

$$\Rightarrow R_{Act/360} = \frac{360}{365} \times R_{Act365}$$

$$\Rightarrow \sigma_N(R_{Act/360}) = \frac{360}{365} \times \sigma_N(R_{Act365})$$

To adjust for different frequencies, one can use the following approximation to relate quarterly rates (R_4) to semiannual (R_2) rates:

$$(1 + R_4/4)^4 = (1 + R_2/2)^2 \Rightarrow \frac{dR_2}{dR_4} = (1 + R_4/4)$$

Using this heuristic, we can set

$$\sigma_N(R_4) \approx \frac{1}{1 + R_4/4} \times \sigma_N(R_2)$$

Putting it together, we have

$$\sigma_N(R_{Q, Act360}) \approx \frac{360/365}{1 + R_{Q, Act360}/4} \sigma_N(R_{SA, 30360})$$

which means that we should be happy to use the standard (SA,30360) vols when selling swaptions on (Q, Act/360) swaps!

For more complicated swaps (amortizing, zero-coupon), the vol adjustment has to be carefully calculated using more advanced techniques (see HJM swaption vol approximation in Chapter 10).

SKEWS, SMILES

In the perfect Black world, asset prices evolve (Normally, Log-Normally) according to a Brownian motion with a single volatility parameter. The price of options then can be obtained once we know this volatility, or alternatively, given a price, we can back out the implied volatility. In practice, it is observed that option prices with same expiration date, but different strikes give rise to different implied Black volatilities. Typically, for options with strikes lower than ATMF, the implied volatility goes up, and this effect is called *skew*. Also out-of-the-money options in either direction (high or low strikes) generally have higher implied Black volatilities than ATMF options. This effect is called *volatility smile*.

The existence of skews and smiles means that the implied distribution of the assets is more complicated than what is posited by Black (Normal, Log-Normal) model, and has given rise to a cottage industry of searching for the *right* model for skew and smile. Among the models proposed are mixture models, constant elasticity of variance (CEV) models, Stochastic volatility models (SABR among them), jump-diffusion models, and fractional Brownian motion models. While each of these models has its merits, they collectively suffer from the fact that they are modeling the wrong thing!

Skews and smiles are predominantly driven by supply and demand. If a majority of clients are worried about higher rates, and are buying high-strike payers to protect themselves, payer swaptions go up in price (and hence in implied vol). Alternatively, if the fear is for low rates, then low-strike receivers go up in premium/vol. On a day-to-day basis, vol traders perceive the skew/smile as a measure of liquidity rather than the implied distribution of rates. Supply/demand patterns change quickly in response to market sentiments/news, and it is implausible to ascribe these changes to the market's view on a meaningful distribution of rates for the life of the option!

Maintaining/Populating Volatility Surface, Cubes

For swaptions, it is customary to maintain a Black *volatility cube*, that is, a volatility for each expiration, swap maturity, and strike. Some desks maintain vols for a series of absolute ($1\%, 1.25\%, 1.5\%, \ldots, 9.75\%, 10\%, \ldots$) strikes, while most desks maintain vols for a series of relative (ATMF, ATMF±25 bp, ATMF±50 bp, ATMF±100 bp, $\ldots$) strikes. A similar procedure is used for caplet vol curves.

As one might imagine, the task of maintaining ATMF volatility surfaces (expiration, swap maturity) and cubes (expiration, maturity, strike) is arduous. Depending on the market, there are 10 to 20 expirations, 10 to 20 maturities, and 10 to 20 strike levels (absolute or relative), hence a rates option trader needs to maintain on the order of 1000 live prices! Given that on a typical trading day, only a few (10 to 20) swaptions and cap/floors trade, most desks keep active watch on certain *anchor* vols, and derive other neighboring vols via linear/ratio interpolation/extrapolation. For example, in USD, 1m2y, 1m5y, 1m10y, 3m10y, 1y1y, and 5y5y can serve as the anchor vols. Once we know these vols, the vol of 1m3y, 1m4y, or 2m10y can plausibly (in the absence of actual markets) be backed out via interpolation.

The market for skews is less active than ATMF options. Most desks select a skew model (SABR, CEV,...) and *calibrate* the few model parameters to any observed skew markets, quoted commonly through *risk-reversals*: the difference between the price an out-of-the-money payer swaption versus an equally out-of-the-money receiver. For Normal dynamics, in the absence of any skew these prices should be the same, as the Normal distribution is symmetric. Hence, when a difference exists, it is indicative of non-Normality or skew. Using these skews markets, volatility traders then populate the cube using these few parameters. Hence the role of skew models is primarily to reduce the dimension of the problem from 1000s to 100s (potentially each expiration/swap-term pair can have its own set of parameters).

SABR Skew Model

The current skew model of choice is the SABR (stochastic alpha, beta, rho) model,[1] as it provides enough, yet not too excessive, number of parameters for each expiration/swap-term pair to fit a variety of smile/skew profiles. It is a combination CEV+stochastic volatility model, and has relatively simple formulae for Black skews based on three parameters: CEV (β) parameter, allowing one to smoothly go from Log-Normal dynamics ($\beta = 1$) to Normal dynamics ($\beta = 0$); vol-of-vol (ν) parameter, allowing one to control/fit the smile (see Figure 7.1); and rate/vol correlation (ρ) parameter, allowing one to control/fit the skew (see Figure 7.2). The "α" term must be backed out via iteration so that ATMF vols are recovered, a good initial guess is

$$\alpha \approx \sigma_{LN}(ATMF)/(1 + \nu^2(2 - 3\rho^2)t_e/24)$$

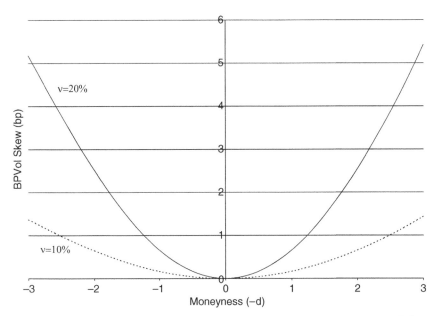

FIGURE 7.1 BPVol Skew $(\sigma_N(K) - \sigma_N(ATMF))$ versus Moneyness $(-d = \frac{K-F}{\sigma_N\sqrt{t_e}})$ in SABR Model with Parameters $(F = 5\%, \sigma_N(F) = 1.00\%, t_e = 1, \beta = 0, \rho = 0)$

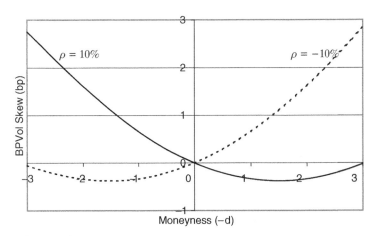

FIGURE 7.2 BPVol Skew $(\sigma_N(K) - \sigma_N(ATMF))$ versus Moneyness $(-d = \frac{K-F}{\sigma_N\sqrt{t_e}})$ in SABR Model with Parameters $(F = 5\%, \sigma_N(F) = 1.00\%, t_e = 1, \beta = 0, \nu = 10\%)$

The SABR formulae are presented below:

$$s = \frac{\alpha}{(FK)^{(1-\beta)/2}} \qquad \phi = \frac{1}{2}\ln(F/K)$$

$$\zeta = \frac{v}{s}\ln(F/K) \qquad x(\zeta) = \ln\frac{\sqrt{1-2\rho\zeta+\zeta^2}+\zeta-\rho}{1-\rho}$$

$$\sigma(K) = \frac{s}{1+[(1-\beta)\phi]^2/3!+[(1-\beta)\phi]^4/5!} \times \frac{\zeta}{x(\zeta)}$$

$$\times \left(1+t_e\left[(\beta-1)^2+\frac{(s/2)^2}{6}+\frac{\rho\beta vs}{4}+\frac{(2-3\rho^2)}{6}(v/2)^2+\cdots\right]\right)$$

$$\sigma_N(K) = \sqrt{FK} \times \frac{s\times(1+\phi^2/3!+\phi^4/5!)}{1+[(1-\beta)\phi]^2/3!+[(1-\beta)\phi]^4/5!} \times \frac{\zeta}{x(\zeta)}$$

$$\times \left(1+t_e\left[(\beta^2-2\beta)+\frac{(s/2)^2}{6}+\frac{\rho\beta vs}{4}+\frac{(2-3\rho^2)}{6}(v/2)^2+\cdots\right]\right)$$

CMS PRODUCTS

A constant maturity swap (CMS) rate is simply the par-swap rate for a given tenor, and a *CMS swap* is the periodic exchange of a CMS rate versus either a fixed rate, or more typically versus Libor. For example, a USD 2-year CMS-10y versus Libor consists of a standard quarterly, Act/360 floating leg based on 3m Libor, versus the quarterly fixing and payment (accrued 30/360) of 10-year par-swap rate on the CMS leg, with both legs spanning 2 years. Since the tenor of the underlying CMS rate does not coincide with the length of the calculation period, the replication argument for plain-vanilla Libor legs does not hold, and one cannot simply discount the forward par-swap rates. Still, there is a strong temptation to do this, and one typically values CMS resets by first calculating the forward swap rate, and then *adjusting* them by a *CMS convexity adjustment*. The term *convexity adjustment* arises in different contexts in interest rate derivatives, and is usually a red flag that a certain level of fudging is going on. Specifically, convexity adjustments are a quick and dirty way of getting the right answer by applying the wrong method, for example discounting the forward rates, for CMS products. This obviously presupposes that we have the right answer, or at least an idea of what the right answer should be!

For CMS-based payoffs, it is first recognized that while the payoff is linear in the underlying CMS rate, a replicating portfolio would consist of forward swap positions. Recalling that receiving in a swap is economically equivalent to paying par for a forward bond, the graph of the forward swap value is a convex function of the underlying swap rate, analogous to the price/yield graph for bonds. For a CMS-based swap, we therefore are hedging a linear payoff (CMS rate) with a nonlinear/convex payoff (forward swap). The hedge for receiving the CMS-rate is to pay in a PV01-equivalent amount of a forward swap. This hedge, however, confers a systematic advantage to the CMS-receiver, the size of which depends on the curvature/convexity of the forward swap versus the swap rate, and the expected size of the deviation of the realized swap rate at reset date versus its forward value. As no free lunch goes untaxed in markets, the CMS-payer will charge the receiver for this free lunch by adjusting the forward swap rate upwards by the convexity adjustment. Note that this adjustment is only used to calculate the PV of future payments, the actual payment on payment date is simply the CMS rate observed at the fixing date (with no adjustment).

The fair level of this CMS convexity adjustment will require a model of the distribution of future swap rates at each reset date in a risk-neutral setting. In lieu of this, the following heuristic argument is invoked to obtain a quick and dirty formula. Using bonds as proxies for swaps, we start with the following Taylor series expansion:

$$P(y) - P(F) = (y - F)P'(y) + 1/2(y - F)^2 P''(y)$$

where F is the forward par-swap rate, and $P(y)$ is the standard bond price-yield formula. It will be recalled that as long as we can ignore stochastic discounting, forward prices must equal expected prices in a risk-neutral world, hence $E P(y) = P(F)$, and

$$0 = (E[y] - F)P'(F) + 1/2 P''(F)E[(y - F)^2]$$

Finally, we approximate

$$E[(y - F)^2] \approx \sigma_N^2 dt$$

to arrive at the following *CMS Convexity Adjustment* Formula:

$$E[y] - F = -\frac{1}{2}\frac{P''(F)}{P'(F)}\sigma_N^2 dt$$

$$= \left[\frac{1}{F} - \frac{N/m}{(1 + F/m)^{N+1} - (1 + F/m)}\right]\sigma_N^2 t_e$$

where N, m are the number and frequency of coupon payments for the underlying *forward* $(C = y = F)$ bond/swap, and t_e is the time to its reset. While very heuristic and approximate, the previous formula due to its simple structure is widely used and in preference to more elaborate models.

CMS Cap/Floors

A CMS cap/floor is similar to Libor cap/floors, but with the payment based on a CMS rate. Traditionally, each caplet has been priced using Black's formula, where the forward swap rate is adjusted by the convexity adjustment, and the stochastic discounting replaced by today's discount factors:

$$E_0[e^{-\int_0^{t_e} r(u,\omega)du} \max(0, S(t_e, \omega) - K)] \approx D(0, t_e) E_0[\max(0, S(t_e, \omega) - K)]$$

where $E_0[\max(0, S(t_e, \omega) - K)]$ is evaluated using Black's formula with appropriate skew-adjusted swaption volatility for the strike, and using the convexity adjusted CMS rate (using ATMF swaption volatility!). As can be seen, while the preceding method gives a quick answer, it leaves one with the uneasy feeling that there are too many approximations/heuristics being used.

Static Replication

As an alternative, we can approximate the CMS caplet payoff $\max(0, S - K)$ as a static portfolio of payer swaptions with different strikes.[2] Specifically, let $K = K_0 < K_1 < \cdots < K_N$, be a sequence of prechosen strikes, and let $P_i(S)$ be the payoff at expiration of an IRR-settled payer swaption with strike K_i:

$$P_i(S) = \frac{\max(0, S - K_i)}{S} \left(1 - \frac{1}{(1 + S/m)^{nm}}\right)$$

The idea is to approximate the CMS caplet's payoff as

$$\max(0, S - K) + \approx \sum_{i=0}^{L} w_i P_i(S)$$

by choosing the weight sequence $\{w_0, \ldots, w_N\}$ so that the difference is small. The price of a CMS caplet is then the weighted sum of the payer swaption prices. This method makes fewer heuristic approximations, as it only requires swaption volatilities and smiles/skews, which are relatively easy to obtain or divine from the market.

Let $C(S) = \sum_{i=0}^{N} w_i P_i(S)$ denote the payoff of the replicating portfolio. One way to define the weights is to ensure that the replicating portfolio exactly matches the CMS caplet on the strikes, that is

$$(1 \leq j \leq N) \qquad C(K_j) = \max(0, K_j - K_0)$$

The w_j's satisfying the previous can be recursively defined as:

$$(0 \leq j < N) \qquad w_j = \frac{(K_{j+1} - K_0) - \sum_{i=0}^{j-1} w_i P_i(K_{j+1})}{P_j(K_{j+1})}$$

The resulting portfolio will upper bound the CMS payoff: $C(S) \geq \max(0, S - K)$. The graph (not to scale) of this approximation is shown in Figure 7.3. A similar procedure can be used to replicate CMS floors via a series of receiver swaptions.

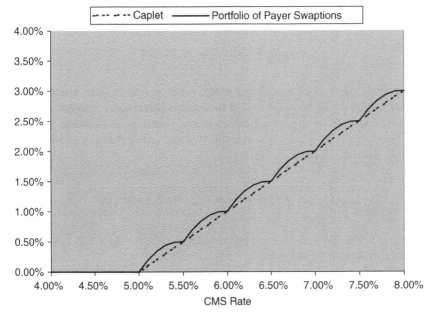

FIGURE 7.3 Payoff of a 5% CMS Caplet and Replicating Portfolio of Payer Swaptions

Having statically replicated a CMS caplet/floorlet via payer/receiver swaptions, we can then invoke put-call parity to value a CMS swap reset:

$$D(0, t_e) \times E_0[S(t_e) - K] = D(0, t_e)E_0[\max(0, S(t_e) - K) - \max(0, K - S(t_e))]$$
$$= \sum_i w_i P_i - \sum_j w'_j R_j$$

where P_i, R_i's are values of IRR-settled payer/receiver swaptions at different strikes.

A final note is that the payoff of the swaption is immediately paid on expiration, while for the CMS products, it is usually paid at the end of the calculation period (typically 3 months later). A simple remedy would be to apply additional discounting to the value of the replicating portfolio(s).

CMS Curve Options

In the past couple of years, options on the slope of swap curve have become popular. These are referred to as *CMS curve options*, as they are simple cap/floors on the diffrence between 2 CMS rates. For example, a CMS 2y-10y curve caplet with strike K is based on the following payoff

$$\max(0, S_{10y}(t_e) - S_{2y}(t_e) - K)$$

The simplest method of evaluating CMS curve products is to use Black's Normal model—Log-Normal would be inappropriate since spreads can go negative, and zero or negative strikes are not uncommon—for the spread: $S_{1,2}(t_e) = S_2(t_e) - S_1(t_e)$, and extract the Normal vol of the spread from the swaption Normal volatilities via:

$$\sigma_N(S_{1,2}) = \sqrt{\sigma_N^2(S_1) + \sigma_N^2(S_2) - 2\rho\sigma_N(S_1)\sigma_N(S_2)}$$

where $\sigma_N(S_1)$, $\sigma_N(S_2)$ are the swaption normal vols for the CMS rates, and ρ is the correlation between them.

Example 7. Consider a 6m caplet on USD CMS-2y/CMS-10y, where the forward 2y, 10y swap rates are 5%, 5.5%, and the 6m-into-2y, 6m-into-10y ATMF swaption Normal volatilities are trading at 120, 100 bp/annum respectively. Using the convexity adjustment formula for the CMS resets, we have

$$E[S_{2y}(2y)] - 5\% = \left[\frac{1}{5\%} - \frac{4/2}{(1 + 5\%/2)^{4+1} - (1 + 5\%/2)}\right](1.20\%)^2 \times 0.5$$

$$= 0.87 \text{ bp}$$

$$E[S_{10y}(2y)] - 5.5\% = \left[\frac{1}{5.5\%} - \frac{20/2}{(1 + 5.5\%/2)^{20+1} - (1 + 5.5\%/2)}\right](1.00\%)^2 \times 0.5$$

$$= 2.34 \text{ bp}$$

to arrive at the convexity adjusted forward spread

$$E[S_{10y}(2y)] - E[S_{2y}(2y)] = 0.5147\%$$

Using a correlation $\rho = 90\%$, we compute the Normal volatility of the spread:

$$\sqrt{(1.20\%)^2 + (1.00\%)^2 - 2(90\%)(1.20\%)(1.00\%)} = 0.529\%$$

For a caplet with strike K equal to the nonadjusted forward spread $K = 50bp$, we can price it as

$$0.1567\% = (0.529\%)\sqrt{0.5}\left[\frac{1}{\sqrt{2\pi}}e^{-d^2/2} + dN(d)\right] \quad d = \frac{0.5588\% - 0.50\%}{(0.529\%)\sqrt{0.5}}$$

The above value, 15.67 cents, has to get discounted by $D(6m)$ to arrive at its today's value.

Contingent Curve Trades

While CMS curve options are the most direct way of taking a view on the slope of the swap curve, one may put on a *conditional* curve trade using European swaptions, since curve trades are usually *directional*: The front end of the swap curve is more volatile than the long end as it is more sensitive to central bank policies, and the front end typically *leads* the long end in either increasing or decreasing rate environments. Therefore, in a tightening (rising rate) environment, the short-term swap rates move more than longer-term swap rates, leading to flattening of the swap curve. This is referred to as *bear-flattening*–"bear" since bond prices are dropping in rising rate environments. Similarly, in an easing (falling rate) environment, short-term rates fall more than long-term rates, leading to *bull-steepening*.

As such, one would want to be in a flattener in bearish environments, while steepeners are preferred in bullish environments.

To be long a steepener, one can either be long the curve via swaps (long the front end, short the back end), using either spot or forward swaps, or own a CMS curve caplet. Instead, one can be in a *conditional* steepener by buying a swaption receiver into the shorter maturity, while selling a swaption receiver into the longer maturity. The size of each swaption is chosen so that if they are both in the money at expiration, each swap will have the same PV01, while the strikes of the swaptions are chosen so that the package is zero-cost: zero-cost bull-steepener (sometimes called conditional or contingent call-call). Similarly, a zero-cost bear-flattener consists of a pair of (in-the-money) PV01-equivalent payer swaptions with strikes chosen to make the package zero-cost.

Example 8. Continuing with the previous example, let us consider a 6m into 2y/10y zero-cost bull-steepener, where the strike of the 6m-into-2y receiver is chosen to be ATMF-25bp (25-low receiver). Ignoring skews, we have $F_{2y} = 5\%$, $F_{10y} = 5.5\%$, $\sigma_{2y} = 120bp$, $\sigma_{10y} = 100bp$, $K_{2y} = 4.75\%$, and we need to solve for K_{10y} to make the package costless. Since each receiver price is computed as

$$Receiver = \text{PVBP(Swap, 6m forward)} \times \text{Black's put formula}$$

and the receiver notionals must satisfy

$$\frac{N_{2y}}{N_{10y}} = \frac{\text{PV01(10y Swap, 6m Forward)}}{\text{PV01(2y Swap, 6m Forward)}}$$

since the underlying forward swaps are close to ATMF, we can assume that

$$PV01(\text{Forward Swap}) \approx PVBP(\text{Forward Swap})$$

In this case, we need to solve for K_{10y} so that

$$\sigma_{2y}\sqrt{0.5}[N'(d_{2y}) - d_{2y}N(-d_{2y})] = \sigma_{10y}\sqrt{0.5}[N'(d_{10y}) - d_{10y}N(-d_{10y})]$$

where

$$d_{2y} = \frac{F_{2y} - K_{2y}}{\sigma_{2y}\sqrt{0.5}} \qquad d_{10y} = \frac{F_{10y} - K_{10y}}{\sigma_{10y}\sqrt{0.5}}$$

Trial and error gives $K_{10y} = 5.3845\%$, which means that we can get into a bull-steepener at a spread of 63.45 bp, that is, 13.45 bp steeper than the forward spread (50bp), which is due to vol of 2y (120) (we are buying) being higher than that of 10y (100bp), which we are selling. This is the typical situation where the market charges one for directionality. If instead the swaption market priced the 2y vol lower than 10y vol, then one could get into a costless bull-steepener at flatter level than forwards.

BOND OPTIONS

While not strictly a "rates" product, bond options are sometimes quoted by flow options desks. The typical expiration for these options is relatively short (a few days or weeks), and are usually priced and hedged using Black's Log-Normal formula, driven by *price volatility*. As the market for bond options is relatively thin, this price volatility is backed out from *yield volatility* using the following heuristic argument: Yield log-volatility σ_y measures a 1 standard deviation percentage change in yields:

$$\sigma_y \approx E\left[\frac{\Delta y}{y}\right]$$

while price log-volatility σ_P measures a 1 standard deviation percentage change in prices:

$$\sigma_P \approx E\left[\frac{\Delta P}{P}\right]$$

One can use Taylor series to relate change in prices due to change in yields:

$$\Delta P \approx \frac{dP}{dy}\Delta y$$

therefore

$$\sigma_P = \frac{1}{P}\frac{dP}{dy}y\sigma_y$$

A common approach is to derive the yield volatility from a similar-maturity swaption volatility using simple regression analysis. For example, when asked to quote a 1m option on the current U.S. treasury 10y bond (CT10), one can perform a regression analysis on the relationship between 10y treasury yields versus 10y swap rates, and multiply the 1m-into-10y swaption volatility by the slope coefficient to arrive at a plausible yield volatility for CT10. By converting this yield vol into price vol, one can then price bond options using Black's Log-Normal formula using *clean* forward and strike prices. Note that as option prices are based on replication using the underlying, the specific bond's financing (repo) rate rather than a generic risk-free rate should be used in Black's formula.

Conditional Swap-Spread Trades

While a swap spread trade involves a cash bond versus a swap, one can also enter into a *conditional* swap spread trade using swaptions and bond options. It is observed that swap spreads are typically *directional*. In falling rate environments, spreads generally "come in" (decrease), while they "go out" in increasing rate environments. To take advantage of this directionality, one would then like to be in a swap-spread widening trade (long cash, pay in swaps) when interest rates are increasing, that is, a bearish-widener. For a given cash bond, this can be achieved by selling a put option on the bond, while buying a PV01-equivalent amount of a payer swaption with maturity identical to a bond: If both options finish in the money, the bond is put to us while we are paying in a matched-maturity swap, that is, we are long the matched-maturity swap spread of the bond when rates are increasing. The strikes of the put and swaption are usually chosen so that the package is costless, typically by selecting one strike higher (in yield) than ATMF, and then solving for the other strike.

To take advantage of directionality in decreasing rate environments, one implements a *bullish-tightener* by selling a call option on the bond and buying a PV01-equivalent (if both options finish in the money) receiver swaption for a matched-maturity swap, with strikes chosen so that the package is costless, resulting in a *zero-cost call/receiver* or bullish-tightener.

A final note that due to relative low liquidity of bond options, most contingent swap-spread trades are implemented using options on treasury futures contracts traded on the Chicago Board of Trade (CBOT), with the future contract equated to cheapest-to-deliver (CTD) issue divided by its conversion factor.

Interest-Rate Exotics

Short-Rate Models

Having milked Black's formula dry for flow products, we need models to price more complicated interest-rate options, prominent among them Bermudan (flexible exercise time) and Asian (path-dependent) options. For non-rate-based assets like equities, closed-form formulae (some exact, and some approximations) exist for some of these options. However, since interest-rate options depend on multiple underlyings (zero-coupon bonds), these formulae are hard to adapt to rate options.

For more complicated interest-rate options, we have to go back to our original framework: risk-neutral valuation, where all prices (underlyings and contingent claims) must satisfy:

$$(0 \leq t \leq T) \qquad C(t) = E_t[e^{-\int_t^T r(u,\omega)du} C(t, \omega)]$$

This compact formula is surprisingly all we need for contingent claim valuation, and is the basis of all interest-rate option models. When applied to interest-rate underlyings, it imposes the following constraint on today's ($t = 0$) discount factors:

$$(0 \leq T) \qquad E_0[e^{-\int_0^T r(u,\omega)du}] = D(0, T)$$

which is loosely called "ensuring no-arbitrage." At all future times $t > 0$, and specifically at option expiry t_e, discount factors can be recovered as

$$(0 \leq t_e \leq T) \qquad E_{t_e}[e^{-\int_{t_e}^T r(u,\omega)du}] = D(t_e, T, \omega)$$

from which we can compute the payoffs of the contingent claim, $C(t_e, \omega)$, as it is a function of the discount curve at that time. Finally, by computing the expected stochastically discounted value of the contingent claim's payoffs, we arrive at its present value:

$$C(0) = E_0[e^{-\int_0^{t_e} r(u,\omega)du} C(t_e, \omega)]$$

All interest-rate models fall within the above framework, and primarily differ in their explicit state space (short rate, or full term structure), and the computational algorithms (tree-based or simulation) used to evaluate it.

A QUICK TOUR

Short-rate models take their state-space as the short-term rate r, as all other quantities can be evaluated from it. The first short-rate models were based on the basic Black-Scholes-Merton dynamics with the underlying asset replaced by the short rate. Specifically, the following dynamics were posited for the short rate:

$$\frac{dr(t, \omega)}{r(t, \omega)} = \mu(t)dt + \sigma(t)dB(t, \omega)$$

with the interpretation that percentage changes in the short rate are driven by a deterministic drift $\mu(t)$ used to ensure the no-arb condition, and driven by increments of a Brownian motion $(dB(t, \omega))$ multiplied by a time-dependent volatility curve $\sigma(t)$, used for recovering the market price of flow options. For the above dynamics, rates are Log-Normally distributed, and while positive (a desirable effect), are boundless. Moreover, there are no closed-form formulas for zero-coupon prices and options.

If instead we assume Normal dynamics

$$dr(t, \omega) = \mu(t)dt + \sigma_N(t)dB(t, \omega)$$

then interest rates are Normally distributed (a better fit to reality), some closed-form formulas can be derived, but interest rates can go negative (a potential undesirable) and are still unbounded.

Interest rates are not unbounded and exhibit mean-reversion. The first simple model to alleviate unboundedness by introducing mean-reversion was proposed by Vasicek,[1] later extended by Hull and White[2] (Hull-White model, Extended-Vasicek model). In this setup, two new parametric curves were introduced: a positive-valued *mean-reversion speed*, $a(t)$, and level $b(t)$:

$$dr(t, \omega) = a(t)[b(t) - r(t, \omega)]dt + \sigma(t)dB(t, \omega)$$

When rates are below mean reversion level, $r(t) < b(t)$, the drift $a(t)[b(t) - r(t)]$ is positive, and interest rates get pulled up. When interest rates are above mean-reversion level, $r(t) > b(t)$, the drift $a(t)[b(t) - r(t)]$ is negative, pushing rates down. When rates are around their mean-reversion levels $r(t) \approx b(t)$, the drift becomes zero, and interest-rates meander around

TABLE 8.1 Common Short-Rate Models

Model	Process Equation
Vasicek	$dr(t, \omega) = a[b - r(t, \omega)]dt + \sigma_N dB(t, \omega)$
Hull-White (Original)	$dr(t, \omega) = a[b(t) - r(t, \omega)]dt + \sigma_N dB(t, \omega)$
Hull-White	$dr(t, \omega) = a(t)[b(t) - r(t, \omega)]dt + \sigma_N(t)dB(t, \omega)$
Ho-Lee	$dr(t, \omega) = a(t)dt + \sigma_N dB(t, \omega)$
Cox-Ingersoll-Ross (CIR)	$dr(t, \omega) = a[b - r(t, \omega)]dt + s\sqrt{r(t, \omega)}dB(t, \omega)$
Black-Derman-Toy (BDT)	$d\ln r(t, \omega) = -\frac{\sigma'(t)}{\sigma(t)}[b(t) - \ln r(t, \omega)]dt + \sigma(t)dB(t, \omega)$
Black-Karasinski (BK)	$d\ln r(t, \omega) = a(t)[b(t) - \ln r(t, \omega)]dt + \sigma(t)dB(t, \omega)$

randomly according to the white noise term dB. While not guaranteeing that interest rates remain positive (interest rates are still Normally distributed), mean-reversion addresses the problem of unbounded interest rates.

A simple extension of Vasicek's model to ensure positive, yet mean-reverting interest rates is to model the logarithm of interest rates rather than the rates themselves:

$$d\ln r(t, \omega) = a(t)[b(t) - \ln r(t, \omega)]dt + \sigma(t)dB(t, \omega)$$

The above dynamic leads to Log-Normal (hence positive), mean-reverting interest rates, and is the basis of Black-Derman-Toy (BDT),[3] and Black-Karasinski (BK)[4,5] models.

Attempts were also made to break away from the Normal/Log-Normal paradigm. Combining the equations for each dynamics, the following *constant elasticity of variance* (CEV) models were introduced:

$$dr(t, \omega) = a(t)[b(t) - r(t, \omega)]dt + \sigma(t)r(t, \omega)^\alpha dB(t, \omega)$$

reducing to Normal (HW-Vasicek) dynamics when CEV parameter $\alpha = 0$, and Log-Normal dynamics when $\alpha = 1$. The Cox-Ingersoll-Ross (CIR) model[6] has the above dynamics with $\alpha = 1/2$, and is also called the square root model. For CIR model, closed-form expressions can be derived for zero-coupon bonds and some options on them. Table 8.1 summarizes the process dynamics for these short-rate models.

DYNAMICS TO IMPLEMENTATION

Positing continuous-time dynamics for short rates is all good and fine to gain an understanding of what is being assumed, and to analyze the behavior of interest rates. In some cases, one can derive closed-form expressions for discount factors, and simple European options. However, in order to price more complicated options, one needs to implement them as a computer program and numerically calculate option prices. For this, the process is discretized, and discrete-time analogs of instantaneous rates, drifts, and vols are used. The process of implementing a discrete-time version of a short-rate model introduces a series of implementation choices and techniques. The process is more of an art, and involves the judicious use of a variety of techniques. The desire is to implement a discretized model that is easy to use, is flexible to handle a variety of instruments, and can recover market prices for liquid flow options, and provides quick Greeks to guide the selection of the replicating portfolio. This is a tall order!

In principle, a multiperiod tree-model is all we need to price interest-rate options. However, since even in the simplest binomial case, the number of nodes doubles after each time step, the computational burden increases exponentially. Instead, we can focus on recombining-tree (lattice) implementation, where the number of nodes increases linearly with each time step. While this implementation is quite efficient, due to recombination, we lose most of the path information, and cannot use these models for path-dependent options. For path-dependent options, the natural implementation is a simulation algorithm, where the risk-neutral integral is evaluated as an approximate sum. Bermudan options, however, are difficult to value in simulation models. Herein lies the main quandary of interest-rate models: *The nonrecombining tree is computationally too onerous, while path-dependent options cannot easily be priced in lattices, and Bermudan options cannot easily be priced in simulation models!*

In practice, one ends up developing a suite of model implementations, each designed to address a particular class of products. For example, for Bermudan options, one develops a lattice/tree implementation calibrated to European swaptions and (hopefully) their skews, while for path-dependent products a simulation implementation is best suited. As much as possible, one should implement models with consistent dynamics, although each type of implementation embeds various techniques/assumptions that may be different from implementation to implementation.

LATTICE/TREE IMPLEMENTATION

A short-rate *tree* model is very similar to a binomial model, where at each time step, each node can lead to new states for short-term interest rates. The number of branches is usually selected to be two (binomial) or three (trinomial). For binomial trees, the number of nodes doubles at each time step, so after n time steps, there are 2^n number of nodes/states. Since the desire is to let the number of time steps get progressively larger, a tree model can quickly (exponentially) outgrow available computational resources.

A lattice is a tree where the nodes recombine, so an up-move followed by a down-move ends up at the same state/node as a down-move followed by an up-move. For lattices, the number of nodes grows linearly as the number of time steps, allowing one to easily increase the number of time steps to achieve better precision.

Starting from a discount factor curve, a typical short-rate lattice implementation proceeds as follows:

1. Time is discretized into lattice-dates: $0 = t_0 < t_1 < \cdots < t_{N+1}$, where usually (but not necessary) the lattice-dates are of equal length, say daily, monthly. The lattice is started by the initial short rate $r(t_0)$ for a deposit over $[t_0, t_1]$:

$$r(t_0) = (1/D(0, t_1) - 1)/(t_1 - t_0)$$

2. At each time t_i, a set of recombining new short rates $r_{i+1}(\omega)$ for deposit period $[t_{i+1}, t_{i+2}]$ are selected for the next time step t_{i+1}, and probabilities are assigned to each branch. The new states and probabilities must jointly ensure the discrete-time no-arb condition required by risk-neutral valuation:

$$D(0, t_{i+2}) = E\left[\frac{1}{1 + r(t_0)dt_0} \frac{1}{1 + r_1(\omega)dt_1} \cdots \frac{1}{1 + r_{i+1}(\omega)dt_{i+1}}\right]$$

$dt_i = t_{i+1} - t_i$ and preserve the posited dynamics (volatility $\sigma(t)$, mean-reversion $a(t)$, $b(t)$, ...) of the short-rate process according to the model. Note that knowing t_{i+1}'s interest rates completely determines t_{i+2}'s discount factor, since r_{i+1} is the interest rate for deposit period $[t_{i+1}, t_{i+2}]$. That's why when generating new r_{i+1}'s, we have a constraint on $D(0, t_{i+2})$. This step is referred to as *inverting the yield curve*.

3. At each node, the implicit discount-factor curve is computed by navigating the sub-lattice emanating from that node. This discount-factor curve can then be used to compute swap values, swap rates, forward rates, and so on.

4. The model parameters are then progressively tweaked, and for each new set of parameters, a new arb-free lattice is reconstructed until the lattice is not only arb-free, but also the lattice price of a set of benchmark flow options (swaptions, cap/floors) match their market prices. This step is called *calibration* and is typically the hardest step.

A calibrated arb-free lattice can then be used to price more exotic interest rate options.

BDT LATTICE MODEL

To make the above concepts concrete, we will show how to construct the Black-Derman-Toy (BDT) lattice model. The basic dynamic for the BDT model is that at each time step, interest rates moves are Log-Normal, according to the time-dependent *local volatility* curve, $\sigma(t)$. (See Figure 8.1.)

Starting with a discount-factor curve, we discretize time into lattice dates, $0 = t_0 < t_1 < \cdots < t_{N+1}$, and also discretize the local volatility curve: $\sigma_i = \sigma(t_i), 0 \leq i < N$. Starting the lattice with

$$r_0 = r(t_0) = (D(0, t_0)/D(0, t_1) - 1)/dt_0$$

let $r_{ij} = r(t_i, \omega_j)$ denote the j-th state at the i-th time t_i. At each time t_i, each node r_{ij} leads to 2 nodes $r_{i+1,j}, r_{i+1,j+1}$ at the next time t_{i+1} with risk-neutral probability of 1/2.

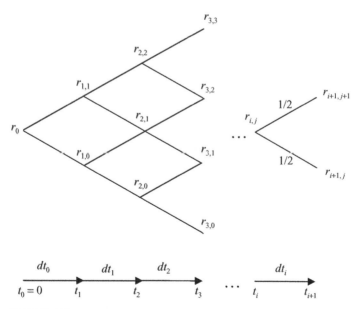

FIGURE 8.1   Black-Derman-Toy (BDT) Lattice for Short Rate

The main dynamic of the BDT lattice is that it is Log-Normal, that is, over each time interval $[t_i, t_{i+1}]$ the log volatility (percent change) of rates is prescribed by the time-dependent volatility $\sigma_i = \sigma(t_i)$. Mathematically, this means

$$Var_{t_i}\left[\frac{1}{dt_i}\ln(\frac{r(t_{i+1}, \omega)}{r(t_i, \omega)})\right] = \sigma_i^2$$

where

$$dt_i = t_{i+1} - t_i \qquad 0 \le i \le N$$

Hence for each node, we must have

$$\sigma_i^2 dt_i = \frac{1}{2}\ln^2\left(\frac{r_{i+1,j+1}}{r_{ij}}\right) + \frac{1}{2}\ln^2\left(\frac{r_{i+1,j}}{r_{ij}}\right)$$
$$- \left[\frac{1}{2}\ln\left(\frac{r_{i+1,j+1}}{r_{ij}}\right) + \frac{1}{2}\ln\left(\frac{r_{i+1,j+1}}{r_{ij}}\right)\right]^2$$

which after a bit of algebra reduces to the following *ratio constraint*:

$$\frac{r_{i+1,j+1}}{r_{i+1,j}} = e^{2\sigma_i\sqrt{dt_i}} = s_i$$

Putting all these ratio constraints together, we can express all the new tree nodes $(r_{i+1,.})$ in terms of the bottom-most node $r_{i+1,0}$:

$$(0 \le i < N)(0 \le j \le i+1) \qquad r_{i+1,j} = r_{i+1,0}e^{2j\sigma_i\sqrt{dt_i}} = r_{i+1,0}s_i^j$$

Therefore at each time interval $[t_i, t_{i+1}]$, fixing the local volatility σ_i, we have one degree of freedom, $r_{i+1,0}$, and one new arb-free constraint:

$$D(0, t_{i+2}) = E\left[\frac{1}{1+r_0 dt_0}\frac{1}{1+r_{1,.}dt_1}\cdots\frac{1}{1+r_{i+1,.}dt_{i+1}}\right]$$

For example, $r_{1,0}$ must satisfy

$$D(0, t_2) = \frac{1/2}{(1+r_0 dt_0)(1+r_{1,0}dt_1)} + \frac{1/2}{(1+r_0 dt_0)(1+r_{1,1}dt_1)}$$
$$= \frac{1/2}{(1+r_0 dt_0)(1+r_{1,0}dt_1)} + \frac{1/2}{(1+r_0 dt_0)(1+r_{1,0}s_1 dt_1)}$$

while $r_{2,0}$ must satisfy

$$
\begin{aligned}
D(0, t_3) &= \frac{(1/2)(1/2)}{(1 + r_0 dt_0)(1 + r_{1,0} dt_1)(1 + r_{2,0} dt_2)} \\
&\quad + \frac{(1/2)(1/2)}{(1 + r_0 dt_0)(1 + r_{1,0} dt_1)(1 + r_{2,1} dt_2)} \\
&\quad + \frac{(1/2)(1/2)}{(1 + r_0 dt_0)(1 + r_{1,1} dt_1)(1 + r_{2,1} dt_2)} \\
&\quad + \frac{(1/2)(1/2)}{(1 + r_0 dt_0)(1 + r_{1,1} dt_1)(1 + r_{2,2} dt_2)} \\
&= \frac{(1/2)(1/2)}{(1 + r_0 dt_0)(1 + r_{1,0} dt_1)(1 + r_{2,0} dt_2)} \\
&\quad + \frac{(1/2)(1/2)}{(1 + r_0 dt_0)(1 + r_{1,0} dt_1)(1 + r_{2,0} s_2 dt_2)} \\
&\quad + \frac{(1/2)(1/2)}{(1 + r_0 dt_0)(1 + r_{1,1} dt_1)(1 + r_{2,0} s_2 dt_2)} \\
&\quad + \frac{(1/2)(1/2)}{(1 + r_0 dt_0)(1 + r_{1,1} dt_1)(1 + r_{2,0} s_2^2 dt_2)}
\end{aligned}
$$

and so on. Notice that the arb-free constraints are nonlinear and a solving routine needs to be used to compute $r_{i,0}$'s.

Arrow-Debreu Prices

As can be seen, the equations and computations quickly become cumbersome after a few time steps. A big part of this complexity is due to repeated calculation of stochastic discounting

$$
E\left[\frac{1}{(1 + r_0 dt_0)} \frac{1}{(1 + r_1(\omega) dt_1)} \cdots \frac{1}{(1 + r_{i-1}(\omega) dt_{i-1})} \right]
$$

to ensure that today's discount factors are recovered.

This computation can be simplified by appealing to *Arrow-Debreu securities*. A (t_i, ω) Arrow-Debreu security has unit payoff at time t_i if and only if a *particular* state ω is realized. For example, a $(t_2, r_{2,1})$ AD-security has a payoff of 1 if we get to state $r_{2,1}$ (the middle state) at time t_2, and zero otherwise. The *Arrow-Debreu Price*, $AD_{i,j} = AD(t_j, \omega_j)$ is today's price of a (t_i, ω_j) AD-security, that is, today's value of unit payoff at time t_i if and only if the j-th state (corresponding to r_{ij}) happens.

Any contingent claim with payoff $C(t_e, \omega)$ can be considered to be a portfolio of Arrow-Debreu securities, with $C(t_e, \omega)$ units of (t_e, ω) AD security for each state. Therefore, today's value of the security is the weighted (by $C(t_e, \omega)$) sum of AD prices:

$$
\begin{aligned}
C(0) &= E\left[\frac{1}{1 + r_0 dt_0} \times \cdots \times \frac{1}{1 + r_{i-1,.} dt_{i-1}} C(t_i, .)\right] \\
&= \sum_{j=0}^{i} AD_{ij} C_{ij}
\end{aligned}
$$

where C_{ij} is the option payoff at time t_i if the j-th state (corresponding to r_{ij}) happens. In particular, if the contingent claim is a t_i-maturity zero-coupon bond (with unit payoff in any state), its price today ($D(0, t_0)$) must satisfy:

$$
\sum_{j=0}^{i} AD_{ij} = D(0, t_i)
$$

Arrow-Debreu prices are related to path integrals and Green's Function. In interest-rate modeling, Jamshidian[7] popularized their use when building interest-rate lattices via a method he coined as *Forward Induction*. His main observation was that for each tree date t_i, if we compute and keep track of $A(t_i, \omega)$, we can easily update it for next period t_{i+1}, and utilize it to ensure that our new interest rates satisfy the no-arb condition. The technique can be summarized as follows: To compute each state's AD price, consider all the one-time-prior nodes that lead to it, and multiply each such node's AD price by probability that it leads to this node, and further multiply it by the prior node's 1-period discount factor (see Figure 8.2). The sum of these gives you the desired AD price:

$$
AD(t_{i+1}, j) = \sum_{k} AD(t_i, k) \frac{P[(t_i, k) \to (t_{i+1}, j)]}{1 + r(t_j, k) dt_i}
$$

Computation of AD prices, while not necessary, greatly simplifies the construction of lattice models and valuation of contingent claims.

Extracting a Discount Factor Curve

This being a short-rate model, we seem to only have access to the short rate at each node. At the same time, we might be interested in valuing a swap, or calculating a swap rate, which would mean that we need a full discount factor curve at each node.

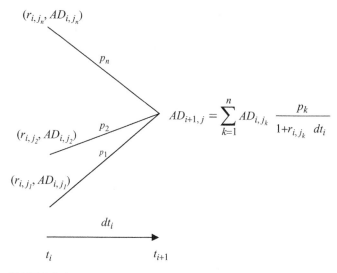

$$AD_{i+1,j} = \sum_{k=1}^{n} AD_{i,j_k} \frac{p_k}{1+r_{i,j_k} \, dt_i}$$

FIGURE 8.2 Updating Arrow-Debreu Prices from One Time-Step to Next

Recall that a risk-neutral model must satisfy

$$(0 \le t_0 \le t_e) \qquad E_{t_0}[e^{-\int_{t_0}^{t_e} r(u,\omega)}] = D(t_0, t_e)$$

for *all* times t_0. The analogous version for a discretized lattice model is

$$(0 \le t_i \le t_j) \qquad E_{t_i}\left[\frac{1}{1+r_i dt_i} \frac{1}{1+r_{i+1} dt_{i+1}} \cdots \frac{1}{1+r_{j-1} dt_{j-1}}\right] = D(t_i, t_j)$$

Having constructed the lattice, we can therefore compute a discount factor curve at each node. Let $D_{ij}(k)$ denote the discount factor at the j-th node at time t_i (corresponding to short-rate r_{ij}) for a dollar to be received at time t_{i+k}. Obviously, $D_{ij}(0) = 1$, and we have:

$$D_{ij}(1) = \frac{1}{1+r_{ij} dt_i}$$

$$D_{ij}(2) = \frac{1/2}{(1+r_{ij} dt_i)(1+r_{i+1,j} dt_{i+1})} + \frac{1/2}{(1+r_{ij} dt_i)(1+r_{i+1,j+1} dt_{i+1})}$$

$$D_{ij}(3) = \frac{(1/2)(1/2)}{(1 + r_{ij}dt_i)(1 + r_{i+1,j}dt_{i+1})(1 + r_{i+2,j}dt_{i+2})}$$

$$+ \frac{(1/2)(1/2)}{(1 + r_{ij}dt_i)(1 + r_{i+1,j}dt_{i+1})(1 + r_{i+2,j+1}dt_{i+2})}$$

$$+ \frac{(1/2)(1/2)}{(1 + r_{ij}dt_i)(1 + r_{i+1,j+1}dt_{i+1})(1 + r_{i+2,j+1}dt_{i+2})}$$

$$+ \frac{(1/2)(1/2)}{(1 + r_{ij}dt_i)(1 + r_{i+1,j+1}dt_{i+1})(1 + r_{i+2,j+2}dt_{i+2})}$$

and so on.

To reduce the computational burden of computing the above, we can instead use the following algorithm to relate t_i's discount factor curves to t_{i+1}'s:

1. Given lattice-dates $0 = t_0 < t_1 < \cdots < t_{N+1}$, start at the last lattice-date (t_N) for which we have short rates, $r_{N,\cdot}$, covering the last deposit period $[t_N, t_{N+1}]$:

$$(0 \le j \le N) \qquad D_{N,j}(0) = 1$$

$$D_{N,j}(1) = \frac{1}{1 + r_{N,j}dt_N}$$

2. Having extracted the discount factor curve $D_{i+1,j}(.)$ for each j-th state at t_{i+1}, move one step back in lattice to t_i, and compute t_i's discount factor curve $D_{ij}(.)$ as follows:

$$(0 \le j \le i) \qquad D_{ij}(0) = 1$$

$$(0 \le k \le N - i) \qquad D_{ij}(k + 1) = \frac{1/2 D_{i+1,j}(k) + 1/2 D_{i+1,j+1}(k)}{1 + r_{ij}dt_i}$$

Since at each node, the short rate can be extracted from the discount factor curve, we can just keep $D_{ij}(\cdot)$ curves at each node alongside the Arrow-Debreu price AD_{ij} for that node. Our lattice then embeds the evolution of the (implicit) discount factor curves rather than just the short rates. Armed with a discount factor curve at each node, we can then compute swap rates, forward rates, swap values, and contingent payoffs on them. For example, pricing a swaption amounts to valuing the underlying swap payoff at each node on the expiration date, and then discounting this (exercised) value to today along each path leading to that node (path-discounting), and averaging over all these paths. Alternatively, we can simply multiply the swaption payoff at each node at expiry by that node's AD price.

Calibration: The Deal-Breaker!

Before we declare victory, and rush off to program the previous algorithms, we need to worry about calibration. So far, the choice of local volatility parameters (σ_i) has been left as arbitrary. *Calibration* involves selecting these parameters so that the lattice price of a selected group of instruments (cap/floors, swaptions) match their market prices. It is of course desirable to have an arb-free lattice that is calibrated to *all* flow instruments: cap/floors, ATMF, and out-of-the-money swaptions, that is, *global calibration*. However, this is almost nearly impossible in practice, and the calibration instruments are judiciously chosen to fit the problem at hand, leading to *local calibration*. For example, for a Libor-in-Arrear swap, the best choice is to calibrate to cap/floors, while for pricing Bermudan swaptions, we need to calibrate to a set of European swaptions.

Calibration is difficult. Indeed, the common experience of many shops is that they get their lattice models up and running in a short time, but spend a long time (or eternity in some cases) to tame the lattice calibration beast. A common practice with varying degree of success is to use nonlinear multi-dimensional optimization methods such as the Levenberg-Marquardt algorithm. However, these methods can easily become unstable, or lead to unrealistic parameters and behavior of short rates. One can help these routines by providing good initial guesses for parameters, at times helped by insights gathered from analyzing the underlying process dynamics (see Appendix B).

One-Year Quarterly Lattice Calibrated to Caplets

To make the previous concepts clear, let us build a 1y quarterly BDT lattice calibrated to quarterly caplets. The inputs to the model are quarterly cash and forward-3m rates, and quarterly ATMF caplet prices, as shown in Table 8.2. We ignore all calendar-related and day-count issues. The resulting arb-free and calibrated BDT lattice is presented in Figure 8.3.

It is helpful to verify that the arb-free condition is satisfied at each time step, and that the lattice is calibrated to each caplet. For example, the parameters $(r_{i,1}, \sigma_0) = (4.84587\%, 9.980\%)$ jointly ensure that the lattice is arb-free:

$$D(0, 6m) = \frac{1}{1 + 5\%/4} \frac{1}{1 + 5.1\%/4} = 0.9752203$$

$$= \frac{1}{1 + 5\%/4} \left[\frac{1/2}{1 + 4.84587\%/4} + \frac{1/2}{1 + 4.84587\%/4 e^{2(9.980\%)\sqrt{0.25}}} \right]$$

TABLE 8.2 BDT Lattice Inputs and Parameters

Calc Period	[0,3m]	[3m,6m]	[6m,9m]	[9m,1y]	[1y,15m]
Fwd Rate	5%	5.1%	5.2%	5.3%	5.4%
Caplet Price (cents)		3.1	6.17	8.69	11.34
Discount Factor	0.9876543	0.9752203	0.9627051	0.9501161	0.9374603
ATMF Caplet LogVol		12.5%	17.5%	20%	22.5%
BDT r_{i0}	5%	4.84587%	4.26620%	3.96676%	3.33522%
BDT σ_i		9.980%	18.928%	18.504%	22.862%

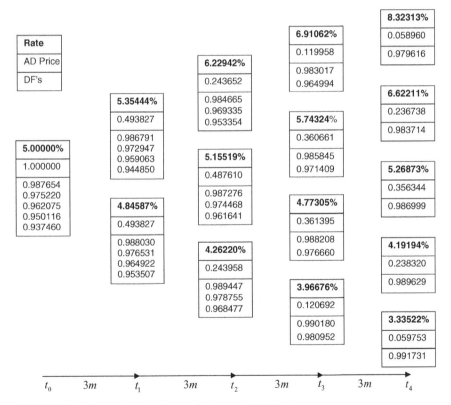

FIGURE 8.3 Example of a Quarterly 1-year BDT Lattice

and the lattice price of $[3m, 6m]$ ATMF $(K = F = 5.1\%)$ caplet matches its market price (3.1 cents, 12.5% implied logvol):

$$[3m,6m] \text{ Caplet Price} = C_{1,0} AD_{1,0} + C_{1,1} AD_{1,1}$$

$$= \frac{(1/4) \max(0, r_{1,0} - K)}{1 + r_{1,0}/4} \times AD_{1,0}$$

$$+ \frac{(1/4) \max(0, r_{1,0} - K)}{1 + r_{1,1}/4} \times AD_{1,1}$$

$$= \frac{(1/4) \max(0, 4.84587\% - 5.1\%)}{1 + 4.84587\%/4} \times \frac{1/2}{1 + 5\%/4}$$

$$+ \frac{(1/4) \max(0, 4.84587\% e^{2(9.980\%)\sqrt{0.25}} - 5.1\%)}{1 + 4.84587\% e^{2(9.980\%)\sqrt{0.25}}/4}$$

$$\times \frac{1/2}{1 + 5\%/4}$$

The reason that the caplet payoff $C_{1,.}$ is written as

$$\frac{1/4 \max(0, r_{1,.} - K)}{1 + r_{1,.}/4}$$

is that each caplet is determined at the beginning of the calculation period, accrued for the length of the calculation period (1/4 in this case), but paid at the end (3m later in this case), so its value at determination date $\frac{1}{4} \max(0, r_{i,.} - K)$ needs to be appropriately discounted by $1/(1 + r_{i,.}/4)$.

In this setup, since the lattice dates are regular (quarterly) and match the calibration instruments' dates (quarterly caplets), we can combine the arb-free and calibration constraints into a series of 1-period 2-dimensional searches for BDT parameter pairs $(r_{i,0}, \sigma_i)$. Moreover, it can be shown that the BDT local volatility $\sigma(t)$ parameter approaches short-term caplet Black logvol as the lattice time-steps get progressively smaller. Hence, a good initial choice for σ_i is the ATMF caplet Black logvol. That is why BDT calibration to caplets is relatively easy, and can (almost) be done *by inspection* of the caplet curve (see Appendix B).

European Swaption

In general, the constraints of arb-free and calibration cannot so easily be combined. For example, if we want the lattice calibrated to a 3m-into-1y semiannual ATMF receiver swaption, at each expiration node $(r_{1,0}, r_{1,1})$, we need to compute the value of the underlying 1y-swap from the corresponding implied discount factor curves $D_{1,0}(.)$, $D_{1,1}(.)$ at those nodes. Each of these discount factor curves depends on the future evolution of the short rates, and hence is a function of current $(r_{1,0}, \sigma_0)$ *and* future $(r_{i,0}, \sigma_i)$ pairs (4 of them for a 1-y swap).

Let's go through the steps of valuing this swaption. We first need to calculate the strike, the ATMF 1y-swap rate in 3 months:

$$K = \text{ATMF} = \frac{D(0, 3m) - D(0, 15m)}{0.5[D(0, 9m) + D(0, 15m)]}$$

$$= \frac{0.98765432 - 0.9374603}{0.5(0.9627051 + 0.9374603)} = 5.28312\%$$

For each node at expiration $(r_{1,0}, r_{1,1})$, we need to evaluate the value of 1y semi-annual 5.28312% receiver swap:

$$R_{1,.} = K/2[D_{1,.}(2) + D_{1,.}(4)] - [D_{1,.}(0) - D_{1,.}(4)]$$

giving us $R_{1,0} = 0.449048\%$ (44.9 cents), $R_{1,1} = -0.44905\%$ (44.91 cents against). Today's value of this receiver swaption is

$$R(0) = \max(0, R_{1,0}) \times AD_{1,0} + \max(0, R_{1,1}) \times AD_{1,1} = 0.22175\%$$

or 22.175 cents, corresponding to Black implied LogVol of 22.16% or Normal vol of 117 bp/annum.

Note that once we have built the lattice and its implied discount factor curves at each node, pricing swaptions (and other instruments) is easy (analysis step). However, building the lattice so that a given swaption has a given price via choice of BDT parameters $(r_{i,0}, \sigma_i)$ (synthesis step, calibration) is difficult.

Libor in Arrears

Continuing along with our example lattice, we will now consider our first exotic, a Libor-in-Arrears swap. This is quite similar to a plain-vanilla swap, except that the floating leg both resets and pays at the end of each calculation period (instead of resetting at the beginning and paying at the end). For example, for a 1-year USD arrears swap, the fixed leg is paid semi-annually (6m, 1y), but the quarterly floating leg is reset based on 3m-Libor in 3m, 6m, 9m, 1y, and paid at the same time (accrued for 3m). Ignoring day-count details, the floating leg has the following 4 cash flows whose today's value can be obtained from the lattice:

$$
\begin{aligned}
CF_1(0) &= r_{1,0}/4 \times AD_{1,0} + r_{1,1}/4 \times AD_{1,1} \\
&= (1/4)[4.84587\% \times 0.49382716 + 5.35444\% \times 0.49382716] \\
&= 1.25930\% \\
CF_2(0) &= r_{2,0}/4 \times AD_{2,0} + r_{2,1}/4 \times AD_{2,1} + r_{2,2}/4 \times AD_{2,2} \\
&= 1.26808\% \\
CF_3(0) &= r_{3,0}/4 \times AD_{3,0} + \cdots + r_{3,3}/4 \times AD_{3,3} \\
&= 1.27601\% \\
CF_4(0) &= r_{4,0}/4 \times AD_{4,0} + \cdots + r_{4,4}/4 \times AD_{4,4} \\
&= 1.28356\%
\end{aligned}
$$

which is the value of the Libor-in-Arrear leg.

While we can use our caplet-calibrated BDT lattice to price arrears swaps, in practice one often resorts to analytical formulae to price them. For example, given the close similarity of an arrears swap to a regular swap, it is often desired to use the same methodology as pricing plain-vanilla swaps (discounting the forward rate), but adjust the forward rate by a small amount to get to the correct value. This adjustment is called the *delay of payment convexity adjustment*. For a Libor-arrears swap, the usual formula used for calculation period $[T_1, T_2]$ is

$$
\text{Convexity Adjustment} = \frac{F^2 \sigma^2 T_1 (T_2 - T_1)}{1 + F \times (T_2 - T_1)}
$$

Table 8.3 compares the lattice's value of the Libor-in-arrears leg versus its value using the above. As we can see, the difference is quite small, and that

TABLE 8.3 Libor in Arrears Swap via BDT Lattice

CalcPeriod	Fwd (F)	LogVol	ConvxAdj (δ) (bp)	$(F + \delta)/4 \times DF$	BDT Price
$[3m, 6m]$	5.1%	12.5%	0.025	1.25932%	1.25930%
$[6m, 9m]$	5.2%	17.5%	0.102	1.26804%	1.26808%
$[6m, 9m]$	5.3%	20.0%	0.208	1.27608%	1.27601%
$[6m, 9m]$	5.4%	22.5%	0.364	1.28352%	1.28356%
Total				5.08693%	5.08695%

is why people use simple convexity adjustment formulae instead of invoking the lattice machinery for Libor-in-arrears swaps. We note however that the difference increases as the reset dates extend further into the future.

CMS-Based Payoffs

While CMS products are usually priced via analytical expressions, we can also price them in a lattice model. Let us consider a 3m-expiration USD ATMF CMS-1y caplet, based on the calculation period $[3m, 6m]$. We first need to calculate the ATMF strike, the 1y semiannual par-swap rate, 3m forward:

$$K = \text{ATMF} = \frac{D(0, 3m) - D(0, 15m)}{0.5[D(0, 9m) + D(0, 15m)]} = 5.28312\%$$

At expiration (3m), for each node, we need to calculate the CMS-1y (semiannual par-swap) rate using the discount factor curve at that node:

$$S_{1.} = \frac{D_{i.}(0) - D_{i.}(4)}{0.5(D_{i.}(2) + D_{i.}(4))}$$

giving us $S_{10} = 4.87199\%$, $S_{11} = 5.75141\%$. The caplet payoff $\max(0, S_{1.} - K)$ will get accrued for 3m and paid 3m later, so today's value of this caplet is 5.705 cents:

$$C(0) = \frac{(1/4)\max(0, S_{10} - K)}{1 + r_{10}/4} \times AD_{10} + \frac{(1/4)\max(0, S_{11} - K)}{1 + r_{11}/4} \times AD_{11}$$
$$= 0.057051\%$$

We can also use the lattice to price resets of CMS-n-year swap. In this case, the payoff for each calculation period $[T_1, T_2]$ is simply the CMS-n-year swap rate observed at T_1, accrued for $T_2 - T_1$, and paid at T_2. For example, today's value of CMS-1y swap for calculation period $[3m, 6m]$ can be computed as

$$\frac{(1/4)S_{10}}{1 + r_{10}/4} \times AD_{10} + \frac{(1/4)S_{11}}{1 + r_{11}/4} \times AD_{11} = 1.288341\%$$

As can be seen, once we have a lattice, we can price any variety of complex payoffs.

HULL-WHITE, BLACK-KARASINSKI MODELS

We have so far focused on the BDT model for expositional purposes, and to highlight the general steps required in building a one-factor short-rate model. BDT/BK models and their multifactor extensions were originally widely used and implemented due to their Log-Normal dynamics, the market's then focus and preference. In the past few years, the default dynamics for interest rates has shifted to Normal, and Hull-White/Vasicek models have regained popularity.

Following original papers by Hull-White, the HW model is usually implemented as a trinomial rather than a binomial lattice. Another difference is that while the BDT implementation fixed up/down probabilities at 1/2, and solved for the states, in most implementations of HW model, both the probabilities and states have to be computed to jointly satisfy the arb-free constraints.

A typical implementation of HW model is as follows.

1. Similar to BDT implementation, we discretize the HW process equation,

$$dr(t, \omega) = a(t)[b(t) - r(t, \omega)]dt + \sigma(t)dB(t, \omega)$$

for lattice dates, $0 = t_0 < t_1 < \cdots < t_{N+1}$, to arrive at discretized mean-reversion speeds, levels, and local volatilities: $a_i = a(t_i)$, $b_i = b(t_i)$, $\sigma_i = \sigma(t_i)$, $dt_i = t_{i+1} - t_i$, $0 \leq i < N$. The mean reversion levels b_i's are used to make the lattice arb-free, while the mean reversion speeds and local volatilities a_i, σ_i are used to calibrate the lattice.

2. Starting from $r_0 = r(t_0) = (D(0, t_0)/D(0, t_1) - 1)/(t_1 - t_0)$, let $r_{ij} = r(t_i, \omega_j)$ denote the j-th state at the i-th time t_i. At each time t_i, each node r_{ij} leads to three nodes as shown in Figure 8.4, with the middle node $r_{i+1,j}$ chosen to ensure that the lattice recombines by setting k to be the closest integer to $r_{ij}(1 - \alpha_i dt_i)/\sigma_i \sqrt{3dt_i}$, and setting

$$r_{i+1,j} = a_i b_i dt_i + k\sigma_i \sqrt{3dt_i}$$

The choice of spacing $dr_i = \sigma_i \sqrt{3dt_i}$ is motivated by lattice stability issues as $dt_i \to 0$, coming from insights of finite-difference disciplines. With this choice, the transition probabilities defined as:

$$p_m = \frac{2}{3} - \frac{(r_{ij}(1 - a_i dt_i) - k\sigma_i \sqrt{3dt_i})^2}{3\sigma_i^2 dt_i}$$

$$p_{u,d} = \frac{1 - p_m}{2} \pm \frac{r_{ij}(1 - a_i dt_i) - k\sigma_i \sqrt{3dt_i}}{2\sigma_i \sqrt{3dt_i}}$$

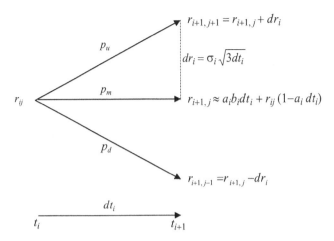

FIGURE 8.4 An Trinomial Lattice Implementation of the Hull-White Model

are all non-negative, and ensure that the process dynamics (local means and volatilities) are respected.

3. Compute AD-prices AD_{i+2}, and solve for b_i so that the arb-free condition is satisfied:

$$\sum_j AD_{i+2,j} = D(0, t_{i+2})$$

4. Calibrate to volatility instruments (cap/floors, swaptions) by tuning the local volatility (σ_i) and mean-reversion speed (a_i) parameters.

Black-Karasinski Model

The Black-Karasinski (BK) model is a generalization of the BDT model, where the mean-reversion speed is allowed to be an arbitrary function—in BDT, it is required to equal $-\sigma'(t)/\sigma(t)$. There is also a close resemblance between the process equation for BK and Hull-White, where $\ln r$ instead of r is diffused. This close resemblance allows one to implement the BK model just like the preceding HW model as a trinomial lattice, with r_{ij}'s replaced by $\ln r_{ij}$'s, and this is usually the approach taken in practice.

SIMULATION IMPLEMENTATION

In a lattice implementation, at each node we have full information as to the short rate and the implied discount factor curve at that state. A contingent claim whose payoff depends only on this information can be valued at that node, and this payoff can be valued today using the node's AD price.

Another class of contingent claims are *path-dependent* options (also called Asian options), whose payoff at each node is not only a function of that node's state, but also the behavior of interest rates for prior nodes that lead to it. For example, the payoff might be the moving average of a particular index, say 3m-Libor, or the running maximum of the index. *Life-time knock-in/knock-out* options are another variety of path-dependent options, where the payoff at expiration is contingent upon an index (or indices) staying within a prescribed range at all times from today to option expiration.

While some analytical formulae or approximations exist for Asian options on simple (one-dimensional) assets such equities, FX,..., for path-dependent interest rate options, one resorts to *simulation* for pricing. This means that we approximate the price

$$C(0) \approx \frac{1}{N} \sum_{i=1}^{N} \frac{1}{1 + r(t_0, \omega_i)dt_0} \times \cdots \frac{1}{1 + r(t_k, \omega_i)dt_k} \times \cdots \times C(t_e, \omega_i)$$

for N randomly selected paths $(\omega_1, \ldots, \omega_N)$. This is called an N-path simulation, and the idea is that as we increase N, the approximation tends to the correct value.

Direct Simulation

There are two main approaches to simulation implementation. The first is to start from the process equation, discretize it for some chosen simulation dates, and simulate this discretized process. A common procedure is to apply Euler's discretization for the Brownian motion component of the process equation:

$$dr(t, \omega) = \mu(t, \omega)dt + \sigma(t, \omega)dB(t, \omega)$$

is implemented as

$$r(t + \Delta t, \omega) - r(t, \omega) = \mu(t, \omega) \times \Delta t + \sigma(t, \omega)X(t, \omega)\sqrt{\Delta t}$$

where $X(t, \omega) \sim N(0, 1)$, although more elaborate discretizations exist. Regardless, the main concern with this procedure is that there are parameters of the discretized process that are not known a priori, and need to be solved for so that the discretized process is arbitrage-free. We saw this in the lattice implementation of the BDT/BK models, where as we try to respect the process equation, we use some of the parameters to ensure that the lattice is arb-free. For simulation implementation, this step is problematic, as it assumes that we know all the parameters and are just generating random paths from the process. The usual remedy is to first simulate the paths, and then shift these simulated paths so that the arb-free conditions are satisfied for these *realized* paths.

Lattice-Sampling

The second method is *sampling a lattice/tree*. For a given model, we first construct an arb-free lattice/tree, and then randomly sample it. Specifically, at each node, only one of its outgoing branches is selected according to the risk-neutral probability of that branch. For example, in a BDT lattice, we flip a fair coin to decide whether we make an up-move or a down-move. For each such randomly selected path, we keep track of the path-dependent option's payoff(s), and whenever there is a payment, we discount it back to today along the short rates on that path. Averaging these path-discounted payoffs gives us the simulation price:

$$C(0) \approx \frac{1}{N} \sum_{i=1}^{N} \frac{1}{1 + r(t_0, \omega_i)dt_0} \times \cdots \frac{1}{1 + r(t_k, \omega_i)dt_k} \times \cdots \times C(t_e, \omega_i)$$

Even in this method, the collection of chosen random paths does not necessarily satisfy the no-arbitrage condition, and one might still have to apply a shift to the simulated paths to ensure no-arbitrage.

Variance Reduction

Simulation pricing suffers from *simulation noise*: It only gives an approximate price, and each simulation run can give a different price. There are a few techniques to reduce simulation noise: antithetic, control variate, importance sampling, low-discrepancy (Sobol, Halton, ...) sequences, and so on. The easiest to implement is antithetic: For an N-path simulation, randomly select the first $N/2$ paths, and generate the remaining paths as the mirror-image of them; whenever you randomly select an up-move for the original path, select a down-move for the mirror-image path. For trinomial branching, the middle branch remains the same for both original and mirror-image paths. (See Figures 8.5 and 8.6.)

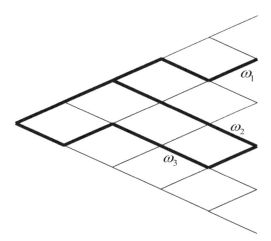

FIGURE 8.5   Three Random Paths in a
Binomial Lattice Sampled for Simulation

Lifetime Knock-Out Option

Consider a single-exercise 1-year 5%-caplet on Libor-3m, with payoff
$\max(0, L_{3m}(1y) - 5\%)$, reset and paid in 1-year, but only if Libor-3m has
not exceeded the knock-out level of 6% from now until the reset date.
The calculation of this caplet based on a 10-path simulation is shown in

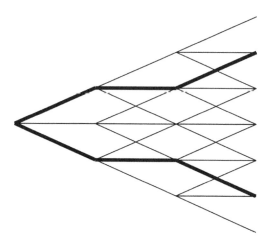

FIGURE 8.6   A Random Path and its Antithetic
Mirror-Image Path

TABLE 8.4 Value of Caplet, max(0, $L_{3m}(1y) - 5\%$), Reset and Paid in 1-Year, With and Without Knock-Out Level of 6%

Path No.	$L_{3m}(0)$	$L_{3m}(3m)$	$L_{3m}(6m)$	$L_{3m}(9m)$	$L_{3m}(1y)$	AD_i	Caplet	Caplet With Knock-Out
1	5.00%	4.27%	2.93%	2.91%	2.65%	0.09631	0.00%	0.00%
2	5.00%	5.38%	5.28%	4.21%	4.34%	0.09518	0.00%	0.00%
3	5.00%	4.95%	5.02%	4.98%	5.64%	0.09516	0.64%	0.64%
4	5.00%	5.84%	5.84%	6.81%	6.79%	0.09434	1.79%	0.00%
5	5.00%	3.81%	4.09%	3.35%	3.78%	0.09604	0.00%	0.00%
6	5.00%	5.35%	6.05%	5.54%	5.58%	0.09470	0.58%	0.00%
7	5.00%	5.77%	5.39%	5.93%	5.28%	0.09466	0.28%	0.28%
8	5.00%	5.39%	5.14%	5.13%	5.13%	0.09500	0.13%	0.13%
9	5.00%	4.59%	5.37%	5.92%	5.85%	0.09494	0.85%	0.85%
10	5.00%	5.92%	5.39%	6.09%	5.83%	0.09459	0.83%	0.00%
							0.48%	0.18%

Table 8.4. Without the knock-out, the value of the caplet is 48 cents:

$$0.48\% = \sum_{i=1}^{10} \max(0, L_{3m}(1y, \omega_i) - 5\%) \times AD_i$$

where

$$AD_i = \frac{1}{10} \frac{1}{(1 + L_{3m}(0)/4) \times \cdots \times (1 + L_{3m}(9m)/4)}$$

However, with the knock-out, the payoff is reduced to 0 for paths 4, 6, 10, reducing the value of the cap to 18 cents.

CHAPTER 9

Bermudan-Style Options

A prominent class of derivatives is the class of *American-style exercise* options, in which the owner of the option has flexibility in choosing the time to exercise. A *true* American-style option allows the owner to exercise the option over *any* time during the exercise window. In interest-rate derivatives, true American-style options are rare, and the flexible-exercise feature is limited to a finite number of dates, typically reset/coupon dates (quarterly, semiannual) of the underlying instrument (bond, swap,...), for example, a 30-year callable bond, callable at par after 10 years, and semiannually thereafter. This class of interest-rate options is known as *Bermudan-style* options.

The general pricing framework for Bermudan-style options is still risk-neutral valuation with t-prices provided as

$$(0 \leq t \leq T) \qquad C(t, \omega) = E_t[e^{-\int_t^T r(u,\omega)du} C(T, \omega)]$$

but augmented to include the owner's option to choose the exercise time. The fixed exercise date $T = t_e$ is replaced by a random exercise time chosen by the owner, $T(\omega)$. The exercise-time decision can be any rule/strategy chosen by the owner, and can depend on the current and history of the asset evolution, but not on the future, that is, it should be *non-anticipative*. In probability theory, the technical term for a nonanticipative strategy is a *stopping time*.

Given such a nonanticipative exercise strategy $T(\cdot)$, we evaluate the option value as follows: For any future random path ω, determine the exercise time $T(\omega)$, evaluate the option payoff at that exercise time and for that path $C(T(\omega), \omega)$, stochastically discount this back to valuation date (t), and average over all paths. This gives the t-value of the option under the given exercise strategy:

$$E_t[e^{-\int_t^{T(\omega)} r(u,\omega)du} C(T(\omega), \omega)]$$

The Bermudan option value is the value of the option under the *optimal* exercise strategy, found by searching over all such nonanticipative strategies:

$$\text{Bermudan } C(t) = \max_T E_t[e^{-\int_t^{T(\omega)} r(u,\omega)du} C(T(\omega), \omega)]$$

BELLMAN'S EQUATION—BACKWARD INDUCTION

Performing the search for the optimal strategy is a daunting task. We first have to enumerate all permissible (nonanticipative) exercise strategies (way too many of them, and quite hard to enumerate), evaluate the option payoff under each such strategy, and calculate the maximum. This is a tall order!

Fortunately, this class of problems has been studied in optimal control theory and dynamic programming disciplines. The most important result from this field is Bellman's equation and its solution, characterizing the optimal strategy and the *optimal value* achieved by it.

In a discrete-time setting, the solution to Bellman's equation (optimal value) can be found via a recursive updating algorithm called *backward induction*. The algorithm goes as follows:

1. For Bermudan exercise dates $t_0 < t_1 < \cdots < t_N$, compute *immediate exercise* values $C(t_i, \omega)$ for each time t_i and state ω. At the last exercise date t_N, compute option value $B(t_N, \omega) = C(t_N, \omega)$.
2. For each prior exercise date, recursively compute $B(t_i, \omega)$:

$$B(t_i, \omega) = \max(C(t_i, \omega), H(t_i, t_{i+1}, \omega))$$

where $H(t_i, t_{i+1}, \omega)$ is the *holding value*, the expected discounted value of the option if held until next exercise date t_{i+1}:

$$H(t_i, t_{i+1}, \omega) = E_{t_i}[e^{-\int_{t_i}^{t_{i+1}} r(u,\omega)du} B(t_{i+1}, \omega)]$$

3. Continue updating $B(t_i, \omega)$ from $B(t_{i+1}, \omega)$ until you get the optimal value at the earliest exercise date, $B(t_0, \omega)$. The t-value of the Bermudan option is then

$$E_t[e^{-\int_t^{t_0} r(u,\omega)du} B(t_0, \omega)] = \max_T E_t[e^{-\int_t^{T(\omega)} r(u,\omega)du} C(T(\omega), \omega)]$$

Notice that backward-induction does not explicitly provide the optimal strategy, just the value of Bermudan option at each node under this (implicit) optimal strategy. Calculation of the hold value, $H(t_i, t_{i+1}, \omega)$—a conditional expectation—is quite easy to implement in lattice/tree models.

That is why most implementations of an interest-rate model are lattice/tree implementations, enabling one to readily tackle Bermudan-exercise options.

Backward Induction in Lattice/Trees

For lattices with tree/lattice-dates $0 = t_0 < t_1 < \cdots < t_{N+1}$, as long as we ensure that the lattice dates include the exercise dates, we can simplify the backward-induction algorithm to obviate the need to calculate $e^{-\int_{t_i}^{t_{i+1}} r(u,\omega)du}$ when computing the hold value. This is accomplished by setting the *immediate-exercise* values $C(t_i, \omega)$ to $-\infty$ for lattice-dates where exercise is not allowed. In this way, we start backward induction at the last lattice date, and apply it to *all* lattice dates (including ones that are not exercise dates) all the way back to today $t_0 = 0$, using the recursive updating formula:

$$H(t_i, t_{i+1}, \omega_j) = \frac{1}{1 + r(t_i, \omega_j)dt_i} \sum_{k=1}^{n} P[(t_i, \omega_j) \to (t_{i+1}, \omega_{j_k})] B(t_{i+1}, \omega_{j_k})$$

The value $B(0, 0)$ is today's value of the Bermudan option.

BERMUDAN SWAPTIONS

A Bermudan swaption is the option to enter into a fixed-maturity (from today) plain-vanilla swap at various points in the future. For example a "1-into-2 5% Berm receiver with semiannual exercise" provides the option holder to enter into a 5% receiver swap maturing 3y from today at any one (and only one) of the following exercise dates:

- 1y from today (entering into a 2y semiannual swap)
- 1y6m from today (entering into 1y6m semiannual swap)
- 2y from today (entering into a 1y semiannual swap)
- 2y6m from today (entering into a 6m semiannual swap)

The exercise frequency (semiannual in this case) usually matches the coupon frequency of the fixed leg. Similarly, a 1-into-2 Bermudan payer swaption ("Berm Payer") provides the option holder to enter into a *payer* swap at any of the preceding exercise dates.

Example 1. 1y-into-2y Bermudan Receiver. To show backward induction in practice, assume that starting with the discount factors shown in Table 9.1, we have built an arb-free calibrated 3y semiannual lattice for 6m-rates shown in Figure 9.1, and we want to price a 1-into-2 Bermudan $K = 5.68038\%$ (semiannual) receiver with semiannual exercise.

TABLE 9.1 Input Curve for Bermudan Pricing via Backward Induction

T	Fwd 6m-Rate	D(0, T)
0	5%	1.0000000
6m	5.1%	0.9756098
1y	5.2%	0.9513503
1y6m	5.3%	0.9272420
2y	5.4%	0.9033045
2y6m	5.5%	0.8795564
3y		0.8560160

To simplify the picture, at each node we are only presenting the 6m-short rate, and the value of *underlying*, that is, receiving $K = 5.68038\%$ for the remaining swap (computed from the node's discount factor curve). As usual, we are ignoring date minutiae and day-count issues.

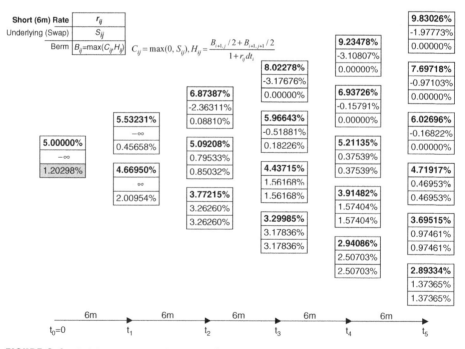

FIGURE 9.1 Pricing a 1y-into-2y Bermudan Receiver Swaption via Backward Induction

Starting at the last exercise date $t_5 = 2y6m$, we compute the value of receiving $K = 5.68038\%$ semiannually for the next 6 months. Therefore, the value of the underlying swap at each node is

$$S(t_5, \omega_j) = K/2 D(t_5, t_5 + 6m, \omega_j) - [D(t_5, t_5, \omega_j) - D(t_5, t_5 + 6m, \omega_j)]$$

and we set the Bermudan option value $B(t_5, \omega_j)$ equal to immediate exercise value $C(t_5, \omega_j) = \max(0, S(t_5, \omega_j))$.

Stepping back to $t_4 = 2y$, we compute the value of receiving $K = 5.68038\%$ semiannually for the next 1y:

$$S(t_4, \omega_j) = K/2[D(t_4, t_4 + 6m, \omega_j) + D(t_4, t_4 + 1y, \omega_j)$$
$$- [D(t_4, t_4, \omega_j) - D(t_4, t_4 + 1y, \omega_j)]$$

and the immediate exercise value $C(t_4, \omega_j) = \max(0, S(t_4, \omega_j))$. The Bermudan option value is the higher of the immediate exercise value and the hold value

$$B(t_4, \omega_j) = \max(C(t_4, \omega_j), H(t_4, \omega))$$

where the hold value is computed as

$$H(t_4, \omega_j) = \frac{B(t_5, \omega_j)/2 + B(t_5, \omega_{j+1})/2}{1 + r(t_4, \omega)dt_4}$$

Continuing similar steps back to today gives us today's value of $B(0, 0) = 1.20298\%$, or 1.20298 *points*.

It is instructive to compare the value of the above Bermudan receiver to the corresponding (1y-into-2y, 1.5y-into-1.5y, 2y-into-1y, 2.5y-into-6m) European receiver swaptions. Since a European swaption can be considered to be a Bermudan with a single-exercise date, we can use the same backward-induction algorithm to price European swaptions, setting the immediate exercise values to $-\infty$ for all lattice dates other than the European single-exercise date. Alternatively, we could price it using Arrow-Debreu prices for each node at expiration date. Regardless, both methods give the same value.

Table 9.2 shows the value of the 1-into-2 receiver computed using AD prices, while Table 9.3 compares the Bermudan receiver to the European receivers. As expected, the value of the Bermudan option is higher than any of the corresponding European swaptions.

TABLE 9.2 Valuing European Swaption Using AD-Prices

State j	6m-Rate r_{ij}	Rcvr Swap S_{ij}	Option Value $C_{ij} = \max(0, S_{ij})$	AD Price AD_{ij}	$C_{ij} \times AD_{ij}$
2	6.87378%	−2.6331%	0.00000%	0.237337	0.00000%
1	5.09208%	0.79533%	0.79533%	0.475675	0.37832%
0	3.77215%	3.26260%	3.26260%	0.238338	0.77760%
1-into-2					1.1559%

TABLE 9.3 Comparison of Bermudan vs European Swaptions

1y-into-2y	1.1559%
1y6m-into-1y6m	0.9166%
2y-into-1y	0.6307%
2y6m-into-6m	0.3057%
Berm	1.20298%

BERMUDAN CANCELABLE SWAPS, CALLABLE/PUTTABLE BONDS

A Bermudan *cancelable swap* is a plain-vanilla swap that can be canceled after some time, and periodically thereafter. For example, a "3-non-call-1y with semiannual exercise" (3nc1, Semi) is a 3-year plain-vanilla swap, where one party has the Bermudan right to cancel the swap at one (and only one) of the following times: 1y, 1y6m, 2y, 2y6m. The Bermudan *cancelation* right is economically equivalent to a Bermudan option to *enter* into an *offsetting* swap, and is modeled and priced as such. Specifically, the following two types of cancelable swaps arise depending on the original position of the owner of the (cancelation) option:

1. Callable: Pay fixed in swap, Own option to cancel = Payer Swap + Own Bermudan Receiver swaption
2. Puttable: Receive fixed in swap, Own option to cancel = Receiver Swap + Own Bermudan Payer swaption

The terminology callable/puttable comes from bonds, where the issuer of a *callable bond* is paying fixed coupons, but can *call* the bond (usually at par) on coupon payment dates after an initial lock-out (noncall) period.

Similarly, a *puttable bond* is one where the owner/investor/lender is receiving fixed coupons, but can *put* the bond (usually at par) back to the issuer after an initial lock-out (non-put) period.

For callables, since the owner of the cancelation option is paying fixed, he needs to compensate the receiver for the option, that is, he has to pay higher than in an otherwise noncallable plain-vanilla swap. The fixed rate K that will make the value of the callable swap (Payer K swap + Bermudan receiver with strike K) zero is called the *callable rate*. The callable rate is therefore higher than the par-swap rate. Similarly, for puttables, since the option-owner has to compensate the payer by receiving below an otherwise nonputtable swap. The *puttable rate* is the fixed rate that will make the value of puttable swap (Receiver K swap + Bermudan payer with strike K) zero, and is lower than the par-swap rate.

Example 2. Using the setup in Example 1, we have calculated the 1y-into-2y $K = 5.68038\%$ Bermudan receiver with semiannual exercise as 1.20298 points. Using today's discount factor curve, let us compute the value of paying the same fixed rate, $K = 5.68308\%$, in a 3y (semiannual) swap:

$$
\begin{aligned}
\text{Pay } K \text{ for } 3y &= -\frac{K}{2}[D(0, 6m) + D(0, 1y) + \cdots + D(0, 3y)] \\
&\quad + [D(0, 0y) - D(0, 3y)] \\
&= -\frac{5.68038\%}{2}[0.9756098 + \cdots + 0.8560160] \\
&\quad + (1 - 0.8560160) \\
&= -1.20998\%
\end{aligned}
$$

which exactly offsets the value of the cancelation option (1-into-2 Berm receiver). Therefore the callable rate is 5.68038%. The callable rate is usually quoted as a spread to the par-swap rate (3y in this case):

$$
S_{3y} = \frac{D(0, 0y) - D(0, 3y)}{0.5(D(0, 6m) + \cdots + D(0, 3y))} = 5.24238\%
$$

so the 3y-nc-1y callable rate is quoted as 43.8 bp ($= 5.68038\% - 5.24238\%$). The broker market for a "3-nc-1" (with semiannual exercise) might then be 43.3-44.3 bp's, implying 43.3 bp *bid*: I *pay* $S_{3y} + 43.3$ bp's and *I* can cancel; and 44.3 bp *offer*: I *receive* $S_{3y} + 44.3$ bp's and *you* can cancel.

One-Time (European) Cancelable Swaps

A *one-time* cancelable swap is simply a package of a swap and a European cancelation swaption (option to enter into offsetting swap). This is simply a Bermudan cancelable swap where the exercise window is reduced to a single date.

European cancelable swaps can be thought of in two ways: a swap plus a cancelation option or a swap with an *extension* option. For example a 3y-nc-1y one-time callable is equivalent to either of the following:

- Pay for 3y, Own a 1y-into-2y European receiver swaption (cancelation option)
- Pay for 1y, Own a 1y-into-2y European payer swaption (extension option)

In either case, the cancelable is a swap+swaption package, and priced as such.

Cancelable Swap—Variations

Armed with a methodology (backward induction for lattices) to price Bermudan cancelation rights, one can price a variety of swaps with different features. For example, a common structure is a cancelable swap where the fixed rate *steps up* according to some schedule (5% for first year, 5.5% for second year, and so on). These structures are generically called step-up callables, and can include step-up or step-down features.

Callable bonds sometimes have an exercise fee schedule. For example a 10y callable bond might be callable after 5y at 105%, after 6y at 104%, and so on. The exercise fee is the amount above par (5 points, 4 points,...), and can have a schedule. It is easy to price cancelable swaps with similar exercise fees, by just replacing the immediate exercise value $C(t_i, \omega) = \max(0, S(t_i, \omega))$ with

$$C(t_i, \omega) = \max(0, S(t_i, \omega) - \text{Fee}(t_i))$$

Another common feature is *notice days*, where the cancelation decision has to be announced a specified number of notice days prior to the coupon payment date. This feature can also easily be priced by ensuring the lattice dates include the notice dates, and pricing a *forward* (offsetting) swap on those notice dates.

BERMUDAN-STYLE OPTIONS IN SIMULATION IMPLEMENTATION

There are situations where a lattice implementation does not exist or is not suited, and we have to resort to an alternate (typically simulation) implementation. For example, the posited dynamics for interest rates might not lend themselves to a lattice (recombining) implementation. This is usually the case when one wants to implement a full term-structure model in the HJM framework. The typical HJM model is non-Markov: an up-move followed by a down-move does not get you to the same place as a down-move followed by an up-move, and hence a tree implementation leads to a nonrecombining tree. A nonrecombining tree implementation will grow exponentially in computation needs as we decrease the time-step size, defeating our desire to achieve good accuracy.

Another instance where a lattice is not suited is for Bermudan-style path-dependent options. For these options, we need to not only know where we are at each state, but how we got there, and a simulation implementation is more natural for their pricing. Of course, we could keep track of each node *and* its history, but then again we are dealing with an exponentially growing number of paths, with its forbidding computational requirement.

For simulation implementation of an interest-rate model, pricing Bermudan-style options is a challenge. This is due to the difficulty of computing the hold value, a *conditional expectation*, at each node. For a simulation implementation, each node has only one path entering *and* exiting it, therefore we cannot compute the *expected* holding value. This is a general problem for any simulation model where computing conditional expectations is quite difficult.

We seem to be at a quandary: In lattice implementations, at each node, we know the full potential future and hence can compute hold value, but do not know how we got to the node (no path information), that is, we know the future, but not the past. For simulation implementations, we know the full path leading to each node, but do not know the node's full potential evolution into the future: We know the past, but not the future! Path-dependent Bermudan-style options bring this quandary to the fore.

To tackle Bermudan-style options in simulation implementation, one can stay with backward induction framework, and try to approximate the hold value. A variety of methods (bundling, stochastic tree/mesh, ...) have been proposed, the most widely implemented being Longstaff/Schwartz's *least-squares in Monte Carlo* (LSM) method.[1] In the LSM method, the hold value is approximated via regression analysis at each node.

Another approach is to abandon backward induction altogether, and directly search for the optimal strategy. For example, we may plausibly assume that the optimal strategy takes the form of a *threshold strategy*: Exercise at time t_i if the option is sufficiently in the money, that is, $C(t_i) > L_i$ for a given sequence of boundary values $\{L_i\}$s. By following this class of strategies, we can compute the option value, and optimize the value by finding the optimal boundary $\{L_i^*\}$s. A commonly used algorithm is to reduce this multidimensional search to a series of recursive one-dimensional searches: Given exercise dates $t_1 < \cdots < t_N$, for a set of simulated paths, start with $L_i^* = \infty$ to ensure that the option is alive until the terminal exercise date. For t_N, find the exercise threshold L_N^*, and fix this threshold as the optimal exercise level if the option is still alive at t_N. Move to the previous exercise date and again find the optimal exercise threshold, subject to the previously found optimal thresholds for future exercise dates. Continue along to the first exercise date, and compute the Bermudan value under these recursively found thresholds.

CHAPTER 10

Full Term-Structure Interest-Rate Models

Short-rate models were the first systematic attempt to break away from Black's formula for pricing interest-rate derivatives. The basic setup was to posit some dynamic for the short rate, $r(t, \omega)$ as

$$(t > 0) \qquad dr(t, \omega) = \mu(t, \omega)dt + \sigma(t, \omega)dB(t, \omega)$$

and then price derivatives $C(t, \omega)$ with a terminal payoff at T using risk-neutral expectation:

$$(0 < t < T) \qquad C(t, \omega) = E_t[e^{-\int_t^T r(u,\omega)du}C(T, \omega)]$$

which results from the martingale condition

$$(0 < t < T) \qquad \frac{C(t, \omega)}{M(t, \omega)} = E_t\left[\frac{C(T, \omega)}{M(T, \omega)}\right]$$

using rolled-over money-market account

$$M(t, \omega) = e^{\int_0^t r(u,\omega)du}$$

as numeraire.

While serving as a consistent arbitrage-free, risk-neutral framework, short-rate models were lacking in providing a clear picture as to the dynamics of the implied discount factors, forward rates, and swap rates. For example, considering the instantaneous forward rate $f(t, T, \omega)$, that is, the forward rate at time t for a forward deposit over $[T, T + dT]$, what can be said about its dynamics? Recalling that

$$(t < T) \qquad f(t, T, \omega) = -\frac{\partial}{\partial T} \ln D(t, T, \omega)$$

the above question boils down to computing the dynamics of

$$-\frac{\partial}{\partial T}\ln E_t[e^{-\int_t^T r(u,\omega)du}]$$

which is quite an arduous task and analytically intractable except for very few specialized dynamics for $r(t, \omega)$. Given that $f(t, T, \omega)$ is a (short-term) proxy for traded instruments such as FRAs and ED futures, the ability to answer this question was of paramount interest to traders and practitioners.

SHIFTING FOCUS FROM SHORT RATE TO FULL CURVE: HO-LEE MODEL

The first known model to tackle the above problem was introduced by Ho and Lee (HL).[1] In their model, rather than starting with the short rate, they started directly by the discount factor *curve*. For this, they discretized today's discount factor curve, and posited a discrete-time dynamic for the discretized curve. Specifically, they considered a series of dates $0 < T_1 < T_2 < \ldots$, and provided the following model:

$$(T_i < T_j) \qquad D(T_{i+1}, T_j, \omega) - D(T_i, T_j, \omega) = \mu(T_i, T_j)dt$$
$$+ \sigma(T_i, T_j, \omega)\Delta(B(T_i, \omega))$$

in a binomial tree setting, and solved for the drift *curve* $\mu(T_i,.)$ for each time T_i to ensure that the tree recombines.

Continuous-time limits of the HL model were soon derived,[2] and challenged by some to be unrealistic. No matter, the important insight of the HL model was that *we can directly start with the full discount factor curve, and evolve the full curve* while ensuring no-arbitrage in a risk-neutral setting. This is in contrast to short-rate models, where the discount factor curve is implicitly derived from the risk-neutral dynamics of the short rate. This shift in focus from short-rate modeling to full curve modeling gave rise to a new paradigm of *full term structure* models.

HEATH-JARROW-MORTON (HJM) FULL TERM-STRUCTURE FRAMEWORK

Following HL's innovation, Heath, Jarrow, and Morton (HJM)[3] considered the dynamics of the full interest-rate curve in a risk-neutral world under general dynamics. Instead of working with the discount factor curve, they chose the equivalent forward rate curve. Note that these two curves are interchangeable, and knowledge of one completely determines the other. In discretized format, we have:

$$f_c(t, [T_1, T_2], \omega) = \frac{1}{T_2 - T_1} \ln(D(t, T_1, \omega)/D(t, T_2, \omega))$$

for continuously-compounded rates. On the other hand, given a series of contiguous forward rates $\{f_c(t, [T_i, T_{i+1}], \omega)\}_i$ with $t = T_0 < T_1 < \dots$, we can compute discount factors:

$$D(t, T_n, \omega) = e^{-\sum_{i=0}^{n-1} f_c(t, [T_i, T_{i+1}], \omega)(T_{i+1} - T_i)}$$

Therefore, *the discount factor curve fully determines the forward-rate curve, and vice-versa*. In either case, by letting the deposit periods $[T_i, T_{i+1}]$ shrink to zero, we get *instantaneous* forward rates, satisfying:

$$D(t, T, \omega) = e^{-\int_t^T f(t, u, \omega) du}$$

$$f(t, T, \omega) = -\frac{\partial}{\partial T} \ln D(t, T, \omega)$$

In this framework, the short rate $r(t, \omega)$ can readily be recovered as $r(t, \omega) = f(t, t, \omega)$, hence as we model the forward rate curve, we are already modeling the short rate. On the other hand, we saw that as we were modeling the short rate, we could compute an *implied* discount factor curve, or its equivalent *implied* forward rate curve. Therefore a short-rate model is an implicit term-structure model, and a term-structure model is an implicit short-rate model. The difference between these modeling paradigms is their state-space: short rate, or the full discount-factor/forward-rate curve.

In the HJM framework, similar to the HL model, we model the evolution of the *full term structure of interest rates*, that is, we evolve a *curve*. The HJM framework takes the forward *curve* $f(t, ., \omega)$ at each time t, and considers its evolution as time t evolves, where ω is the generic random future evolution of the curve. Note that this is a doubly indexed system consisting of the valuation/calendar time t, and the forward time T. At each point of time t, and for each potential future state ω, the forward curve $f(t, ., \omega)$ represents the series of (contiguous) forward rates, one for each forward date $T > t$.

For instantaneous forward rates $f(t, T, \omega)$, the general HJM framework posits the following process:

$$df(t, T, \omega) = \mu(t, T, \omega)dt + \sigma(t, T, \omega)dB(t, \omega)$$

for a 1-factor dynamic where $dB(t, \omega)$ are interpreted as increments of independent Brownian motions. At each time t, we have a system of process equations (one for each forward date T), and these series of systems have to be solved by $\mu(t, T, \omega)$ to ensure risk neutrality.

DISCRETE-TIME, DISCRETE-TENOR HJM FRAMEWORK

As in short-rate models, any computer implementation of the HJM-based model will be based on discretized versions of the continuous time-evolution of the instantaneous forward rates. While each discretization (one for t, one for T) can be arbitrary, for the sake of notational brevity, we will present the discretized version of HJM by letting $\{0 = \tau_0 < \tau_1 < \cdots < \tau_n\}$ be a *common* discretization of the t and T axes. Let f_{ij} denote the discretized continuously compounded forwards:

$$(0 \le i \le j) \qquad f_{ij}(\omega) = f_c(\tau_i, [\tau_j, \tau_{j+1}], \omega)$$

that is, the continuously compounded forward rate at calendar time τ_i for a deposit over the forward period $[\tau_j, \tau_{j+1}]$. The continuously compounded short rate $r_i(\omega) = r(\tau_i, \omega)$ can easily be recovered from the forward rate: $r_i(\omega) = f_{ii}(\omega)$.

Focusing on a one-factor model, the discretized version of the process equation for forwards becomes

$$(0 \le i < j) \qquad f_{i+1,j}(\omega) = f_{ij}(\omega) + \mu_{ij}(\omega)d\tau_i + \sigma_{ij}(\omega)X_i(\omega)\sqrt{d\tau_i}$$

where $d\tau_i = \tau_{i+1} - \tau_i$, and X_i's form a *white noise* (independent, mean 0, variance 1) sequence, that is, a discretization of the term $dB(t, \omega)$ (continuous-time white noise).

We have left σ_{ij} as a general and potentially random sequence. For Log-Normal dynamics, we can let $\sigma_{ij}(\omega) = s_{ij} \times f_{ij}(\omega)$ for some deterministic sequence $\{s_{ij}\}$, with the interpretation that s_{ij} is the Log-Normal volatility over the interval $[\tau_i, \tau_{i+1}]$ of the forward rate f_{ij}. Similarly, for Normal dynamics, we can let $\sigma_{ij}(\omega) = s_{ij}$ for some deterministic sequence of Normal (BPVol) volatilities. The doubly indexed surface $\sigma(t, T, .)$ or its discretized version s_{ij} is called the *forward-forward volatility surface*.

The discretized zero-coupon bond prices (discount factors) are denoted by D_{ik}, where D_{ik} denotes the τ_i-price of the τ_k-maturity zero-coupon bond. We have

$$(0 \le i \le k) \qquad D_{ik}(\omega) = e^{-\sum_{j=i}^{k-1} f_{ij}(\omega)d\tau_j}$$

Similarly, the discretized money-market numeraire becomes:

$$(0 \le i \le k) \qquad M_i(\omega) = e^{\sum_{j=0}^{i-1} r_j(\omega)d\tau_j} = e^{\sum_{j=0}^{i-1} f_{jj}(\omega)d\tau_j}$$

where $M_i(\omega) = M(\tau_i, \omega)$ denotes the τ_i-value of value of unit investment in a money-market account initiated today, $\tau_0 = 0$, and periodically rolled over at the prevalent short-term rates.

The risk-neutrality constraint is that bond prices for all maturities relative to the numeraire are martingales, that is, their expected value in the future is their current value. This constraint can be expressed as 1-period conditional expectation as follows:

$$(0 \le i < k) \qquad E_{\tau_i}\left[\frac{D_{i+1,k}(\omega)}{M_{i+1}(\omega)}\right] = \frac{D_{ik}(\omega)}{M_i(\omega)}$$

Expressing discount factors in terms of forward rates, and noting that

$$(0 \le i) \qquad M_{i+1}(\omega) = M_i(\omega)e^{f_{ii}(\omega)d\tau_i}$$

the above becomes

$$E_{\tau_i}\left[\frac{e^{-\sum_{j=i+1}^{k-1} f_{i+1,j}(\omega)d\tau_j}}{M_i(\omega)e^{f_{ii}(\omega)d\tau_i}}\right] = \frac{e^{-\sum_{j=i}^{k-1} f_{ij}(\omega)d\tau_j}}{M_i(\omega)}$$

Canceling the M_i terms from both sides, and invoking the process equation for the forward rates ($f_{i+1,j} = f_{ij} + \cdots$), we get

$$E_{\tau_i}\left[e^{-\sum_{j=i+1}^{k-1}\left[f_{ij}(\omega) + \mu_{ij}(\omega)d\tau_i + \sigma_{ij}(\omega)X_i(\omega)\sqrt{d\tau_i}\right]d\tau_j}\right] = e^{f_{ii}(\omega)d\tau_i} \times e^{-\sum_{j=i}^{k-1} f_{ij}(\omega)d\tau_j}$$

$$= e^{-\sum_{j=i+1}^{k-1} f_{ij}(\omega)d\tau_j}$$

which after cancelation of $e^{-\sum f_{ij}}$ terms from both sides, gives us

$$E_{\tau_i}\left[e^{-\sum\limits_{j=i+1}^{k-1}\left[\mu_{ij}(\omega)d\tau_i + \sigma_{ij}(\omega)X_i(\omega)\sqrt{d\tau_i}\right]d\tau_j}\right] = 1$$

$$\Rightarrow e^{d\tau_i \sum\limits_{j=i+1}^{k-1}\mu_{ij}(\omega)d\tau_j} = E_{\tau_i}\left[e^{-X_i(\omega)\sqrt{d\tau_i}\sum\limits_{j=i+1}^{k-1}\sigma_{ij}(\omega)d\tau_j}\right]$$

or equivalently,

$$d\tau_i \sum\limits_{j=i+1}^{k-1}\mu_{ij}(\omega)d\tau_j = \ln E_{\tau_i}\left[e^{-X_i(\omega)\sqrt{d\tau_i}\sum\limits_{j=i+1}^{k-1}\sigma_{ij}(\omega)d\tau_j}\right]$$

The drifts can now be solved for:

$$(0 \le i < k) \qquad \mu_{ik}(\omega) = \frac{1}{d\tau_i d\tau_k}\ln\frac{E_{\tau_i}\left[e^{-X_i(\omega)\sqrt{d\tau_i}\sum\limits_{j=i+1}^{k}\sigma_{ij}(\omega)d\tau_j}\right]}{E_{\tau_i}\left[e^{-X_i(\omega)\sqrt{d\tau_i}\sum\limits_{j=i+1}^{k-1}\sigma_{ij}(\omega)d\tau_j}\right]}$$

Note that the preceding hold for any white noise sequence. For example, if we recall the random-walk origin of Brownian motion, X_i becomes a binomial r.v., $X_i = \pm 1$ with probability $1/2$. In this case, we get

$$\mu_{ik}(\omega) = \frac{1}{d\tau_i d\tau_k} \ln \frac{\cosh(\sqrt{d\tau_i} \sum_{j=i+1}^{k} \sigma_{ij}(\omega) d\tau_j)}{\cosh(\sqrt{d\tau_i} \sum_{j=i+1}^{k-1} \sigma_{ij}(\omega) d\tau_j)}$$

where $\cosh(x) = (e^x + e^{-x})/2$. On the other hand, if we let the X_i to be standard Normal, $X_i \sim N(0, 1)$, then the terms in the numerator and denominator are LN r.v.'s, and we can compute the expectation ($E[LN(\mu, \sigma^2)] = e^{\mu + \sigma^2/2}$) to get

$$\mu_{ik}(\omega) = \frac{1}{2} \frac{1}{d\tau_k} \left[\left(\sum_{j=i+1}^{k} \sigma_{ij}(\omega) d\tau_j \right)^2 - \left(\sum_{j=i+1}^{k-1} \sigma_{ij}(\omega) d\tau_j \right)^2 \right]$$

By letting $\max_i |d\tau_i| \to 0$, the above converges to

$$\mu(t, T, \omega) = \frac{1}{2} \frac{\partial}{\partial T} \left(\int_t^T \sigma(t, u, \omega) du \right)^2 = \sigma(t, T, \omega) \int_t^T \sigma(t, u, \omega) du$$

which is the HJM drift in continuous time (see Appendix C).

This explicit expression for the required drifts for posited volatilities of the forward rate curve was missing (hard to get) in the short-rate paradigm. Armed with this result, we can start from today's forward curve, $f(0, T)$, posit some volatility structure $\sigma(t, T, \omega)$ for calibration to option markets, and go ahead and construct models for the evolution of the forward/discount curve in a risk-neutral setting. Today's price of any derivative with payoff at T can then be computed as the expected discounted value of its future payoff(s):

$$C(0) = E \left[e^{-\int_0^T f(u, u, \omega) du} C(T, \omega) \right]$$

FORWARD-FORWARD VOLATILITY

Other than having the full term structure as its state-space, the HJM framework allows direct access to the volatilities of each forward rate. Recall that $\sigma(t, T)$ is interpreted as the volatility over time $(t, t + dt)$ of a forward rate with term $(T, T + dT)$. In practice, the volatility surface $\sigma(t, T, \omega)$ or its discretized version is parameterized as

$$\sigma(t, T, \omega) = \sigma_N(t, T)$$

for Normal dynamics, and

$$\sigma(t, T, \omega) = \sigma(t, T) \times f^\alpha(t, T, \omega)$$

for CEV dynamics with parameter α, reducing to Log-Normal dynamics when $\alpha = 1$.

One plausible parameterization is to require forward-forward vol $\sigma(t, T)$ to be a function of *remaining* maturity $T - t$, leading to so-called *homogeneous* volatility surface. This parameterization in practice does not recover caplet vols, and instead is often modified to a *semihomogeneous* format:

$$\sigma(t, T) = A(t)B(T - t)$$

with $B(T - t)$ set to the calibrated caplet curve, and $A(t)$ used for calibration.

No matter what the particular parameterization (if any), the deterministic forward-forward volatility surface $\sigma(t, T), \sigma_N(t, T)$ are then used to calibrate the HJM model to liquid volatility instruments. This is aided by the fact that most simple instruments have a distinct *volatility signature*. For example, we can identify the T-expiry caplet volatility for the forward rate spanning $[T, T + dT]$ as

$$\sqrt{\frac{1}{T} \int_0^T \sigma^2(t, T)dt}$$

while for a midcurve option, that is, an option on a forward rate with expiry strictly before the effective date of the forward rate, the relevant volatility is

$$\sqrt{\frac{1}{t_e} \int_0^{t_e} \sigma^2(t, T)dt} \qquad t_e < T$$

Figure 10.1 shows the volatility signature of a few simple products. For a given set of calibration instruments, we can calibrate our model to their market prices by the judicious tweaking of their volatility signature. This is usually done by discretizing the forward-forward surface into piecewise flat levels, and using the collection of these forward-forward volatility buckets as

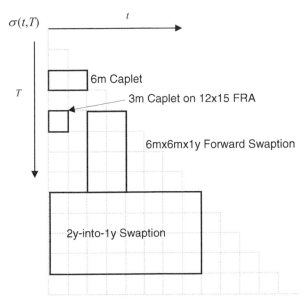

FIGURE 10.1   Volatility Signature of Instruments on a
Quarterly/Quarterly Forward-Forward Volatility Surface

implicit free parameters for calibration. Alternatively, one can parameterize
the surface via a functional form driven by a few parameters, and apply
more formal optimization techniques for calibration.

Forward Vol and Bermudans

A *forward swaption* straddle is a swaption straddle whose strike is set to the
ATMF swap rate at a future strike-setting date. For example, a 6mx6mx1y
forward swaption is a 6m-into-1y swaption straddle whose strike is set in
6m. Note that 6m expiry of the underlying swaption is from the strike date,
so 1y from today. Since until the strike setting, the floating strike remains
ATMF, the value of a forward swaption is directly a function of the implied
forward volatility, and these are also referred to as *forward vol* contracts.
We have shown the volatility signature of 6mx6mx1y forward swaption in
Figure 10.1.

These forward swaption volatilities are of particular interest for pricing
Bermudan cancelable swaps, as the hold versus immediate-exercise decision is directly affected by the implied forward vol. As an example, consider a 1-year into 1-year Bermudan swaption with semi-annual (1y, 1y6m)

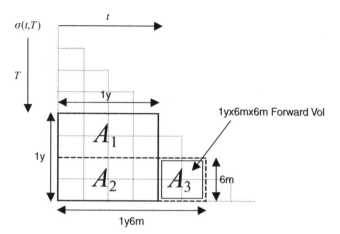

FIGURE 10.2 Relationship Between European, Bermudan, and Forward Volatilities

exercise. The underlying European swaptions are 1y-into-1y and 1y6m-into-6m, and we will require that our model be calibrated to these swaptions. We know that the Bermudan option has to be higher than these two European swaptions, with the excess value coming from delaying exercise at first opportunity (1-year) to the later one (1y6m), but only if the expected hold value is greater than the immediate exercise value. This expected hold value is directly a function of the 1yx6mx6m forward vol (area A_3), as shown in Figure 10.2. If most of the 1y1y volatility ($A_1 + A_2$) is assigned to its first two quarterly forward rates (A_1), then to maintain 1y6m-6m volatility ($A_2 + A_3$) would require back-loading the volatility into 1yx6mx6m bucket (A_3), thereby increasing the value of the Bermudan. The forward-forward volatility surface then allows us to relate European and Bermudan swaption prices via forward vols, and can serve as a rich/cheap signal if their prices result in implausible forward vols.

Swaption Calibration

While caplet volatilities can easily be computed from the volatility surface, swaption volatilities, while having a clear signature, are harder to compute. There do exist however good analytical approximations that relate swaption volatilities to forward-forward vols. Starting with a generic HJM framework,

$$df(t, T, \omega) = \mu(t, T, \omega)dt + \sigma(t, T, \omega)dB(t, \omega)$$

let us discretize the T axis: $0 = T_0 < T_1 < T_2 < \ldots$ and write the continuous-time process equations for these discretized forward rates $f_i(t, \omega) = f(t, [T_i, T_{i+1}], \omega)$:

$$df_i(t, \omega) = \mu_i(t, \omega)dt + \sigma_i(t, \omega)dB(t, \omega)$$

We can relate other rates to these forward rates. For example, if we have used a semiannual discretization, then a semiannual forward swap rate, with effective date $\tau_1 = 2$-years from now, and maturity date $\tau_3 = 3$-years from now (a 1-year par swap rate, 2-years forward) can be written as

$$S(t, [2y, 3y], \omega) = \frac{D(t, 2y, \omega) - D(t, 3y, \omega)}{1/2(D(t, 2y6m, \omega) + D(t, 3y, \omega))}$$

$$= \frac{1 - \dfrac{1}{(1 + f_4(t, \omega)/2)(1 + f_5(t, \omega)/2)}}{1/2\left[\dfrac{1}{(1 + f_4(t, \omega)/2)} + \dfrac{1}{(1 + f_4(t, \omega)/2)(1 + f_5(t, \omega)/2)}\right]}$$

For a given rate, $S(t, [\tau_1, \tau_2], \omega)$ with effective/maturity dates τ_1, τ_2, let us summarize its relationship to our discretized rates via a function g:

$$S(t, [\tau_1, \tau_2], \omega) = g(f_0(t, \omega), f_1(t, \omega), \ldots)$$

To compute the Normal volatility of S over a period $[t_1, t_2]$, we must calculate:

$$\sigma_N(t_1, t_2) = \sqrt{\frac{1}{t_2 - t_1} Var[S(t_2, [\tau_1, \tau_2], \omega) - S(t_2, [\tau_1, \tau_2], \omega)]}$$

while its Log volatility is

$$\sigma(t_1, t_2) = \sqrt{\frac{1}{t_2 - t_1} Var \ln \frac{S(t_2, [\tau_1, \tau_2], \omega)}{S(t_2, [\tau_1, \tau_2], \omega)}}$$

In either case, we need the dynamics for S. Using Ito's Lemma (see Appendix A), we have:

$$dS(t, \omega) = \frac{\partial g}{\partial t}dt + \sum_i \frac{\partial g}{\partial f_i}df_i + \frac{1}{2}\sum_{i,j} \frac{\partial^2 g}{\partial f_i \partial f_j}df_i df_j$$

$$= \mu_S(t, \omega)dt + \sum_i \frac{\partial g}{\partial f_i}\sigma_i(t, \omega)dB(t, \omega)$$

We will first *assume* that we can ignore the effects of the drift μ_S. With this assumption, we can focus on the second term to compute the Normal volatility:

$$Var[S(t_2, [\tau_1, \tau_2], \omega) - S(t_2, [\tau_1, \tau_2], \omega)] = Var \int_{t_1}^{t_2} \sum_i \frac{\partial g}{\partial f_i}(t, \omega)\sigma_i(t, \omega)dB(t, \omega)$$

$$= E \int_{t_1}^{t_2} \left[\sum_i \frac{\partial g}{\partial f_i}(t, \omega)\sigma_i(t, \omega) \right]^2 dt$$

$$= \int_{t_1}^{t_2} E \left[\sum_i \frac{\partial g}{\partial f_i}(t, \omega)\sigma_i(t, \omega) \right]^2 dt$$

where the second equality follows from Ito's isometry and the fact that Ito integrals are martingales (mean 0).[4]

In order to evaluate the preceding equation, we *assume* that we can *freeze-forward* the pesky stochastic terms, that is, replace the stochastic terms inside the expectation with their (today's) forward values. For example, if we are using Normal dynamics for the forwards, we can let σ_i's be deterministic functions of time:

$$\sigma_i(t, \omega) = \sigma_i(t)$$

and all that remains are $\frac{\partial g}{\partial f_i}(t, \omega)$ random terms. In this case, the freeze-forward method gives

$$(t_2 - t_1)\sigma_N^2(t_1, t_2) = \int_{t_1}^{t_2} \left[\sum_i \frac{\partial g}{\partial f_i}(0)\sigma_i(t) \right]^2 dt$$

$$= \sum_{i,j} \frac{\partial g}{\partial f_i}(0) \frac{\partial g}{\partial f_j}(0) \int_{t_1}^{t_2} \sigma_i(t)\sigma_j(t)dt$$

The above integral can now be computed numerically, or if we have discretized the forward-forward vols are piecewise flat, computed as sums.

Similarly, we can let each forward have deterministic log volatility

$$\sigma_(t, \omega) = \sigma_i(t) f_i(t, \omega)$$

to come up with the following approximate formula for swaption log volatility

$$Var \ln \frac{S(t_2, [\tau_1, \tau_2], \omega)}{S(t_1, [\tau_1, \tau_2], \omega)} = \sum_{i,j} \frac{\partial g}{\partial f_i}(0) \frac{\partial g}{\partial f_j}(0) \frac{f_i(0) f_j(0)}{S^2(0, [\tau_1, \tau_2])} \int_{t_1}^{t_2} \sigma_i(t) \sigma_j(t) dt$$

The above formulas provide a good first-order approximation for swaption volatilities, greatly aiding in calibration of HJM models.

MULTIFACTOR MODELS

The HJM framework can easily be extended to be multifactor. For this, we allow the evolution of the forward curve to be driven by multiple independent Brownian drivers, $dB_i(t, \omega)$, each affecting the evolution by its own volatility impact $\sigma_i(t, T, \omega)$:

$$df(t, T, \omega) = \mu(t, T, \omega)dt + \sum_i \sigma_i(t, T, \omega)dB_i(t, \omega)$$

We can rewrite the dynamics as

$$df(t, T, \omega) = \mu(t, T, \omega)dt + \sigma(t, T, \omega) \sum_i \rho_i(t, T, \omega)dB_i(t, \omega)$$

where

$$\sigma(t, T, \omega) = \sqrt{\sum_i \sigma_i^2(t, T, \omega)}$$

$$\rho_i(t, T, \omega) = \frac{\sigma_i(t, T, \omega)}{\sigma^2(t, T, \omega)}$$

and satisfy

$$\sum_i \rho_i^2(t, T, \omega) = 1$$

Reexpressing the multifactor dynamics in this way allows us to separate the volatility $\sigma(t, T, \omega)$ from the factor/correlation structure $\rho_i(t, T, \omega)$. A common way of extracting the factor structure is based on a historical study of movements of the term structure using principal component analysis (PCA).

Model Correlations

Similar to swaption vols, we can derive approximations for the correlation of different swap rates. Starting with the multifactor dynamics of the discretized forwards,

$$df_i(t, \omega) = \mu_i(t, \omega)dt + \sum_{l=1}^{N} \sigma_{l,i}(t, \omega)dB_l(t, \omega)$$

we can derive approximate expressions for the correlation between their changes (percent, absolute) during some time window $[t_1, t_2]$. For example, given two swap rates S_1, S_2, let us summarize the quote mechanics of each swap rate in two functions $g_{1,2}$.

Using Log-Normal vols for the forwards:

$$\sigma_{l,i}(t, \omega) = \sigma_{l,i}(t) \times f_i(t, \omega)$$

we can compute the correlation of percentage changes (sometimes called log-correlation) of S_1, S_2:

$$\rho_{S_1,S_2}(t_1, t_2) = \frac{\text{Cov}\left[\ln \frac{S_1(t_2)}{S_1(t_1)}, \ln \frac{S_2(t_2)}{S_2(t_1)}\right]}{\sigma_{S_1}(t_1, t_2)\sigma_{S_2}(t_1, t_2)}$$

by forward-freezing the stochastic terms to get:

$$\text{Cov}\left[\ln \frac{S_1(t_2)}{S_1(t_1)}, \ln \frac{S_2(t_2)}{S_2(t_1)}\right] = \sum_{i,j} \frac{\partial g_1}{\partial f_i}(0)\frac{\partial g_2}{\partial f_j}(0)\frac{f_i(0)f_j(0)}{S_1(0)S_2(0)} \int_{t_1}^{t_2} \sum_{l=1}^{N} \sigma_{l,i}(t)\sigma_{l,j}(t)dt$$

Similarly, using Normal vols for the forwards

$$\sigma_{l,i}(t, \omega) = \sigma_{l,i}(t)$$

provides the following approximation for the correlation on the absolute changes of two swap rates:

$$\rho_{S_1,S_2}(t_1, t_2) = \frac{\text{Cov}\,[S_1(t_2) - S_1(t_1), S_2(t_2) - S_2(t_1)]}{\sigma_{S_1}(t_1, t_2)\sigma_{S_2}(t_1, t_2)}$$

where

$$\text{Cov}\,[S_1(t_2) - S_1(t_1), S_2(t_2) - S_2(t_1)] = \sum_{i,j} \frac{\partial g_1}{\partial f_i}(0)\frac{\partial g_2}{\partial f_j}(0) \int_{t_1}^{t_2} \sum_{l=1}^{N} \sigma_{l,i}(t)\sigma_{l,j}(t)dt$$

While the previous expressions might look formidable, they are relatively easy to compute, especially if the forward-forward vol buckets are piecewise flat, where the integrals can be replaced by summations.

The ability to investigate the implied correlations between various rates as an explicit function of the assumed dynamics is one of the features of the HJM models. Of course, one could always calculate the model-implied correlations for any model, but for HJM-based models, these calculations are more explicit and in terms of more intuitive quantities such as forward-forward vol buckets, and factor structures.

HJM FRAMEWORK TYPICALLY LEADS TO NONRECOMBINING TREES

HJM models in general do not admit a lattice implementation, that is, an up-move followed by a down-move does not lead to the same state as a down-move followed by an up-move. This is usually referred to the typical HJM model being *non-Markovian*, and is the consequence of the drifts having stochastic terms in them.

HJM models are hence typically implemented via simulation models, with simulation noise controlled through a variety of variance reduction techniques. The simulation implementation can then easily be used to price European-style and path-dependent interest-rate derivatives, can easily be augmented to handle multifactor dynamics for richer dynamics of interest rates or to incorporate stochastic volatility for skews/smiles. As simulation renders itself easily to parallel processing and distribution among idle workstations, and its accuracy improves as $1/\sqrt{N}$ for an N-path simulation, it has become the method of choice for general HJM models. Bermudan options, however, are difficult in simulation models, and one has to resort to approximation techniques like LSM method in Chapter 9 to compute the hold value.

Alternatively, in order to avoid simulation, one can focus on the subclass of HJM models that *are* Markovian, or can be made Markovian through the addition of a few state variables. The former approach typically leads to Normal models (similar in dynamics to Hull-White) and were introduced by Cheyette[5] and Ritchken and colleagues,[6] while the second approach has been investigated by Ritchken[7] among others.

Log-Normal Instantaneous-Forwards Lead to Explosive Behavior

All is not well in HJM-land: The first volatility structure considered by HJM was for Log-Normal dynamics. For this, they considered the simplest Log-Normal model where all instantaneous forward rates at all times have the same constant volatility σ:

$$(0 \leq t \leq T) \qquad df(t, T, \omega) = \mu(t, T, \omega)dt + \sigma \times f(t, T, \omega)dB(t, \omega)$$

To their chagrin, HJM could prove that even for this simple Log-Normal model, forward rates can *explode*, that is, there is a positive probability that forward rates can diverge to $+\infty$!

It turns out that the main reason for this behavior is that we are assuming that the *instantaneous* forward rates are Log-Normally distributed. If instead, we focus on discretized forward rates, they remain bounded. This result was established by Sandman and colleagues,[8] where they showed that discretized rates remained bounded even under Log-Normal dynamics. Sandman and colleagues' result allayed some of the "explosive" fears, and led to wider implementation of HJM framework, under what has become known as *market models*, where the term *market* is meant to emphasize that the *discretized* rather than the *instantaneous* forward rates are modeled. We will discuss these models and their specification through the forward-measure lens in the next chapter.

CHAPTER **11**

Forward-Measure Lens

We have so far focused on risk-neutral valuation using the intuitive "money-market" numeraire. In this framework, the main pricing operator is

$$(0 < t < T) \qquad C(t, \omega) = E_t[e^{-\int_t^T r(u,\omega)du} C(T, \omega)]$$

which we have interpreted as the expected value of terminal option payoff, when stochastically discounted back to valuation date. Written another way,

$$(0 < t < T) \qquad \frac{C(t, \omega)}{M(t, t, \omega)} = E_t\left[\frac{C(T, \omega)}{M(t, T, \omega)}\right]$$

where $M(t, T, \omega) = e^{\int_t^T r(u,\omega)du}$ is the value of a money-market account with initial unit deposit at time t, and continually rolled over until T along the series of instantaneous short rates $r(u, \omega)$. Since $M(t, t, \omega) = 1$, the above two formulae are equivalent. However, the second formula highlights the required martingale property: It states that having chosen the money-market account as the currency (numeraire), then all relative prices in the future should have 0 expected P&L. This requirement pins down the risk-neutral probabilities used when taking expected values.

NUMERAIRES ARE ARBITRARY

Derivatives prices being *relative* prices, it turns out that a more general result holds, stating that no matter what the chosen currency/numeraire, then relative prices of all assets (underlyings and derivatives) with respect to that numeraire should have 0 expected P&L, that is, relative prices should be martingales. Of course, different numeraires give rise to different risk-neutral probabilities, and one has to use the one consistent with the

201

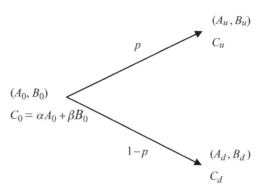

FIGURE 11.1   Binomial Model for Two
Random Assets

chosen numeraire. However, this arbitrariness of the numeraire allows one
to choose it judiciously for the problem at hand to simplify or justify pricing
formulae.

Change of Numeraires and Likelihood Ratios

To motivate and clarify the change of numeraires, let us go back to our basic
building-block model: A 1-period binomial setting. Instead of a loan and the
underlying, let us replace the loan with a general asset, so that there are two
traded assets, A, B, and a t_e-expiry European-style contingent claim C that
can depend on these two assets, as shown in Figure 11.1.

Our goal is to set up a replicating portfolio consisting of (α, β) units of
(A, B) that replicate the option payoff at expiration t_e:

$$\alpha A_{\{u,d\}} + \beta B_{\{u,d\}} = C_{\{u,d\}}$$

The preceding is two equations and two unknown portfolio holdings (α, β),
so we can solve for them to get

$$\alpha = \frac{B_d}{A_u B_d - A_d B_u} C_u + \frac{-B_u}{A_u B_d - A_d B_u} C_d$$

$$\beta = \frac{-A_d}{A_u B_d - A_d B_u} C_u + \frac{A_u}{A_u B_d - A_d B_u} C_d$$

to arrive at today's price of contingent claim:

$$C(0) = \alpha A_0 + \beta B_0$$
$$= \frac{A_0 B_d - A_d B_0}{A_u B_d - A_d B_u} C_u + \frac{A_u B_0 - A_0 B_u}{A_u B_d - A_d B_u} C_d$$

A bit of algebra reexpresses the above in our desired format:

$$\frac{C(0)}{A(0)} = p_A \frac{C_u}{A_u} + (1 - p_A) \frac{C_d}{A_d} \qquad p_A = \frac{A_u(A_0 B_d - A_d B_0)}{A_0(A_u B_d - A_d B_u)}$$

which looks like a martingale constraint: If we choose asset A as the numeraire, then all relative prices have zero expected P&L. All that remains is to show that p_A is a probability: $0 \le p_A \le 1$.

Note that the above formula holds for any contingent claim, in particular, when it (trivially) replicates the asset B, $C_{\{u,d\}} = B_{\{u,d\}}$. In this case, we get

$$\frac{B(0)}{A(0)} = p_A \frac{B_u}{A_u} + (1 - p_A) \frac{B_d}{A_d}$$

or equivalently,

$$1 = p_A \frac{B_u / A_u}{B_0 / A_0} + (1 - p_A) \frac{B_d / A_d}{B_0 / A_0}$$

We will use the preceding equation to characterize when p_A is a probability.

An arbitrage opportunity exists if one can create positive gain with no risk. Existence of arbitrage can be reduced to the following prototypical situation: Create a costless portfolio at time 0 by selling short A_0 units of asset B and buying B_0 units of asset A for zero up front cost: $-A_0 B_0 + B_0 A_0$. At expiration t_e, own B_0 units of asset A which can trade at A_u or A_d depending on which state is realized, and simultaneously owe A_0 units of asset B, which can trade at B_u or B_d, respectively. The value of the portfolio is either $B_0 A_u - A_0 B_u$ in the (A_u, B_u)-state, or $B_0 A_d - A_0 B_d$ in the (A_d, B_d)-state. Since it cost 0 up front to construct this portfolio, the portfolio value at each up/down-state is the P&L.

If both of these are nonnegative, with at least one positive, then the P&L is never negative and sometimes positive. Existence of arbitrage opportunity is then equivalent to

$$B_0 A_u - A_0 B_u \ge 0 \Leftrightarrow \frac{B_u / A_u}{B_0 / A_0} \le 1$$

and

$$B_0 A_d - A_0 B_d \geq 0 \Leftrightarrow \frac{B_d/A_d}{B_0/A_0} \leq 1$$

with strict inequality ($<$ instead of $\leq$) in at least one of them. Now if p_A is a probability, $0 \leq p_A \leq 1$, we arrive at a contradiction:

$$1 = p_A \frac{B_u/A_u}{B_0/A_0} + (1 - p_A)\frac{B_d/A_d}{B_0/A_0}$$
$$< p_A + (1 - p_A) = 1!$$

We have just shown that existence of arbitrage implies that p_A cannot be a probability, or stated otherwise, *if p_A is a probability, then there is no arbitrage.* The converse also holds: *If there is no arbitrage, then p_A is a probability,* but its proof requires a deep result from functional analysis (Hahn-Banach Theorem leading to Separating Hyperplane Theorem) and is beyond the scope of this text.[1] In summary, *Lack of arbitrage is equivalent to p_A being a probability.*

What would happen if we chose the asset B as the numeraire? In this case, we have

$$\frac{C(0)}{B(0)} = p_B \frac{C_u}{B_u} + (1 - p_B)\frac{C_d}{B_d} \qquad p_B = \frac{B_u(B_0 A_d - B_d A_0)}{B_0(B_u A_d - B_d A_u)}$$

and lack of arbitrage is equivalent to p_B being a probability. In either case, the value of the contingent claim is the same, equal to its replicating portfolio. The choice of numeraire does not change the option value; it simply is a way of getting to the same result via different—but equivalent—ways.

A bit of algebra shows that

$$p_A/p_B = (A_u/A_0)/(B_u/B_0)$$
$$(1 - p_A)/(1 - p_B) = (A_d/A_0)/(B_d/B_0)$$

that is, for each future state, the ratio of the two probabilities—their *likelihood ratio*—is related to the corresponding relative asset values. This property on the likelihood-ratio can be formalized as follows: Let $P_A(t, \omega)$ denote the probability measure induced by numeraire A for the future date t:

$$P_A(t, \omega) = \begin{cases} p_A & \omega \text{ is "u" (up-state)} \\ 1 - p_A & \omega \text{ is "d" (down-state)} \end{cases}$$

Similarly, let $P_B(t, \omega)$ denote the probability measure induced by numeraire B:

$$P_B(t, \omega) = \begin{cases} p_B & \omega \text{ is "u" (up-state)} \\ 1 - p_B & \omega \text{ is "d" (down-state)} \end{cases}$$

We have the following relationship on their likelihood ratio:

$$\frac{P_A(t, \omega)}{P_B(t, \omega)} = \frac{A(t, \omega)/A(0)}{B(t, \omega)/B(0)}$$

As was done in Chapter 5, we can extend the above setup to multiple periods, using the binomial model as the building block. For an N-period setup $\{t_0 = 0 < t_1 < \cdots < t_N\}$, the replicating portfolio has to be rebalanced, but will be self-financing, and all our previous results hold with the slight modification to keep track and identify the numeraire:

$$(0 \le t_i \le t_N) \qquad \frac{C(t_i, \omega)}{\text{Num}(t_i, \omega)} = E_{t_i}^{\text{Num}} \left[\frac{C(t_N, \omega)}{\text{Num}(t_N, \omega)} \right]$$

which in the limit leads to the following continuous-time version:

$$(0 \le t \le T) \qquad \frac{C(t, \omega)}{\text{Num}(t, \omega)} = E_t^{\text{Num}} \left[\frac{C(T, \omega)}{\text{Num}(T, \omega)} \right]$$

Moreover, the likelihood ratio property remains and can be used to identify and compute the probabilities when switching from one numeraire to other. In a discrete-state setting, we have

$$(0 \le t) \qquad \frac{P_A(t, \omega)}{P_B(t, \omega)} = \frac{A(t, \omega)/A(0)}{B(t, \omega)/B(0)}$$

while for a continuous-state setting, probability measures are expressed in terms of their density functions: $P_A = \int f_A$, and the condition above is written as

$$(0 \le t \le T) \qquad \frac{f_A}{f_B}(t, \omega) = \frac{dP_A}{dP_B}(t, \omega) = \frac{A(t, \omega)/A(0)}{B(t, \omega)/B(0)}$$

where the term $\frac{dP_A}{dP_B}$ is the generalized version of the likelihood ratio, called the *Radon-Nikodym derivative*. It is easy to see $\frac{dP_A}{dP_B}(t, \omega)$ is itself a martingale under P_B, and the *change of numeraire formula*[2] is usually written as:

$$(0 \le t \le T) \qquad \frac{dP_A}{dP_B}(t, \omega) = \frac{A(t, \omega)/A(0)}{B(t, \omega)/B(0)} = E_t\left[\frac{A(T, \omega)/A(0)}{B(T, \omega)/B(0)}\right]$$

where the expectation is taken under P_B probability.

FORWARD MEASURES

Other than interesting mathematical identities, how do the above results help us? The answer is *forward measures*. Recall that using the money-market account as the numeraire leads to the following formula:

$$(0 \le T) \qquad C(0) = E_0^M[e^{-\int_0^T r(u,\omega)du} C(T, \omega)]$$

which requires computing the expected value of the *stochastically discounted payoffs*.

Let us now consider a claim $C(t, \omega)$ that has a single payoff at a fixed future date T^*. For example, a t_e-expiration caplet on 3m-Libor has a final payoff on $T^* = t_e + 3m$. Instead of the money-market account, let us choose as numeraire the price of a T^*-maturity zero-coupon bond $D(t, T^*, \omega)$. Corresponding to this numeraire, we have to ensure risk neutrality, that is, we have to make sure that relative prices are martingales:

$$(0 \le t \le T \le T^*) \qquad E_t^{T^*}\left[\frac{C(T, \omega)}{D(T, T^*, \omega)}\right] = \frac{C(t, \omega)}{D(t, T^*, \omega)}$$

where the superscript in E^{T^*} shows the dependence of the probability set used on this particular numeraire. In particular, by setting $t = 0$, and $T = T^*$, we have

$$E_0^{T^*}\left[\frac{C(T^*, \omega)}{D(T^*, T^*, \omega)}\right] = \frac{C(0)}{D(0, T^*)}$$

where since $D(T^*, T^*, \omega) = 1$, gives us:

$$C(0) = D(0, T^*)E_0^{T^*}[C(T^*, \omega)]$$

which is the expected value of the option payoff discounted using *today's* discount factors. This validates part of the common market practice of pulling the stochastic discounting outside the expectation, and simply calculating the expected value of the option payoff, and then multiplying it by today's discount factor to the payment date as is done in Black's Formula for caplets and European swaptions.

The probability set P^{T*} used in computing E^* is called the T^*-*forward measure* to distinguish it from the probability set P^M used when using the money-market account as the numeraire, the latter loosely called risk-neutral measure. The name forward-measure comes from the following observation: For any tradeable asset A with no interim cash flows, the T^*-forward value of an asset at time t, $F_A(t, T^*)$ satisfies:

$$F_A(t, T^*, \omega) = \frac{A(t, \omega)}{D(t, T^*, \omega)} = E_{T^*}\left[\frac{A(T^*, \omega)}{D(T^*, T^*, \omega)}\right] = E_{T^*}[A(T^*, \omega)]$$

since $D(T^*, T^*, \omega) = 1$. Hence, under P^{T^*} the expected value at T^* is the T^*-forward value of the asset.

This result also extends to any T^*-maturity *simple* rate. Let $f(t, [T_s, T^*], \omega)$ be the simple forward rate for deposit period $[T_s, T^*]$. At its settlement date T_s, this is simply the cash rate for a deposit from T_s to T^*. Recall the relationship between forward rates and discount factors:

$$f(t, [T_s, T^*], \omega) = \frac{D(t, T_s, \omega)/D(t, T^*, \omega) - 1}{T^* - T_s}$$

For any chosen numeraire, all tradeable assets (including any T-maturity zero-coupon bond) relative to it must have no expected P&L. For our particular $D(t, T^*)$ numeraire, this martingale constraint requires:

$$(0 \le u \le t) \qquad E_u^{T^*}\left[\frac{D(t, T, \omega)}{D(t, T^*, \omega)}\right] = \frac{D(u, T, \omega)}{D(u, T^*, \omega)}$$

Applying the above constraint to the T_s-maturity zero, we have:

$$
\begin{aligned}
E_u^{T^*} f(t, [T_s, T^*, \omega) &= E_u\left[\frac{1}{T^* - T_s}\left(\frac{D(t, T_s, \omega)}{D(t, T^*, \omega)} - 1\right)\right] \\
&= \frac{1}{T^* - T_s}\left(E_u\left[\frac{D(t, T_s, \omega)}{D(t, T^*, \omega)}\right] - 1\right) \\
&= \frac{1}{T^* - T_s}\left(\frac{D(u, T_s, \omega)}{D(u, T^*, \omega)} - 1\right) \\
&= f(u, [T_s, T^*], \omega)
\end{aligned}
$$

In particular, setting $u = 0$, this means that from today until its settlement T_s, the expected value of the $[T_s, T^*]$-rate is its today's forward value $f(0, [T_s, T^*])$, that is, the distribution remains centered at today's value, and is driftless. In particular, the expected settlement value (at time T_s) of any $[T_s, T^*]$ rate is today's forward rate for that period:

$$f(0, [T_s, T^*]) = E_{T_s}^{T^*}[f(T_s, [T_s, T^*], \omega)]$$

Considering the diffusion dynamics for $f(t, [T_s, T_w], \omega)$ under the P^{T^*} measure,

$$df(t, [T_s, T^*], \omega) = \mu(t, \omega)dt + \sigma(t, [T_s, T^*], \omega)dB^{T^*}(t, \omega)$$

the above argument shows that the drift term $\mu(t, \omega)$ is zero, that is,

$$df(t, [T_s, T^*], \omega) = \sigma(t, [T_s, T^*], \omega)dB^{T^*}(t, \omega)$$

BGM/JAMSHIDIAN RESULTS

All that remains to justify Black's Normal/Log-Normal caplet formula is to ensure that under this T^*-forward measure, the driftless (centered at today's forwards) distribution of the $f(T_s, [T_s, T^*], \omega)$ is Normal/Log-Normal. A sufficient condition is to *assume* that volatility parameters are nonrandom. Specifically, to attain Log-Normal dynamics, it suffices to have

$$\frac{df(t, [T_s, T^*], \omega)}{f(t, [T_s, T^*], \omega)} = \sigma(t, T_s)dB^{T^*}(t, \omega)$$

for a nonrandom/deterministic log volatility curve $\sigma(., T_s)$. In this case, the distribution of the rate at any expiration date $t_e \leq T_s$ is Log-Normal:

$$\frac{f(t_e, [T_s, T^*], \omega)}{f(0, [T_s, T^*])} \sim LN\left(-\frac{1}{2}\bar{\sigma}^2 t_e, \bar{\sigma}^2 t_e\right)$$

where

$$\bar{\sigma} = \sqrt{1/t_e \int_0^{t_e} \sigma^2(t, T_s)dt}$$

leading to Black's Log-Normal formula for caplets:

$$C(0) = D(0, T^*)E_0^{T^*}[\max(0, f(t_e, [T_s, T^*], \omega) - K)]$$
$$= D(0, T^*)[f(0, [T_s, T^*])N(d_1) - K N(d_2)]$$
$$d_{1,2} = \frac{\ln(f(0, [T_s, T^*])/K)}{\overline{\sigma}\sqrt{t_e}} \pm 1/2\overline{\sigma}\sqrt{t_e}$$

Similarly, to attain Normal dynamics, it suffices to have

$$df(t, [T_s, T^*], \omega) = \sigma_N(t, T_s)dB^{T^*}(t, \omega)$$

for a nonrandom/deterministic Normal volatility curve $\sigma_N(., T_s)$. In this case, the distribution of the rate at any expiration date $t_e \leq T_s$ is Normal:

$$f(t_e, [T_s, T^*], \omega) \sim N(f(0, [T_s, T^*]), \overline{\sigma}_N^2 t_e)$$

where

$$\overline{\sigma}_N = \sqrt{1/t_e \int_0^{t_e} \sigma_N^2(t, T_s)dt}$$

which leads to the familiar Black's Normal formula for caplets:

$$C(0) = D(0, T^*)E_0^{T^*}[\max(0, f(t_e, [T_s, T^*], \omega) - K)]$$
$$= D(0, T^*)\overline{\sigma}_N\sqrt{t_e}[N'(d) + dN(d)]$$
$$d = \frac{f(0, [T_s, T^*]) - K}{\overline{\sigma}_N\sqrt{t_e}}$$

The conditions to recover Black's Log-Normal formula for caplets were presented and popularized in a series of papers by Brace-Gartarek-Musiela (BGM)[3] (see Appendix C).

A similar procedure can be used to justify Black-type formula for pricing swaptions. Jamshidian[4] used the forward annuity price as the numeraire, and showed that pricing a swaption under the probabilities induced by this numeraire (called the forward-swap measure, or swap measure) is equivalent to evaluating the expected option payoff under this measure, and multiplying it by today's value of this forward annuity, identical to how Black's formula is used in practice. With the additional assumption that the swap rate under this swap measure is Normal/Log-Normal, we recover exactly the market-standard Black's Normal/Log-Normal formula for European swaptions.

DIFFERENT MEASURES FOR DIFFERENT RATES

The BGM result applied to a series of contiguous forward rates naturally leads to the BGM term-structure model: Having discretized the forward curve into a series of maturity dates $0 < T_1 < \cdots < T_{N+1}$, the contiguous forward rates $f([T_i, T_{i+1}]$—each considered under its own forward-T^{i+1}-measure—are easy to calibrate to caplets, as the root-mean-square (RMS) average of model parameter $\sigma(t, T_i)$ or $\sigma_N(t, T_i)$ must equal the implied Black Log-Normal or Normal caplet vol bootstrapped from ED/Cap prices in the market. Therefore, for each T_i, one can come up with a deterministic curve $\sigma(., T_i)$ and ensure the RMS average equals the bootstrapped caplet curve. Trivially, setting $\sigma(t, T_i)$ to bootstrapped caplet vol for all t satisfies the condition, but one can (and typically does) use a piecewise constant (where the $\int \sigma(t, T_s)$ becomes $\sum \sigma_i(T_s)$ for a sequence of volatility levels), or an easily-integrable parametric shape. This flexibility in the timing of volatilities can be used to calibrate to other instruments (European swaptions). This model was proposed by BGM, dubbed the Libor-market-model (LMM) to distinguish it from forward-measure models based on swap rates, the latter called the swap market model (SMM). Strictly speaking, BGM—taking its state variables as a series of forward rates rather than the short rate—*is a subclass of HJM models*, with a specific volatility structure that would lead to Log-Normal dynamics for each rate when viewed under that rate's associated forward-measure.

Forward Measures Are Interrelated

The joint relation between different forward measures can be characterized via the numeraire change formula by their likelihood ratios. For example, let us consider 2 successive forward rates: $f(t, [T_{k-2}, T_{k-1}], \omega)$ and the next contiguous rate $f(t, [T_{k-1}, T_k], \omega)$. Under BGM,

$$\frac{df(t, [T_{k-2}, T_{k-1}], \omega)}{df(t, [T_{k-2}, T_{k-1}], \omega)} = \sigma(t, T_{k-2})dB^{T_{k-1}}(t, \omega) \text{ under } P^{T_{k-1}}$$

$$\frac{df(t, [T_{k-1}, T_k], \omega)}{df(t, [T_{k-1}, T_k], \omega)} = \sigma(t, T_{k-1})dB^{T_k}(t, \omega) \text{ under } P^{T_k}$$

The change of numeraire formula gives us:

$$\frac{dP^{T_{k-1}}}{dP^{T_k}}(t,\omega) = E_t\left[\frac{D(T_{k-1}, T_{k-1}, \omega)/D(0, T_{k-1})}{D(T_{k-1}, T_k, \omega)/D(0, T_k)}\right]$$

$$= \frac{1 + (T_k - T_{k-1})f(t, [T_{k-1}, T_k], \omega)}{1 + (T_k - T_{k-1})f(0, [T_{k-1}, T_k])}$$

An application of Girsanov's Theorem (see Appendix C) uses the preceding likelihood ratio to relate the Brownian motions $dB^{T_{k-1}}, dB^{T_k}$ associated with the forward measures:

$$dB^{T_{k-1}}(t,\omega) = dB^{T_k}(t,\omega) - \frac{(T_k - T_{k-1})f(t, [T_{k-1}, T_k], \omega)}{1 + (T_k - T_{k-1})f(0, [T_{k-1}, T_k])} \text{ under } P^{T_k}$$

The above recurrence relationship suggests a way of tackling multirate exotics:

1. Having discretized the forward curve into $0 = T_0 < T_1 < \cdots < T_{N+1}$, start with the last Brownian driver $dB^{T_{N+1}}$, and evolve it.
2. Evolve the forward rate $f(t, [T_k, T_{k+1}], \omega)$ according to its dynamics $\sigma(t, T_k)$ under the driver $dB^{T_{k+1}}$.
3. Use the already obtained evolution for the Brownian driver $B^{T_{k+1}}(t, \omega)$ and $f[t, [T_k, T_{k+1}], \omega)$ to compute (not evolve) the previous Brownian driver dB^{T_k}.
4. Repeat steps 2 and 3 until you get to the first forward rate.
5. Price each cash flow of any multirate exotic by computing the expected value of the each cash flow at its payment date, and multiplying it by today's discount factor to the payment date.

This formulation of the BGM model is known as BGM under the *terminal measure*. An alternative formulation of BGM is to consider the evolution of a discretized money-market account and relate the evolution of all forward rates to it using the previous recurrence equation. This can be done and is referred to as BGM under *spot measure*.[5] Regardless of which measure (terminal, spot) we use in BGM, the evolution of the Brownian drivers affecting the individual forwards is not Markovian due to the stochastic terms in their drifts, and a tree implementation is nonrecombining. Hence, the BGM model is most commonly implemented via a simulation model, with the spot measure chosen due to its numerically more stable behavior.

"CLASSIC" OR "NEW IMPROVED": PICK YOUR POISON!

The relative ease of calibration in the BGM term-structure model initially raised the hope of ability to price complex interest-rate exotics in a single arbitrage-free framework that renders itself to easy calibration. However, this relative ease of calibration is exactly the Achilles' heel of the model. The key concept is that each forward rate *under its own forward measure* is easy to calibrate, and hence complex derivatives that solely depend on that particular rate can easily be priced. However, as most exotics depend on multiple forward rates, this gain is limited. To price multirate exotics, we need to simultaneously evolve all the interrelated Brownian drivers under their own interrelated measures, and compute the expected value of the payoff. The problem could still be tackled if the Brownian drivers were independent, or followed a given correlation structure; however, for BGM, these Brownian motions are interrelated, and their correlation structure depends on the realized path of the forward rates. Hence, no analytical solution exists for their dynamics, and need to be numerically calculated, typically via a simulation implementation.

To wit, by considering each forward rate under its own measure, the thorny arbitrage-free dynamics of each forward rate is transferred to its own measure: For single-rate derivatives, this is a gain, but for multirate derivatives, the thorny dynamics come back to the fore, as we have to consider the joint relationship of these forward measures. Hence, as far as multirate derivatives are concerned, we have simply delayed or transferred the computational task.

As stated before, BGM and associated Market models are a subclass of HJM models, with their term structure dynamics specified through the forward-measure lens. The choice of BGM or discretized HJM is mostly academic. To see this, let us consider BGM under spot measure. The discretized forward rates have elegant properties under each rate's forward measure, but complicated stochastic drifts under any single measure. The general BGM model is non-Markovian, and hence it is best implemented as a simulation model. In any finite-sample simulation run, all arbitrage-free conditions, calibration constraints, and derivatives prices are *approximate*. Hence when simulated, BGM loses almost all the beauty of exact cap calibration under the forward measure. Braving on, the realized simulation paths can be jiggled/tuned to exactly satisfy the arbitrage-free conditions, and calibration constraints can either exactly or approximately be satisfied. Even with this, we still end up with an approximate price for the derivative, clouded by simulation noise. Further ingenuity (variance reduction) allows us to reduce the remaining simulation noise, but not eliminate it. Moreover, we still have to grapple with pricing early exercise for Bermudan options in a simulation model, using heuristic algorithms such as LSM. Compare this with the simulation implementation of a discrete-time, discrete-tenor HJM model under the money-market measure, and all the previous remarks and challenges hold.

On the other hand, because BGM is a subclass of HJM models, it shares many of its strengths: Choice of the more intuitive discretized forward *curve* rather than the short rate as its state-space; access to a flexible and relatively intuitive forward-forward volatility surface for volatility calibration; ability to posit more general dynamics than Log Normal, say Normal or CEV, to aid in skew/smile calibration; and easy adaptation to multifactor and stochastic vol dynamics, especially in simulation implementation.

CHAPTER 12

In Search of "The" Model

The rates markets have experienced explosive growth over the last 25 years, starting with the first interest-rate swaps in the 1980s to the introduction of swaptions in mid-1980s and structured note programs in the early 1990s. While in the early days, swaps were thought and explained via comparative advantage theories, these were soon replaced by the current arbitrage-free arguments relating them to discount and forward curves. As such, other than the date-related minutiae and shifting of focus from prices to rates, the pricing of swaps are not that different from bonds. For simple interest-rate derivatives, many option pricing formulae and concepts were borrowed from equities and co-opted to interest rates. However, callable bonds and the evolving structured note programs in the early 1990s necessitated a more thorough approach, leading to various term structure models based on either the short-rate or the full-term structure.

MIGRATION TO FULL-TERM STRUCTURE MODELS

In the early days, with the large margins associated with newfangled products, it was sufficient to have some model—however rudimentary—that could price complex payoffs. Most firms in the early 1990s started with a short-rate model, either BDT/BK with multifactor extensions, or a Hull-White model. These models were adequate for pricing simple interest-rate products and Bermudans in the tree implementation, and path-dependent options in simulation implementation, although the underlying dynamics and parameterizations were not optimal. It was understood that the embedded dynamics in a short-rate model were limited, since the short-rate determines the full term structure at each time, and hence payoffs that depend on multiple parts of the yield curve are not adequately represented in these models. In the early 1990s, the HJM framework started to get adopted, but this framework generally required a simulation implementation and therefore was not optimal for pricing Bermudans. With the migration of the structured products from the United States to Europe and then Asia, European banks became the dominant players in structured products, and research staff and quants in these firms utilized the newly developed BGM/LMM framework as their modeling platforms. As discussed, these models are a subclass of the HJM framework and share the advantages and disadvantages (non-Markovian) of these models.

IMPLEMENTATION ERA

By the late 1980s, most of the theoretical work for interest-rate modeling was done, and since then, we have mostly been in the implementation stage. Indeed, most of the new work in interest-rate modeling is on implementation tricks and ideas rather than a rethinking or reformulation of the basic risk-neutral valuation paradigm. As we have shown, despite the ever-increasing complexity of interest-rate models, they are simply instances of risk-neutral valuation, the core elements of which—dynamic replication—can be understood in a simple two-step binomial model.

As interest-rate modeling requires the evolution of the full term structure, there are few analytical results, and most models need to get implemented via computer programs. The problem of implementing a reasonable and consistent model that can handle a variety of products while calibrated to observed market prices has been and remains challenging. While in the early 1990s, many of the implementation tricks for interest-rate models were regarded as company secrets, and people in the know were loathe to discuss or publish them, most of these techniques have by now made it into public domain. With the rotation of the same cast of quants within various firms, this tribal knowledge has almost become universally known and deployed. Nowadays, the competitive advantage of a firm's pricing and risk-management capabilities for interest rates is not in their underlying model per se, but in the efficient implementation and speed of obtaining prices and intuitive risk measures.

MODEL VERSUS MARKET: LIQUIDITY AND CONCENTRATION RISK

As we have seen, most interest-rate models are based on arbitrage arguments in idealized settings. These arbitrage arguments are in a sense extrapolation guides: A contingent claim's payoffs can be replicated via dynamically rehedged financed positions in the underlyings, and hence the price of a derivative is the value of its replicating portfolio. Of course, the onus for the seller of a contingent claim is to construct and maintain the replicating portfolio, and rebalance it in real-world dynamics, which often differ significantly from the simple assumed dynamics. Moreover, even if one is truly invested in a replicating portfolio, the price of the option versus that of the replicating portfolio can diverge in response to changing market liquidity. Regardless of the true worth of the replicating portfolio, the whole can differ significantly from the sum of the parts, and one can end up in "In Philadelphia, it is worth 50 bucks!" situation.

With this in mind, one should take the model price of any instrument with a grain of salt, and take provisions for the period of time that one is on the hook for them. This, however, is easier said than done: With the increased competition for any high-margin product, the impetus for trading them at ever-decreasing margins to stay in business is too large to ignore, and the reserve cushion quickly evaporates. Moreover, the compensation structure for many traders incentivizes them to book and extract up front as much mark-to-model profit as possible.

For most rates products, the flows are typically one-way, and there is no natural or meaningful way of laying off the risk. This results in large one-way inventories of risks that are held in trading books, with the only valuation available being the model price. Risk and control groups should be vigilant in putting concentration limits on risks, although these groups are generally viewed as cost centers, and despite much touting of their autonomy and expertise, their oversight is unfortunately usually inadequate and perfunctory.

COMPLEXITY RISK

Another problem with derivatives and especially interest-rate derivatives is their increasing complexity. While an argument can be made that derivatives allow for the fair distribution of risk to those able to understand and willing to take it, the distribution can also result in complexity not appreciated by the end users, with each intermediating party assuming that due diligence has been performed by other links in the transmission chain. The common wisdom of "If you don't understand it, don't buy it" is too often ignored by end-users of interest-rate derivatives, as there is too much temptation of picking up deceptively easy extra yield in exchange for knowing or unknowing selling of volatility, which is the core tradeoff embedded in most structured products.

The sell-side is not immune to complexity, as most senior management of broker-dealer firms have little understanding of the risks in their trading books, be it simple time decay of their options book to the more complicated volatility or correlation risk. Keeping it simple is easier said than done though, as the lure of high margin products and bragging ability to be a "full-service" shop tempts many firms to delve into financial products and risks for which they are not adequately resourced, usually resulting in loss a couple of years down the road.

REMAINING CHALLENGES

As far as interest-rate models are concerned, the challenge continues to remain in the implementation arena. To date, no single model has emerged as "the" model, and most firms rely on a suite of models, each perfected to handle a class of products (Bermudans, Asians), with the potential danger of inconsistent dynamics between models. While cognizant of the potential for intermodel arbitrage, in the absence of any convincing alternatives, most firms still deploy multiple models.

The full-term structure paradigm of HJM can in principle serve as "the" framework for the consistent pricing and risk management of all interest-rate products. However, due to its general non-Markovian nature, its most natural implementation is via a nonrecombining tree. This implementation, however, suffers from the curse of dimensionality, and will persist even as computational horsepower becomes cheaper, since there is a commensurate need for more pricing accuracy due to falling margins. The other common implementation is simulation, but as discussed, pricing early-exercise features remains a challenge for simulation. While much progress has been made in applying new techniques for the implementation of these models, there is still room for improvement, as the pricing, risk-management, and calibration issues of models for multiasset, path-dependent with Bermudan exercise features will continue to require ever more implementation ingenuity.

Taylor Series Expansion

In this appendix, we review the Taylor Series expansion formula from ordinary analysis. This expansion is commonly used to relate sensitivities (risk, PV01, convexity) to profit and loss (P&L) for financial instruments (bonds, swaps, ...), as shown in Chapters 1 and 6. The much-dreaded Ito's Lemma used in Chapters 10 and 11 is basically Taylor Series expansion in a stochastic setting, and can be easily used in practice via a *multiplication table*.

FUNCTION OF ONE VARIABLE

For a function of one variable, $f(x)$, the Taylor Series formula is:

$$f(x + \Delta x) = f(x) + f'(x)\Delta x + 1/2 f''(x)(\Delta x)^2 + \ldots + 1/n! f^{(n)}(x)(\Delta x)^n + \ldots.$$

where $f'(x)$ is the first derivative, $f''(x)$ the second derivative, $f^{(n)}(x)$ the n-th derivative, and so on. In practice, we usually just use the first two derivatives, and ignore the effect of the remaining *higher-order* terms:

$$f(x + \Delta x) - f(x) = f'(x)\Delta x + 1/2 f''(x)(\Delta x)^2 + \text{Higher Order Terms}$$

For example, considering the Price-Yield formula for bonds, we have:

$$P(y + \Delta y) - P(y) \approx P'(y)\Delta y + 1/2 P''(y)(\Delta y)^2$$

$$= \text{PV01} \times \frac{\Delta y}{0.0001} + 1/2 \times \text{Convexity} \times (\Delta y)^2$$

FUNCTION OF SEVERAL VARIABLES

A similar formula holds for functions of several variables $f(x_1, \ldots, x_n)$. This is usually written as

$$f(x_1 + \Delta x_1, \ldots, x_n + \Delta x_n) = f(x_1, \ldots, x_n)$$

$$+ \sum_{i=1}^{n} \frac{\partial f}{\partial x_i}(x_1, \ldots, x_n)\Delta x_i$$

$$+ 1/2 \sum_{i=1}^{n} \sum_{j=1}^{n} \frac{\partial f}{\partial x_i}(x_1, \ldots, x_n)\frac{\partial f}{\partial x_j}(x_1, \ldots, x_n)\Delta x_i \Delta x_j$$

$$+ \text{Higher Order Terms}$$

For example, using Black's Formula, the expected P&L of an option is usually computed by considering the first-order terms and only one second-order term (gamma), ignoring all others:

$$C(F + \Delta F, \sigma + \Delta \sigma, t + \Delta t) - C(F, \sigma, t) \approx \frac{\partial C}{\partial F}\Delta F + \frac{\partial C}{\partial \sigma}\Delta \sigma + \frac{\partial C}{\partial t}\Delta t + 1/2 \frac{\partial^2 C}{\partial F^2}(\Delta F)^2$$

$$= \text{Delta} \times \Delta F + 1/2 \times \text{Gamma} \times (\Delta F)^2$$

$$+ \text{Vega} \times \Delta \sigma + \text{Theta} \times \Delta t$$

ITO'S LEMMA: TAYLOR SERIES FOR DIFFUSIONS

Ito's Lemma is basically Taylor series expansions for stochastic diffusions. For a given diffusion $X(t, \omega)$ driven by

$$dX(t, \omega) = \mu(t, \omega)dt + \sigma(t, \omega)dB(t, \omega)$$

consider a function $f(t, X(t, \omega))$. Ito's Lemma allows one to compute the diffusion for $f(t, X)$ by following Taylor series expansion for two variables, and employing the following simple *multiplication rule:*[1]

$\times$	dt	$dB(t, \omega)$
dt	0	0
$dB(t, \omega)$	0	dt

In particular, it means that we only need to keep first-order terms and only one second-order term $(dB \times dB = dt)$, ignoring all other terms.

Starting with

$$dX(t, \omega) = \mu(t, \omega)dt + \sigma(t, \omega)dB(t, \omega)$$

we proceed formally with Taylor Series for a function of two variables $f(t, X)$, and ignore all terms with order higher than 2, or any term with $(dt)^2$ or $dt \times dB$:

$$
\begin{aligned}
df(t, X(t, \omega)) &= \frac{\partial f}{\partial t}dt + \frac{\partial f}{\partial X}dX(t, \omega) + 1/2\frac{\partial^2 f}{\partial X^2}(dX(t, \omega))^2 \\
&= \frac{\partial f}{\partial t}dt + \frac{\partial f}{\partial X}[\mu(t, \omega)dt + \sigma(t, \omega)dB(t, \omega)] + 1/2\frac{\partial^2 f}{\partial X^2}\sigma^2(t, \omega)dt \\
&= \left[\frac{\partial f}{\partial t} + \frac{\partial f}{\partial X}\mu(t, \omega) + 1/2\frac{\partial^2 f}{\partial X^2}\sigma^2(t, \omega)\right]dt + \frac{\partial f}{\partial X}\sigma(t, \omega)dB(t, \omega)
\end{aligned}
$$

The most common application of Ito's Lemma in finance is to start with the following dynamics for proportional (percent changes) of an asset:

$$\frac{dA(t, \omega)}{A(t, \omega)} = \mu dt + \sigma dB(t, \omega)$$

where the drift μ and volatility σ are constant numbers. Therefore,

$$dA(t, \omega) = \mu(t, \omega)dt + \sigma(t, \omega)dB(t, \omega)$$

where

$$\mu(t, \omega) = \mu \times A(t, \omega)$$
$$\sigma(t, \omega) = \sigma \times A(t, \omega)$$

Considering $f(t, A(t, \omega)) = \ln A(t, \omega)$, we notice $\frac{\partial}{\partial t}f = 0$ since f is not a direct function of t, and recalling

$$\frac{d}{dx}\ln(x) = 1/x, \qquad \frac{d^2}{dx^2}\ln(x) = -1/x^2$$

from ordinary calculus, Ito's Lemma gives us:

$$d\ln(A(t,\omega)) = df(t,\omega)$$

$$= \left[\frac{1}{A(t,\omega)} \times \mu \times A(t,\omega) - 1/2\frac{1}{A^2(t,\omega)} \times \sigma^2 \times A^2(t,\omega)\right]dt$$

$$+ \left[\frac{1}{A(t,\omega)} \times \sigma \times A(t,\omega)\right]dB(t,\omega)$$

$$= (\mu - \sigma^2/2)dt + \sigma dB(t,\omega)$$

Integrating both sides, we have

$$\ln A(t,\omega) - \ln A(0,\omega) = (\mu - \sigma^2/2)t + \sigma \int_0^t dB(t,\omega)$$

$$= (\mu - \sigma^2/2)t + \sigma(B(t,\omega) - B(0,\omega))$$

$$= (\mu - \sigma^2/2)t + \sigma B(t,\omega)$$

since a Brownian motion is started at 0, $B(0,\omega) = 0$. Recalling that a standard Brownian motion is Normally distributed, $B(t,\omega) \sim N(0,t)$, we get:

$$A(t,\omega) = A(0,\omega)e^{(\mu-1/2\sigma^2)t+\sigma N(0,t)}$$

that is, $A(t,\omega)/A(0)$ is Log-Normal: $A(t,\omega)/A(0) \sim LN((\mu - \sigma^2/2)t, \sigma^2 t)$, $E A(t,\omega) = A(0)e^{\mu t}$. Note that if the process for A is drift less, that is, $\mu = 0$, then $dA(t,\omega) = \sigma A(t,\omega)dB(t,\omega)$, and $E A(t,\omega) = A(0)$. In this case, A(t) has zero expected change and is a martingale.

Mean-Reverting Processes

The process equation for the Hull-White, BDT/BK models in Chapter 8, and the Ho-Lee model in Chapter 10 can be expressed as a generalized Ornstein-Uhlenbeck process:

$$dx(t, \omega) = [\mu(t) - a(t)x(t, \omega)]dt + \sigma(t)dB(t, \omega)$$

$$\Rightarrow dx(t, \omega) + a(t)x(t, \omega)dt = \mu(t)dt + \sigma(t)dB(t, \omega)$$

where for the Hull-White/Ho-Lee models $x(t, \omega) = r(t, \omega)$, while for the BDT/BK models $x(t, \omega) = \ln r(t, \omega)$. Multiplying both sides by the integrating factor

$$A(t) = e^{\int a(u)du}$$

we get

$$A(t)dx(t, \omega) + a(t)A(t)x(t, \omega)dt = \mu(t)A(t)dt + \sigma(t)A(t)dB(t, \omega)$$

$$\Rightarrow d[A(t)x(t, \omega)] = \mu(t)A(t)dt + \sigma(t)A(t)dB(t, \omega)$$

$$\Rightarrow A(s)x(s, \omega) - A(t)x(t, \omega) = \int_t^s \mu(u)A(u)du + \int_t^s \sigma(u)A(u)dB(u, \omega)$$

$$\Rightarrow x(s, \omega) = \frac{x(t, \omega)A(t)}{A(s)} + \frac{1}{A(s)}\int_t^s \mu(u)A(u)du + \frac{1}{A(s)}\int_t^s \sigma(u)A(u)dB(u, \omega)$$

Since the increments of Brownian motion, $dB(t, \omega)$, are independent and Normal, $x(s, \omega)$ is conditionally Normal (conditioned on $x(t, \omega)$):

$$x(s, \omega) \sim N\left(\frac{x(t, \omega)A(t)}{A(s)} + \frac{1}{A(s)}\int_t^s \mu(u)A(u)du, \frac{1}{A^2(s)}\int_t^s \sigma^2(u)A^2(u)du\right)$$

Moreover, $\int_t^T x(s, \omega)ds$ is also conditionally normal:[1]

$$\int_t^T x(s, \omega)ds \sim N\left(x(t, \omega)A(t)\int_t^T \frac{ds}{A(s)} + \int_t^T \left(\int_t^s \mu(u)\frac{A(u)}{A(s)}du\right)ds, V(t, T)\right)$$

where

$$V(t, T) = E_t\left[\int_t^T \int_t^T \frac{1}{A(s)}\frac{1}{A(r)}\int_t^s \sigma(u)A(u)dB(u, \omega)\int_t^r \sigma(v)A(v)dB(v, \omega)drds\right]$$

$$= \int_t^T \int_t^T \frac{1}{A(s)}\frac{1}{A(r)}\left(\int_t^s \int_t^r \sigma(u)\sigma(v)A(u)A(v)E_t[dB(u, \omega)dB(v, \omega)]\right)drds$$

$$= \int_t^T \int_t^T \frac{1}{A(s)}\frac{1}{A(r)}\left(\int_t^{min(r,s)} \sigma^2(u)A^2(u)du\right)drds$$

where we have used the following property of Ito differentials:

$$E_t[dB(u, \omega)dB(v, \omega)] = \begin{cases} du & \text{if } u = v \\ 0 & \text{otherwise} \end{cases}$$

NORMAL DYNAMICS

For the Vasicek/Hull-White/Ho-Lee models, $r(t, \omega) = x(t, \omega)$, this means that the short rate is Normally distributed, and that discount factors are Log-Normally distributed. In particular,

$$D(t, T, \omega) = E_t[e^{-\int_t^T r(s, \omega)ds}]$$

$$= e^{-r(t,\omega)A(t)\int_t^T \frac{ds}{A(s)} - \int_t^T \left(\int_t^s \mu(u)\frac{A(u)}{A(s)}du\right)ds + \frac{1}{2}V(t, T)}$$

Recall that instantaneous forward rates are related to discount factors as

$$f(t, T, \omega) = -\frac{\partial}{\partial T}\ln D(t, T, \omega)$$

therefore,

$$f(t, T, \omega) = \frac{r(t, \omega)A(t)}{A(T)} + \frac{1}{A(T)}\int_t^T \mu(u)A(u)du - \frac{1}{2}\frac{\partial}{\partial T}V(t, T)$$

Rearranging the previous, we have

$$\int_t^T \mu(u)\,A(u)\,du = A(T)\,f(t, T, \omega) - r(t, \omega)\,A(t) + \frac{1}{2}A(T)\frac{\partial}{\partial T}V(t, T)$$

Setting $t = 0$, and differentiating both sides with respect to T, we obtain the following expression for the arb-free drift:

$$\mu(T) = \frac{\partial}{\partial T}f(0, T) + a(T)\,f(0, T) + \frac{1}{2}a(T)\frac{\partial}{\partial T}V(0, T) + \frac{1}{2}\frac{\partial^2}{\partial T^2}V(0, T)$$

The above expression can be further simplified when the mean-reversions and volatilities are constant. In particular, for Hull-White with constant mean-reversion speed and volatilities, $a(t) = a, \sigma(t) = \sigma$, we have

$$\mu_{HW}(T) = ab(T) = \frac{\partial}{\partial T}f(0, T) + af(0, T) + \frac{\sigma^2}{2a}(1 - e^{-2aT})$$

while for the Ho-Lee model $(a(t) = 0, \sigma(t) = \sigma)$, we have

$$\mu_{HL}(T) = \frac{\partial}{\partial T}f(0, T) + \sigma^2 T$$

Note that since $A(.), \mu(.), V(.)$ are all deterministic functions of time, the short rate $r(t, \omega)$ at each time t completely determines the full-forward *curve* $f(t, ., \omega)$!

Euro-Dollar Convexity Adjustment

As discussed in Chapter 3, due to the daily settlement, the implied rate in the ED future contract is not the same as the forward rate, and dominates it by an amount called the ED convexity adjustment. In order to compute this convexity adjustment, we observe that the implied futures rate is the expected value of the short rate at contract expiry. This can be shown by observing that at any time t, its payoff on the next period is $F(t + dt) - F(t)$, hence the value of the future contract at t is

$$E_t\left[\frac{F(t + dt, \omega) - F(t, \omega)}{1 + r(t, \omega)dt}\right]$$

Since at each time, the futures price is chosen so that the contract has zero value, $F(t)$ must satisfy

$$F(t, \omega) = E_t[F(t + dt, \omega)]$$

Since at expiry t_e, $F(t_e, \omega) = r(t_e, \omega)$, using law of iterated expectation, we have

$$F(0) = E_0[r(t_e, \omega)]$$

Using the Ho-Lee Model, we have

$$dr(t, \omega) = \left[\frac{\partial}{\partial t}f(0, t) + \sigma^2 t\right] dt + \sigma_V \times dB(t, \omega)$$

$$\Rightarrow r(t, \omega) \sim f(0, t) + 1/2\sigma_N^2 t^2 + N(0, \sigma_N^2 t)$$

leading to the convexity adjustment formula

$$E_0[r(t, \omega)] - f(0, t) = 1/2\sigma_N^2 t^2$$

LOG-NORMAL DYNAMICS

For BDT/BK models, $x(t, \omega) = \ln r(t, \omega)$, which means that short rates are Log-Normal, and discount factors are "log-log-normal" or "doubly exponential." In this case, we cannot derive explicit analytical expressions for discount factors and/or forward rates, and the arb-free drift $\mu(.)$—while deterministic—cannot be analytically solved for and is left as an *implicit* function.

However, we can still derive some analytical expressions for the Log-Volatility of the short rate:

$$\sigma_{[t,T]} = \sqrt{\frac{1}{T-t}\text{Var}_t\left[\ln\left(\frac{r(T, \omega)}{r(t, \omega)}\right)\right]}$$

$$= \sqrt{\frac{1}{T-t}\int_t^T \sigma^2(u)e^{-2\int_u^T a(v)dv}du}$$

Recall that for a BK model, the mean-reversion speed $a(t)$ is an arbitrary function of time, while for a BDT model, it is related to the local volatility curve:

$$a(t) = -\frac{\sigma'(t)}{\sigma(t)} = -\frac{d}{dt}\ln\sigma(t)$$

therefore,

$$\sigma_{[t,T]} = \sqrt{\frac{1}{T-t}\int_t^T \sigma^2(u)e^{-2\int_u^T a(v)dv}\,du}$$

$$= \sqrt{\frac{1}{T-t}\int_t^T \sigma^2(u)e^{2\int_u^T \ln'(\sigma(v))dv}\,du}$$

$$= \sqrt{\frac{1}{T-t}\int_t^T \sigma^2(u)\frac{\sigma^2(T)}{\sigma^2(u)}\,du}$$

$$= \sigma(T)$$

that is, for a BDT model, the local volatility is the same as the horizon/ average volatility! Since the caplet curve gives direct information on $\sigma_{[t,T]}$, this implies that BDT models are relatively easy to calibrate to caplets.

Girsanov's Theorem and Change of Numeraire

The change of numeraire formula in Chapter 11 relates the risk-neutral probability sets when switching numeraires via their likelihood ratios (Radon-Nikodym derivative):

$$\frac{dP_A}{dP_B}(t, \omega) = \frac{A(t, \omega)/A(0)}{B(t, \omega)/B(0)}$$

When working with diffusions, Girsanov's Theorem uses the same likelihood ratios to relate Brownian motions under one probability to another. We will use the following version of it.[1]

Girsanov's Theorem

Let $B_1(t, \omega)$ be a Brownian motion under a probability measure P_1: $B_1(t, \omega) \sim N(0, t)$ under P_1. Define a new probability measure P_2 related to P_1 through their likelihood ratios as follows:

$$\frac{dP_2}{dP_1}(t, \omega) = e^{-\int_0^t \gamma(s,\omega)dB_1(u,\omega)-1/2\int_0^t \gamma^2(s,\omega)ds}$$

for a random process $\gamma(s, \omega)$. Then subject to some regularity conditions on $\gamma(s, \omega)$, the process $B_2(t, \omega)$ defined as

$$B_2(t, \omega) = B_1(t, \omega) + \int_0^t \gamma(s, \omega)ds$$

(or $dB_2(t, \omega) = dB_1(t, \omega) + \gamma(t, \omega)dt$ in differential format) is a Brownian motion under P_2: $B_2(t, \omega) \sim N(0, t)$ under P_2.

CONTINUOUS-TIME, INSTANTANEOUS-FORWARDS HJM FRAMEWORK

As for short-rate models, the original HJM formulation of their framework was in continuous time and in terms of *instantaneous* forward rates, related to discount factors as follows:

$$(0 \le t \le T) \qquad D(t, T, \omega) = e^{-\int_t^T f(t,u,\omega)du}$$

$$f(t, T, \omega) = -\frac{\partial}{\partial T} \ln D(t, T, \omega)$$

We assume the following general dynamics for the 1-factor (can easily be generalized to multifactor) evolution of the forward rate and discount factors:

$$dD(t, T, \omega) = \mu_D(t, T, \omega)dt + \sigma_D(t, T, \omega)dB^M(t, \omega)$$

$$df(t, T, \omega) = \mu_f(t, T, \omega)dt + \sigma_f(t, T, \omega)dB^M(t, \omega)$$

where $B^M(t, \omega)$ is a standard 1-dimensional Brownian motion under the money-market measure.

Applying Ito's Lemma to the discount factor process, and taking liberties with the interchange of limits, we get

$$df = -\frac{\partial}{\partial T}\left[\frac{dD}{D} - \frac{1}{2}\left(\frac{dD}{D}\right)^2\right]$$

$$= -\frac{\partial}{\partial T}(\mu_D - 1/2\sigma_D^2)dt - \frac{\partial}{\partial T}\sigma_D dB^M$$

Matching terms, we have

$$\mu_f(t, T, \omega) = -\frac{\partial}{\partial T}\left(\mu_D(t, T, \omega) - 1/2\sigma_D^2(t, T, \omega)\right)$$

$$\sigma_f(t, T, \omega) = -\frac{\partial}{\partial T}\sigma_D(t, T, \omega)$$

Expressing σ_D in terms of σ_f, we have

$$\sigma_D(t, T, \omega) = -\int_t^T \sigma_f(t, u, \omega)du$$

The risk-neutral martingale constraint is that the *return* on all tradeable assets (zero-coupon bonds) must equal the short rate, that is, $\mu_D(t, T, \omega) = r(t, \omega)$. We get

$$\mu_f(t, T, \omega) = -\frac{\partial}{\partial T}\left(\mu_D(t, T, \omega) - 1/2\sigma_D^2(t, T, \omega)\right)$$

$$= 1/2\frac{\partial}{\partial T}\sigma_D^2(t, T, \omega)$$

$$= \sigma_D(t, T, \omega)\frac{\partial}{\partial T}\sigma_D(t, T, \omega)$$

$$= \sigma_f(t, T, \omega)\int_t^T \sigma_f(t, u, \omega)du$$

We arrive at the continuous-time version of the HJM drifts:

$$df(t, T, \omega) = \left[\sigma_f(t, T, \omega)\int_t^T \sigma_f(t, u, \omega)du\right]dt + \sigma_f(t, T, \omega)dB^M(t, \omega)$$

Forward and Money-Market Measures in HJM Framework

A simple application of Girsanov's Theorem is to relate the forward and money-market measures in the HJM framework. Starting with HJM process equations for discount factors under the money-market measure,

$$\frac{dD(t, T, \omega)}{D(t, T, \omega)} = r(t, \omega)dt + \sigma_D(t, T, \omega)dB^M(t, \omega)$$

we have

$$\frac{D(t, T, \omega)}{D(0, T, \omega)} = e^{\int_0^t (r(u,\omega)-1/2\sigma_D^2(u,T,\omega))du+\int_0^t \sigma_D(u,T,\omega)dB^M(u,\omega)}$$

When switching numeraires from the money-market account to a T^*-maturity zero-coupon bond, we are switching the measure from P^M to P^{T^*}. We have

$$\frac{dP^{T^*}}{dP^M}(t, \omega) = \frac{D(t, T^*, \omega)/D(0, T, \omega)}{M(t, \omega)/M(0)}$$

$$= e^{-1/2\int_0^t \sigma_D^2(u,T^*,\omega)du-\int_0^t -\sigma_D(u,T^*,\omega)dB^M(u,\omega)}$$

By Girsanov's Theorem, the process $B^{T^*}(t, \omega)$ defined by

$$dB^{T^*}(t, \omega) = -\sigma_D(t, T^*, \omega)dt + dB^M(t, \omega)$$

is a Brownian motion under P^{T^*}.

BGM RESULT

Fixing a maturity T^*, the simple forward rate $f(t, [T_s, T^*], \omega)$ over $[T_s, T^*]$ is related to the instantaneous forwards $f(t, T, \omega)$ by

$$f(t, [T_s, T^*], \omega) = \frac{1}{\delta}[D(t, T_s, \omega)/D(t, T^*, \omega) - 1]$$

$$= \frac{1}{\delta}(e^{\int_{T_s}^{T^*} f(t, T, \omega)dT} - 1)$$

where $\delta = T^* - T_s$.

Starting with the process equations for instantaneous forwards in the HJM framework under the money-market measure:

$$df(t, T, \omega) = \left[\frac{\partial}{\partial T}\left(1/2\sigma_D^2(t, T, \omega)\right)\right]dt + \left[-\frac{\partial}{\partial T}\sigma_D(t, T, \omega)\right]dB^M(t, \omega)$$

we apply Ito's Lemma first to $X = \int_{T_s}^{T^*} f(t, T, \omega)dT$:

$$d\int_{T_s}^{T^*} f(t, T, \omega)dT = \int_{T_s}^{T^*} df(t, T, \omega)dT$$

$$= \int_{T_s}^{T^*}\left(\left[1/2\frac{\partial}{\partial T}\sigma_D^2(t, T, \omega)\right]dt - \frac{\partial}{\partial T}\sigma_D(t, T, \omega)dB^M(t, T, \omega)\right)dT$$

$$= \left(\int_{T_s}^{T^*} 1/2\frac{\partial}{\partial T}\sigma_D^2(t, T, \omega)dT\right)dt + \left(\int_{T_s}^{T^*} -\frac{\partial}{\partial T}\sigma_D(t, T, \omega)dT\right)dB^M(t, \omega)$$

$$= 1/2[\sigma_D^2(t, T^*, \omega) - \sigma_D^2(t, T_s, \omega)]dt$$
$$- [\sigma_D(t, T^*, \omega) - \sigma_D(t, T_s, \omega)]dB^M(t, \omega)$$

Having found dX, since $f(t, [T_s, T^*], \omega) = \frac{1}{\delta}(e^X - 1)$, another application of Ito's Lemma gets us:

$$df(t, [T_s, T^*], \omega) = \frac{1}{\delta}d(e^X - 1)$$

$$= \frac{e^X}{\delta}[d(X) + 1/2(dX)^2]$$

$$= \frac{e^X}{\delta}(\sigma_D(t, T_s, \omega) - \sigma_D(t, T^*, \omega))[-\sigma_D(t, T^*, \omega)dt + dB^M(t, \omega)]$$

$$= \left[\left(\frac{1}{\delta} + f(t, [T_s, T^*], \omega)\right)(\sigma_D(t, T_s, \omega) - \sigma_D(t, T^*, \omega))\right]dB^{T^*}(t, \omega)$$

where we used the relationship between the money market and forward Brownian motions

$$dB^{T^*}(t, \omega) = -\sigma_D(t, T^*, \omega)dt + dB^M(t, \omega)$$

for the last equality. Notice that under the T^*-measure, the forward rate has no drift.

The BGM result is to set the pesky term in square brackets to a deterministic function of time multiplying the forward rate:

$$\left[\left(\frac{1}{\delta} + f(t, [T_s, T^*], \omega)\right)(\sigma_D(t, T_s, \omega) - \sigma_D(t, T^*, \omega))\right] = f(t, [T_s, T^*], \omega) \times \sigma(t, T_s)$$

In this case, we get

$$\frac{df(t, [T_s, T^*], \omega)}{f(t, [T_s, T^*], \omega)} = \sigma(t, T_s)dB^{T^*}(t, \omega)$$

resulting in Log-Normal distribution of the rate at any expiration date $t_e \leq T_s$.

Similarly, to attain Normal dynamics, it suffices to have

$$\left[\left(\frac{1}{\delta} + f(t, [T_s, T^*], \omega)\right)(\sigma_D(t, T_s, \omega) - \sigma_D(t, T^*, \omega))\right] = \sigma_N(t, T_s)$$

for a deterministic curve $\sigma_N(t, T_s)$ to arrive at Normal dynamics. In this case, we get

$$df(t, [T_s, T^*], \omega) = \sigma_N(t, T_s)dB^{T^*}(t, \omega)$$

resulting in the Normal distribution of the rate at any expiration date $t_e \leq T_s$.

Notes

CHAPTER 5   Derivatives Pricing: Risk-Neutral Valuation

1. F. Black and M. Scholes, "The Pricing of Options and Corporate Liabilities," *Journal of Political Economy* 81 (1973): 637–659.
2. J.C. Cox, S.A. Ross, and M. Rubinstein, "Option Pricing: A Simplified Approach," *Journal of Financial Economics* 7 (1979): 229–263.
3. J.M. Harrison and D.M. Kreps, "Martingales and Arbitrage in Multi-Period Securities Markets," *Journal of Economic Theory* 20 (1979): 381–408.
4. J.M. Harrison and S.R. Pliska, "Martingales and Stochastic Integrals in the Theory of Continuous Trading," *Stochastic Processes and Their Applications* 11 (1981): 215–260.
5. H. Geman, N. El Karoui, and J-C. Rochet, "Changes of Numeraire, Changes of Probability Measure, and Option Pricing," *Journal of Applied Probability* 32 (1995): 443–458.

CHAPTER 6   Black's World

1. F. Black, "The Pricing of Commodity Contracts," *Journal of Financial Economics*, 31 (1976): 167–179.

CHAPTER 7   European-Style Interest-Rate Derivatives

1. P.S. Hagan, D. Kumar, A.S. Lesniewski, and D.E. Woodward, "Managing Smile Risk," *Wilmott Magazine* (2002); 84–108.
2. G. Amblard and J. Lebuchox, "Models for CMS Options," *Euro Derivatives/Risk Magazine* (September 2000): 68.

CHAPTER 8   Short-Rate Models

1. O. Vasicek, "An Equilibrium Characterization of the Term Structure," *Journal of Financial Economics* 5 (1977): 177–188.
2. J. Hull and A. White, "Bond Option Pricing Based on a Model for the Evolution of Bond Prices," *Advances in Futures and Options Research* 6 (1993): 1–13.

3. F. Black, E. Derman, and W. Toy, "A One-Factor Model of Interest Rates and Its Application to Treasury Bond Options," *Financial Analysts Journal* 46 (1990): 33–39.

4. F. Black and P. Karasinski, "Bond and Option Pricing When Short Rates are Log-Normal," *Financial Analysts Journal* 47 (1991): 52–59.

5. K. Back. *A Course in Derivative Securities: Introduction to Theory and Computation.* (New York: Springer, 2005): 300–302.

6. J.C. Cox, J.E. Ingersoll, and S.A. Ross, "A Theory of the Term Stucture of Interest Rates," *Econometrica* 53 (1985): 385–407.

7. F. Jamshidian, "The One-Factor Gaussian Interest Rate Model: Theory and Implementation," *Working Paper, Merrill Lynch Capital Markets* 1988.

CHAPTER 9   Bermudan-Style Options

1. F.A. Longstaff and E.S. Schwartz, "Valuing American Options by Simulation: A Simple Least-Squares Approach," *Review of Financial Studies* 14 (2001): 113–147.

CHAPTER 10   Full Term-Structure Interest-Rate Models

1. T.S.Y. Lee and S.-B. Lee, "Term Structure Movements and the Pricing of Interest Rate Contingent Claims," *Journal of Finance* 41 (1986): 1011–1029.

2. Philip H. Dybvig, "Bond and Bond Option Pricing Based on the Current Term Structure," *Mathematics of Derivative Securities*, Cambridge University Press, 1997: 271–292.

3. D. Heath, R. Jarrow, and A. Morton, "Bond Pricing and the Term Structure of Interest Rates: A New Methodology," *Econometrica* 60 (1992): 77–105.

4. B. Oksendal. *Stochastic Differential Equations*, 3rd ed. (New York: Springer-Verlag, 1992): 19.

5. O. Cheyette, "Markov Representation of the Heath-Jarrow-Morton Model," *Presented at UCLA Workshop of the Future of Fixed Income Financial Theory* 1992.

6. P. Ritchken and L. Sankarasubramanian, "Volatility Structures of Forward Rates and Dynamics of the Term Structure," *Mathematical Finance* 5 (1995): 55–72.

7. A. Li, P. Ritchken, and L. Sankarasubramanian, "Lattice Models for Pricing American Interest Rate Options," *Journal of Finance* 50 (1995): 719–737.

8. K. Sandmann and D. Sondermann, "A Note on the Stability of Log-Normal Interest Rate Models and the Pricing of Eurodollar Futures," *Mathematical Finance* 7 (1997): 119–128.

CHAPTER 11   Forward-Measure Lens

1. N.H. Bingham and R. Kiesel, *Risk-Neutral Valuation: Pricing and Hedging of Financial Derivatives* (New York: Springer, 2004): 19–20..

2. H. Geman, N. El Karoui, and J-C. Rochet, "Changes of Numeraire, Changes of Probability Measure, and Option Pricing," *Journal of Applied Probability* 32 (1995): 443–458.

3. A. Brace, D. Gartarek, and M. Musiela, "The Market Model of Interest Rate Dynamics," *Mathematical Finance* 7 (1997): 127–154.

4. F. Jamshidian, "Libor and Swap Market Models and Measures," *Finance and Stochastics* 1 (1997): 261–291.

5. N.H. Bingham and R. Kiesel, *Risk-Neutral Valuation: Pricing and Hedging of Financial Derivatives* (New York: Springer, 2004): 361.

APPENDIX A Taylor Series Expansion

1. B. Oksendal, *Stochastic Differential Equations*, 3rd ed. (New York: Springer-Verlag, 1992): 33.

APPENDIX B Mean-Reverting Processes

1. S. Karlin and H. Taylor, *A First Course in Stochastic Processes*, 2nd ed. (San Diego: Academic Press, 1975): 384.

APPENDIX C Girsanov's Theorem and Change of Numeraire

1. B. Oksendal, *Stochastic Differential Equations*, 3rd ed. (New York, Springer-Veralg, 1992): 126.

Index

volatility surface
  forward-forward, 188, 191–197,
    199, 213

when-issued, 7
WI. *See* when-issued

yield curve
  inverting, 155
  trade, 15

yield to maturity, 5
yield volatility, 147–148

Z spread, 54–55
zero coupon bond, 4, 10
zero rate, 27
  continuously compounded,
    27
zero-coupon swap, 53–54
  spread, 53–54

Printed and bound by CPI Group (UK) Ltd, Croydon, CR0 4YY

23/04/2025

14661008-0001